MEDIEVAL TEXTS

GENERAL EDITORS

V. H. Galbraith, R. A. B. Mynors and C. N. L. Brooke

HUGH THE CHANTOR

The History of the Church of York

1066–1127

Hugh the Chantor

The History of the Church of York

1066-1127

Translated from the Latin
and with Introduction by

Charles Johnson C.B.E. F.B.A.
sometime Scholar of Trinity College, Oxford

Thomas Nelson and Sons Ltd
London Edinburgh Paris Melbourne Johannesburg
Toronto and New York

THOMAS NELSON AND SONS LTD
Parkside Works Edinburgh 9
36 Park Street London W1
312 Flinders Street Melbourne C1

302-304 Barclays Bank Building
Commissioner and Kruis Streets
Johannesburg

THOMAS NELSON AND SONS (CANADA) LTD
91-93 Wellington Street West Toronto 1

THOMAS NELSON AND SONS
19 East 47th Street New York 17

SOCIÉTÉ FRANÇAISE D'ÉDITIONS NELSON
97 rue Monge Paris 5

———

First published 1961

CONTENTS

INTRODUCTION

I

THE sixty-one years covered by the narrative of Hugh 'the chantor' were eventful both for Europe and for England. In Europe, they began the 'Contest between the Empire and the Papacy'. Hildebrand, who had already been the pope's right-hand man, succeeded to the papacy as Gregory VII (1073–85). He tried to suppress clerical marriage and simony; and the latter involved the question of lay investiture, which was not settled till near the end of the period. The power of Rome over the western church was consolidated: new monastic orders were formed (like the Augustinian Canons) from the secular clergy, while the Cluniac and Cistercian movements reformed the Benedictine monks. And the whole of Christendom was roused in the first Crusade (A.D. 1095–9). Meanwhile the French monarchy was growing, and the German princes becoming more independent of the empire.

In England, William I was adapting the English kingdom to a stronger and more centralized pattern of government. Both he and his successors set limits to papal interference. The two metropolitan churches had both suffered catastrophe in the earliest years of the period, and both were re-established under the care of archbishops brought over from Normandy. The contest for the primacy may seem a petty matter against the background of general history, but incidents in the story illustrate the nature of more important events.

II

Hugh Sottovagina or Sottewain, commonly known as Hugh the chantor, is said by the author of the first Chronicle

of the archbishops of York to have been a counsellor (*neces-sarius consiliarius*) of the first four Norman archbishops of York [1] and so was probably a canon as early as A.D. 1100, though he does not speak of the chapter as *nos* till 1108, when Thomas II became archbishop. He was precentor and archdeacon of York in 1133, and accompanied archbishop Thurstan at his visitation of St Mary's abbey, which resulted in the foundation of Fountains in 1138.[2] He is mentioned as precentor in Thurstan's grant to Fountains abbey of woodland at 'Herleshow' (Ripon), which Farrer dates 1139–40.[3] Osbert of Bayeux had then succeeded him as archdeacon. He wrote a poem on the Battle of the Standard, at which he is said to have been present.[4] Very near the same time (1138–9), while still archdeacon of York, he wrote a letter to Roger, prior of Durham, attesting the remission by archbishop Thurstan to all churches in the province of York of the synodals (i.e. payments for chrism).[5] His seal, which is appended to the original letter, represents him seated, with a book in his left hand and a rod (?) in his right. He wears 'an alb or cassock with a short vestment, without sleeves, worn over it in form not unlike a short chasuble'.[6] (Perhaps the upper vestment, which seems more like a cape than a chasuble, is his almuce as a canon.) The year of his death is not known but his obit was celebrated on 4 July.[7] He had been succeeded as precentor by William of Eu (de Augo) before Thurstan's resignation (25 Jan. 1140).[8] It is therefore probable that Hugh died in 1139. Two other members of the family, Arnulf and Thomas, became canons of York, and there seems some reason to think that they had their home in Richmondshire,[9] possibly at Gilling.

---

[1] Raine, *Historians of the Church of York*, ii. 355   [2] *Monasticon*
[3] Farrer, *Early Yorkshire Charters*, i. 63-4. See also Clay, *York Minster Fasti* (1958-60).   [4] Raine, u.s. II. xiii   [5] ibid.
[6] D. & C. of Durham, Treasury, 2-4, Ebor, 6. Described by Dr. C. H. Hunter Blair in 'Catalogue of Durham Seals' (offprint from *Archaeologia Aeliana*, 3rd Ser., vols. VII to XVII), II, No. 3285, and Plate 61
[7] Raine, u.s. II. xiiii
[8] Farrer, *Early Yorkshire Charters*, i. 131   [9] *op. cit.* iv. 117

Hugh's narrative suggests that he was not only much concerned in maintaining the liberties of his church as against Canterbury, but also accompanied his archbishop into exile and on his visit to Rome. It is tempting to find an allusion to himself when he says 'one of us'. Though his treatise is a party pamphlet, it is valuable for its dates and places, as may be seen in Farrer's 'Outline Itinerary of Henry I'.[1] It has a special value as showing how the period of the 'Contest of Empire and Papacy'—the adjustment of the boundaries between the Church and the State (which is even now not complete)—appeared to one of the humbler sharers in the struggle. We find a layman being consecrated bishop of Geneva to forestall the appointment by the excommunicated emperor of an adherent of the antipope. The story of the election of William de Corbeil emphasizes both the resentment of the secular clergy at the election of a series of Benedictine or Cluniac popes [2] and the hollowness of the papal victory in the matter of investitures.[3] On the latter point Hugh quotes with approval the opinion of Ivo of Chartres : on the former it may be enough to recall that he wrote a satirical poem against the Cluniacs, not foreseeing that his hero Thurstan was to die as a Cluniac at Pontefract. Canon Raine, who edited his treatise for the Rolls Series, laments his neglect to give us a character sketch of Thurstan, a description of the journey to Rome, or an account of the rise of the Yorkshire monastic houses. But within his limited field he does much to give solidity to historical characters. We can feel the statesmanship of Lanfranc, the combination of affection and opposition in the relations of Henry I and Thurstan, and the

---

[1] *English Historical Review*, xxxiv. 303-82, 505-79 (also issued separately with Index)

[2] On this point see Eadmer's letter to the prior and convent of Worcester on the election of a successor to Bishop Theulf (ob. 1123) (Wharton, *Angl. Sacr.* ii. 235).

[3] Mr R. W. Southern has pointed out to me that Hugh, writing *c.* 1127, says nothing of the question of homage, which had been an important point in 1107.

sympathy of one civil servant with another shown by William de Warelwast, the blind bishop of Exeter, to the exiled Thurstan in the papal court at Valence. We note how Henry I pleads the 'custom of the realm' when he uses William I's control over papal letters (like the later praemunire) to exclude the papal legate and to nullify the effect of papal bulls. Neither pope nor king, however, dares to play his last card: excommunication and interdict on the one hand, and adherence to an antipope on the other. It will also be observed that the popes do their best to encourage appeals to Rome, and the king to prevent them, and that the bulls in favour of York lay stress on the institution of St Gregory, while those in favour of Canterbury insist on the confirmation of its privileges without prejudging the case at issue. There are also some matters of practice which deserve attention. Thus the bulls in favour of Thurstan appear to have been sent to him and left to him to serve on the persons addressed. Again, light is thrown on the part which laymen (*ex officio* illiterate) play in the king's council: his decisions are influenced by Robert, count of Meulan, his main counsellor in both ecclesiastical and secular affairs, and Nigel d'Aubigny, the local justiciar of Yorkshire and Northumberland. Another person who appears in an unfamiliar light is Ranulf Flambard, though some of his old unscrupulousness is seen in his effort to make a fine with the king (including the customary 'Queen's gold') to obtain 'justice and canonical judgment' for the church of York.

III

The concluding paragraphs of Hugh's treatise imply that it was finished in 1127, and this is confirmed by the fact that Ranulf Flambard, who died 5 September 1128, is referred to throughout as a living person. We have few indications of the

method by which it was compiled. The documents quoted
were, no doubt, preserved among the chapter muniments at
York. We can only guess to what extent he had to rely on his
own memory, or whether he kept notes of his travels and of the
proceedings of which he was himself a witness.

The earliest manuscript of his work occupies ff. 1-31 of the
great cartulary of York Minster, the *Registrum Magnum Album*,
preserved in the Chapter Library at York. This is a handsome
manuscript of the fourteenth century, measuring 14 in. × 9½ in.,
and divided into four parts which have been bound together
so as to form one thick volume. These parts are of 71, 100,
100, and 118 ff. respectively, and contain charters, papal
bulls of privilege, and documents of title to the various possessions of the Minster. The binding appears to be contemporary,
and is of oak (?) boards with a leather cover which was probably
white. It is in need of repair, but retains some of the cords to
which the leaves were sewn, and the ends of the leather straps
by which it was closed let into the wooden covers. Prefixed
to the numbered folios are an extract from Domesday Book and
an index to the contents. The end-papers (or rather end-
parchments) are taken from a legal manuscript, presumably a
glossed text of the Civil Law, dealing with the rights of wards.
The title of Hugh's treatise is rubricated, and the initial
capitals of the sections have been left blank for rubrication
but not completed. The transcription is in a good hand but
somewhat unintelligent. There are some marginal notes
apparently contemporary, calling attention to points in the
text, such as the names of the four archbishops or the remission
of synodals by Thurstan. Others are in a hand of the seven-
teenth century, giving readings of words badly written in the
manuscript, or, occasionally, indicating points of interest, such
as Hugh's estimate of Gilbert the Universal as a lawyer. One
on the first page reads *Auctor Hugo cantor Eboracensis: eum
laudat et sequitur Th. Stubs.* It seems possible that these notes

were added by the transcriber of the seventeenth-century copy of the treatise in Gale MS o.10.35, at Trinity College, Cambridge. The reference is to the anonymous first part of the chronicle of the archbishops printed by Roger Twysden in 1652 under the name of the writer who continued it from 1147 to 1373.

The treatise was first printed in *Historians of the Church of York*, II (*Rolls Series*, London, 1886), by Canon James Raine. His text, though accurate on the whole, uses modernized spelling. In the present edition the medieval forms have been restored from a photograph of the MS.

IV

The theme of Hugh's treatise is the contest for the primacy of Britain between the sees of Canterbury and York. This was not merely a question of precedence, as may be seen in the importance attached by William I to the action of Gregory VII in 1079 in subjecting the metropolitan see of Rouen to the primacy of the archbishop of Lyons, a step which marked the increasing control of the apostolic see over the whole of the Western Church. Though the two archbishops were necessarily the protagonists, their respective churches were equally, if not more deeply, involved in the struggle. Throughout Hugh's narrative, the suffragans of Canterbury and monks of Christ Church are represented as urging the archbishops to maintain their superiority; while the chapter of York encouraged their archbishops to offer a firm resistance. A subsidiary subject, which from time to time obscures the main theme, is the effort of the Scottish Church to escape from the control of its nominal metropolitan, the church of York, and to become a separate province with St Andrews as its archbishopric.

The canonical claim of the church of York was simple and

logical. St Gregory the Great had instructed Augustine in a letter of 22 June 601 to establish two archbishoprics, London and York, each with twelve suffragans. Augustine himself was to have the *pallium*, as also was the future archbishop of York. During Augustine's life, he was to have control over all priests in Britain; but after his death, the archbishop of York was to be independent of the archbishop of London. The senior archbishop in date of consecration was to have precedence. A subsequent decree of Honorius I had provided that, on the death of either of the archbishops, the survivor should consecrate his successor. This, they held, had been the state of things in the time of Aldred, the last English archbishop of York; and the demand by the archbishop for a profession of submission was uncanonical and fraudulent.

The claim of Canterbury (in the extreme form in which it appeared to Eadmer [1]) was that its archbishop was the successor of Augustine as fully as the pope was of St Peter, and therefore the inheritor of the powers granted to him. (The popes of the eleventh century constantly argued that their decisions were in that sense apostolic.) Moreover, no archbishop of York had had the *pallium* between Paulinus (625–33) and Egbert (732–66). The constitution of St Gregory was *nil ad rem*, since it only equated York with London, not Canterbury. Theodore of Tarsus had undoubtedly had jurisdiction throughout Britain.

Canterbury certainly had the weaker case on paper. But historically the position was very different. Augustine had not appointed an archbishop of York. The mission of Paulinus had left no permanent effect, and Egbert (732 or 734 to 766) was probably the first archbishop of York after him. There was no doubt that the archbishops of Canterbury, both Theodore of Tarsus and his successors, had repeatedly intervened in the affairs of the northern province. The commanding position

[1] *Hist. Nov.* p. 277

of Aldred in 1066 was due to the equivocal standing of Stigand as archbishop of Canterbury, which left Aldred as the only person who could properly crown William I. It was not therefore unreasonable in Lanfranc to claim the primacy in 1070, though he may have exceeded his rights in demanding a profession of submission and an oath, which the York party held not to be due from one metropolitan to another, but only to the pope.

Archbishop Aldred died 11 September 1069, a week before his cathedral was burned down. Stigand was deposed at the Council of Easter, 1070. So, when Thomas of Bayeux was chosen to succeed Aldred, and Lanfranc Stigand, the latter had to be consecrated by his own suffragans. Thomas came to Canterbury for consecration, but refused to make the profession demanded by Lanfranc. He was, however, persuaded to make a personal profession to Lanfranc, reserving the question of the submission of the see to the pope's decision. Both archbishops went to Rome together, and the question was remitted to be determined by a Legatine Council in England. The council, which was a joint meeting of the legates, the archbishops and clergy of both provinces, and the king's court, held two meetings; at Winchester at Easter (8 April 1072) and at Windsor at Whitsuntide (27 May); a letter of Lanfranc to Alexander II [1] reports the proceedings of the first meeting and the submission of archbishop Thomas. It seems possible that the second meeting was a Legatine Council to confirm the earlier proceedings in the *Curia Regis* at Winchester.[2] This was done and, for the time, settled the question; though the chapter of York asserted that the charter thus circulated gave an untrue account and that the great seal had been fraudulently attached. The matter had been brought

---

[1] H. Boehmer, *Die Fälschungen Erzbischof Lanfranks von Canterbury* (Leipzig, 1902), pp. 169-73
[2] The original letter preserved at Canterbury only mentions the first meeting (*Regesta Regum Anglo-Normannorum* (Oxford, 1913), i, No. 65).

before William I just before his last visit to Normandy, and he had promised to deal with it on his return. Hugh's account, however, of Lanfranc's argument in advising the king not to allow York to be independent, viz. the danger of York becoming he head of a hostile kingdom, seems to show that the real reason for the council's decision was political, and that the charge of forgery was nonsense. Hugh tells us that on Lanfranc's death Thomas refused to consecrate Anselm as 'primate of all Britain.'[1]

The charter of 1072 was the strong point in the Canterbury case throughout the struggle which followed. It is unnecessary to recapitulate Hugh's narrative of the successive attempts of archbishops Thomas I, Gerard, and Thomas II to escape from the domination of Canterbury and of Thurstan's ultimate success, counterbalanced though it was by the temporary concession to William of Corbeil of the papal legation to England, which developed into the permanent advantage of the Canterbury primate as *legatus natus*. His account is confirmed in its main details by Eadmer in his *Historia Novorum*, which presents the case from the Canterbury side, as does William of Malmesbury, following him, in his *Gesta Pontificum*. Eadmer insists on the voluntary submission of archbishops Thomas I and Thomas II,[2] and cites the words of the profession of the latter (made during the vacancy of the see of Canterbury), while he suppresses the charter of Henry I which saves the liberties of the church of York. He also asserts that Paschal II, by a bull dated Benevento, 12 December 1101, ordered Gerard to make his profession to Anselm,[3] and that Gerard, in 1107, solemnly recognized that the profession which he had made as bishop of Hereford held good for his archbishopric of York.[4] He also consistently describes the archbishop of York

---

[1] Eadmer contradicts this, saying that the words objected to were 'metropolitan of all Britain', and that 'primate' was substituted to satisfy Thomas. [2] *Hist. Nov.* pp. 10, 210
[3] ibid. p. 216 [4] ibid. p. 187

as a suffragan of Canterbury in his records of consecrations.[1]
He asserts (and Hugh denies) that Anselm excommunicated
Thomas II, if he should fail to make his profession before
being consecrated.[2] He also quotes Anselm's letter to Paschal
II on Thomas's recalcitrant conduct and Paschal's carefully
guarded reply in his bull dated Benevento, 12 October 1108.[3]
He also identifies the bishop who testified to the profession of
Thomas I of submission to Anselm, as Samson, bishop of
Worcester, father of Thomas II.[4] His account of Thurstan
agrees in the main with Hugh's, though he asserts that Thurstan
promised Henry I not to be consecrated by the pope when he
attended the council of Rheims in 1119.[5] He also relates
cardinal Peter Pierleone's visit to Canterbury, and his inspec-
tion of copies of the privilegia said to have been destroyed in
the fire of 1067.[6] These were possibly the 'Lanfranc forgeries'
subsequently produced at Rome in 1123 and laughed out of
court,[7] which appear to have been prepared about 1120.
Eadmer also tells us that Thurstan was forbidden to perform
divine service outside his province when restored to his see in
1121.[8]

Eadmer's ill-starred promotion to St Andrews is part of
the story of the Scottish church, though it has its place in the
York and Canterbury dispute, since Thurstan, then in exile,
protested to Henry I against the consecration of Eadmer as
bishop of St Andrews by the archbishop of Canterbury,[9] thus
adding to Eadmer's natural bias against him. It is not clear

[1] e.g. *Hist. Nov.* pp. 74, 187   [2] ibid. p. 296
[3] ibid. pp. 201-2. The letter shows that the bishop of London was also
trying to obtain a *pallium*; which throws a sidelight on the Canterbury
claim that York and London were equally designed by St Gregory as
metropolitan sees subordinate to Canterbury.
[4] ibid. p. 208   [5] ibid. p. 255   [6] ibid. p. 296
[7] On this subject see H. Boehmer, *Die Fälschungen Erzbischof Lanfranks
von Canterbury* (Leipzig, 1902), and A. J. Macdonald, *Lanfranc* (Oxford,
1926), pp. 271-91. I am indebted to Mr R. W. Southern for allowing me
to see his paper on the subject later published in the *English Historical
Review*, lxxiii. 193-226 (1958). He agrees with Macdonald in exonerating
Lanfranc and placing the date of the forgeries about 1120.
[8] *Hist. Nov.* p. 291   [9] ibid. p. 283

what was the precise legal position of the archbishops of York as metropolitans of Scotland. Archbishop Ralph, writing to Calixtus II in 1119, claims that Aidan, the first bishop of Lindisfarne, was a bishop in the Scottish church before he came to Northumbria, and that Durham was therefore not a suffragan see of York,[1] but of Canterbury, in virtue of Augustine's supremacy over all British bishops. The bishop of Glasgow was also claimed by Canterbury for the same reason.[2] On the other hand Turgot, bishop of St Andrews, was consecrated at York in 1109 by Archbishop Thomas II, and Hugh names three bishops of Glasgow consecrated at York and three bishops of Orkney; but there is no evidence that bishops of other Scottish sees recognized York as their metropolitan see. Eadmer ascribes his nomination to St Andrews to the reluctance of King Alexander to acknowledge the jurisdiction of York.[3] The question arose again in 1126, when Thurstan, then at Rome, claimed John, bishop of Glasgow, as his suffragan, while a deputation of Scottish bishops, then also at Rome, were attempting to obtain the *pallium* for the bishop of St Andrews, and so make Scotland into a separate province. This was opposed by Thurstan on the ground that Scotland was feudally dependent on England, as its king did homage to the English king. Decision was accordingly deferred, in hopes of a compromise, and after an interview between King David and Henry I after Christmas, 1126, was allowed to drop. Scotland was not formally independent of York till near the end of the century.

[1] Raine, *Historians of the Church of York*, ii. 234
[2] ibid. ii. 241. The case against York is forcibly stated in a letter by Nicholas (probably Nicholas prior of Worcester) to Eadmer in 1120, advising him to obtain consecration from the pope. (Printed in Wharton's *Anglia Sacra*, ii. 234-6, from Corpus Christi College, Cambridge, MS. C.C.C.C. 371, p. 7)
[3] *Hist. Nov.* p. 282

B

LATIN TEXT
and
ENGLISH TRANSLATION

F.1 De adventu W[illelmi] ducis Normannie in Angliam, et succes-
sivo modo tam Cantuarienses quam Eboracenses archiepiscopos invicem consecrandi, et subieccione episcoporum
Scocie et Insularum debita ecclesie, et augmento pre-
bendarum in dignitate earum, et multiplici processu
domini Thurstani Eboracensis archiepiscopi et Cantua-
riensium episcoporum super quadam subieccione indebite
expetita et defensa potenter.[a]

CASUS [b] adversos et infortunia acerba que post devictam
a W[illelmo] Normannorum duce Angliam urbi Eborace
et ecclesie contigerunt, si quis omnia velit enarrare,
plena est dolore narracio et prolixa; verum ex hiis
aliqua perstringere ad id quod intendimus res admovet.

1069   Dux prefatus, Anglia debellata, in regem elevatus
est, et ab Aldredo, venerabili archiepiscopo Eboracen-
sium, consecratus et coronatus. Civitas autem Eboraca
et tota regio circa, quamquam regi datis obsidibus de
pace servanda, infidelis tamen exstitit et adversa, et
nequiter et violenter perniciosa; quapropter a Francigenis ferro, fame, flamma destructa est. Incensa
quoque et Beati Petri metropolis ecclesia et ornamenta
illius, carte et privilegia combusta vel perdita fuerunt.
Aldredus [c] archiepiscopus . . . defunctus est. Ipse quidem
de Wigornensi sede in metropolim Eboracam translatus,
quendam monachum suum, nomine Wlstan, ordinavit
episcopum, et duodecim villas sibi retinuit. Reliquas
vero W[lstano] episcopo, tanquam vicario suo, reliquit.

[a] Written in large red letters
[b] The 'C' is om., a space being left for an illuminated letter.
[c] An erasure, over which is written 'Aldredus'

HUGH THE CHANTOR

Of the coming to England of William, duke of Normandy.
How the archbishops of Canterbury and York used to
consecrate each other in turn. The subjection to York
of the bishops of Scotland and of the Isles. Prebends
raised to be dignities. The complicated suit between
Thurstan, archbishop of York, and the Canterbury
bishops about the subjection, claimed unduly by the
latter and powerfully resisted.

THE man who would relate all the unhappy accidents
and bitter misfortunes which befell the city and church
of York after the conquest of England by William, duke
of Normandy, would find his story both painful and
tedious. But my purpose in writing leads me to give
a brief account of some of them.

When the duke had conquered England, he became 1069
king, and was consecrated and crowned by Aldred, the
venerable archbishop of York. But the city of York
and the whole district round it, in spite of having given
hostages to the king for keeping the peace, was disloyal,
wickedly and violently hostile, and was on that account
destroyed by the French with the sword, famine, and
flames. The metropolitan church of St Peter was also
burned, and its ornaments, charters, and privileges
consumed or lost. Archbishop Aldred . . . died. He had
been translated from Worcester to the metropolitan
see of York, and appointed one of his monks [at Wor-
cester], Wulstan by name, to be bishop. He kept
twelve manors for himself, but left the others to bishop
Wulstan as his vicar.

Rex vero dedit archiepiscopatum cuidam capellano suo, clerico quidem eleganti et plurima sciencia pollenti, honesto et honestatis amico, Thome Baiocensis ecclesie thesaurario, cuius sciencie et honestatis, et elegancie preconium per omnes Galliarum provincias et longe ultra frequens resonabat.

Stigandus autem Cantuariensis archiepiscopus, qui et simul Wintoniensis episcopus et cenobiorum aliquot abbas erat, paulo post, propter hoc et alia sibi obiecta per legatos sedis Apostolice, rege volente, degradatus est.[1] Erat et ipse possessionum multarum dives plurimum, auri vero et argenti supra modum.[2] Que omnia remanencia [regi] eum copiose ditaverunt, et confirmatum est regnum in manu eius. Cantuariensem archiepiscopatum dedit rex cuidam seniori, nomine Lanfranco, sciencia et religione famoso, sub cuius magisterio de Gallie, Germanie, Italie finibus omnes fere didicerant, inter quos et prefatus Thomas, quicunque tunc temporis sciencie litterarum aliquantum nomen habebat. Hunc et ideo regi placuit ad quod potuit dignius promovere, quod eum primum abbatem fecerat in Cadomensi monasterio Sancti Stephani, quod ipse fundaverat. Tunc non potuit servari illa consuetudo a papa Honorio inter Cantuariensem et Eboracensem archiepiscopos instituta, ut altero decedente successor eius ab altero superstite vicissim consecraretur. Lanfrancus, licet posterius investitus, a suffraganeis suis prius consecratus est. Thomas ab eo consecrari requisivit. Ille vero renuit nisi subieccionis professionem ei faceret. Quod ille ex F.iv iure ecclesie sue se non debere / dicens, non consecratus dicessit, rem, sicut erat, regi denuncians. Rex primo moleste accipiens, remisit eum ad archiepiscopum

---

[1] Easter 1070. The legates were Ermenfrid, bishop of Sion and cardinals John and Peter.

[2] *Ipse* can hardly be the king, as Raine suggests. It seems more likely that a line has been dropped, and that Stigand's wealth enriched the king.

But the king gave the archbishopric to one of his chaplains, Thomas, treasurer of the church of Bayeux, a distinguished and very learned clerk, honourable and loving honour in others, renowned throughout the provinces of Gaul for his learning, honour, and distinction.

Now Stigand, archbishop of Canterbury who was also bishop of Winchester and abbot of more than one abbey, was soon afterwards degraded with the king's consent for that plurality and for other charges against him, by the papal delegates.[1]   He was also very rich, with great possessions, and had gold and silver beyond measure.[2]   All this left behind amply enriched the king, and the kingdom was established in his hands.

The king gave the archbishopric of Canterbury to an elderly man called Lanfranc, famous for his learning and piety, who had been the master of almost everyone in France, Germany, or Italy (including Thomas), who had then any considerable reputation as a man of letters.   The king had another reason for wishing to promote him as highly as he could, since he had made him the first abbot of his own foundation of St Stephen's, Caen.   It was impossible this time to observe the custom ordained by Pope Honorius for the archbishops of Canterbury and York, that when either of them died his successor should be consecrated by the other. Lanfranc, the later to be invested, was consecrated first by his own suffragans.   Thomas then applied to him for consecration, but he refused unless Thomas would make profession of subjection to him.   Thomas said that the rights of his church forbade him to do so, and departed without consecration, reporting the actual state of the case to the king.   William was annoyed at first, and sent him back to the archbishop with orders

cum mandato ut eum professione non exacta consecraret, set nec tunc quidem voluit. Venit igitur
ad regem. Interrogatus ab eo cur Eboracensem electum
non consecrasset, respondit Eboracensem ecclesiam Cantuariensi debere subici, et electum illius ordinandum
ordinatori suo profiteri : porro utile esse ad regni
integritatem et firmitatem conservandam, ut Britannia
tota uni quasi primati subderetur ; alioquin contingere
posse, vel suo vel successorum suorum tempore, ut de
Dacis, seu Norensibus, sive Scotis, qui Eboracam navigio
venientes regnum infestare solebant, unus ab Eboracensi archiepiscopo et a provincie illius indigenis mobi-
libus et perfidis rex crearetur, et sic regnum turbatum
scinderetur. Talis opinio de Lanfranco apud Norman-
nos habebatur quod quicquid astrueret non aliter
debere esse iudicaretur. Erat quidem ipse vir bonus
et sapiens, sed plus quam decebat monacum glorie et
dignitatis appetens. Persuasionibus illius rex novus
credulus, donis et pollicitacionibus plurimis distractus
est. Sicut quidam sapiens ait, 'plerumque regie vo-
luntates ut nunc mentes, sic sunt mobiles, sepe ipse
adverse sibi'.

Loquens igitur rex Eboracensi electo, primo precibus, blandiciis, promissis, efficere conatus est ut consecracionem suscipiens professionem faceret, propter regni
unitatem et pacem, sicut ei persuasum erat. Ille regi
respondit nec debere, nec canonicum esse, regno quidem nec honestum nec utile. Iratus itaque rex dixit
ei quod odium eius perpetuo haberet ; comminatus est
eciam quod nec quisquam de sui generis propinquis in
Anglia nec in Normannia remaneret, si non personaliter, saltem L[anfranco], profiteretur. Ut Scriptura

to consecrate him without insisting on the profession,
but Lanfranc still refused. He came to the king, who
asked him why he had not consecrated the archbishop-
elect of York. He replied that the church of York
ought to be subject to that of Canterbury, and its elect
awaiting ordination make his profession to his ordinary.
Moreover, that it was expedient for the union and
solidarity of the kingdom that all Britain should be
subject to one primate; it might otherwise happen, in
the king's time or that of one of his successors, that some
one of the Danes, Norwegians, or Scots, who used to
sail up to York in their attacks on the realm, might be
made king by the archbishop of York and the fickle and
treacherous Yorkshiremen, and the kingdom disturbed
and divided. Lanfranc's reputation with the Normans
was such that whatever he suggested was thought certain to be right. He was certainly a good and wise man,
but more eager for glory and honour than befitted a
monk. The king, inexperienced and impressionable, was
moved by his arguments, and by his many gifts and
promises. As a wise man says, 'The wills of kings, and
their minds too, are mostly changeable and often contra-
dictory'.

So the king spoke to the archbishop elect and began
to try, by prayers, coaxing, and promises, to induce him
to make his profession and be consecrated for the sake
of unity and peace as he himself had been advised.
Thomas replied that he ought not to do it; it was
neither canonically right, nor was it either honourable
or expedient for the kingdom. The king then lost his
temper and said he should hate him for ever; and
threatened that none of Thomas's near kinsmen should
stay in England or Normandy, unless he, at least, made
his profession personally to Lanfranc. As it is written,

dicit, 'sicut rugitus leonis, sic terror regis'.[1] Timuit
domini sui et regis clericus suus et familiaris odium
incurrere; pertimuit non tam suum quam suorum exilium. Multi vero dissuadentes ei prius et confortantes
[si] non faceret ipsi sibique modo timentes, quidam
vero assentatorie regi faventes consiliabantur, suade-
bant, instabant ut regie voluntati obsequeretur. Sic
ergo consilio deceptus, minis territus, invitus et dolens
tandem facere concessit. Multi audierunt eum postea
dicentem se nullatenus hoc concessisse si sine capcione
putasset Angliam exire.

Ventum est igitur Cantuariam ut consecraretur;
ubi cum iuxta morem examinacionis L[anfrancus] archiepiscopus Th[omam] electum consecrari paratum in-
terrogaret: 'Vis esse subiectus sancte Cantuarie ecclesie,
et michi et successoribus meis?', paulisper attendens,
flens, et suspirans sic respondit: 'Tibi subiectus ero,
quamdiu vixeris, successoribus tuis minime, nisi iudi-
cante summo pontifice'. Cumque rogaretur ut cartam
professionis a Cantuariensibus scriptam legeret, et archiepiscopo traderet, ille nec legit nec tradidit. Adhuc
supersunt aliqui qui hoc et viderunt et audierunt.

A primordio Christianitatis in Eboracensi urbe semper paritas dignitatis extiterat inter Cantuariensem et
Eboracensem ecclesias.

Nequam regis ecclesie retribucio. Illa enim in regem consecrando exaltavit; ipse eam subdendo humiliavit. Audistis immanem et superbam prelacionis et
elacionis ambicionem. Audite monachorum, si vere

---

[1] Prov. 20 : 2

'The fear of a king is as the roaring of a lion'.[1] The
king's clerk and household servant was afraid to arouse
the anger of his lord and master; though he was less
afraid of his own exile than of that of his kinsmen.
Moreover many who had at first advised him not to
give way and supported him, being now afraid both for
him and for themselves if he should not make his
profession—some of them by way of flattery to the king
—advised, persuaded, and pressed him to conform to
the king's will. Misled by bad advice and terrified by
threats, he at last sadly and unwillingly yielded. Many
people afterwards heard him say that he would never
have so given way if he had thought he could leave
England without being arrested.

He came to Canterbury to be consecrated. There,
as he was ready for consecration and Lanfranc questioned
him according to the customary form of examination,
'Wilt thou be subject to the holy church of Canterbury,
and to me and my successors?'; he paused a moment,
wept, and answered with a sigh 'I will be subject to
thee as long as thou livest, but not to thy successors,
unless the pope shall so judge'. And when he was asked
to read the charter of profession written by the Canterbury scribes and deliver it to the archbishop, he neither
read it nor delivered it. There are still some people
living who saw and heard this.

From the very beginning of Christianity in the city
of York, the churches of Canterbury and York had been
equal in dignity.

It was a shabby return for the king to make to the
church. It had exalted him by consecrating him as
king: he humiliated it by making it subject. So ends
the shocking story of the ambition of a proud prelate.
Now you shall hear the foul and deceitful sacrilege of

monachorum, turpem et dolosam possidendi impietatem,
F.2 iniuste et violenter assecutam subieccionem. Mo/nachi
Cantuarienses cartam scripserunt, et regis sigillo surrepcione et dolo acquisito sigillaverunt, causam scilicet
ventilatam esse inter duos archiepiscopos coram rege
et episcopis et primoribus Anglie, et ostensum et cognitum esse Eboracensem archiepiscopum Cantuariensi
debere cum iuramento professionem facere.[1] Set propter
amorem regis L[anfrancus] T[home] sacramentum remisit, non preiudicans successoribus suis. Quod quam
veri dissimile sit, quam ficticium,[a] ex hoc facile perpendi
potest, quod nec abbas episcopo suo, nec episcopus
metropolitano subieccionem iureiurando promittit, soli
summo pontifici, ex consuetudine Romane ecclesie
metropolite ; et qui palleis utuntur, quando ipsa sus-
cipiunt, obedienciam et fidelitatem iurant. Plurima
autem carte illius exempla miserunt in ecclesias et
monasteria ut in armariis conservarentur.

Contigit vero post aliquot annos[2] quod rege in
Normanniam transfretare parato, ambo archiepiscopi
usque ad Wectam insulam eum persecuti sunt. Ibi
dictum fuit regi cartam illam sic esse scriptam et sigil-
latam. Quod moleste accipiens, coram utroque archiepiscopo dixit per se factum non esse, et si T[homas]
archiepiscopus aliquid propter amorem et timorem regis
dispensative et personaliter vel temporaliter fecerat,
nolebat illud Eboracensi ecclesie preiudicium fieri. Ipsum vero T[homam] archiepiscopum blande deprecatus
est ut interim patienter ferret, et, si Deus illi redire
permitteret, inter duos archiepiscopos rem iuste et
canonice disponeret. Hoc plures audierunt, inter quos
et Rann[ulphus], qui nunc usque superest, Dunelmensis

---

[a] fictiti, MS

[1] 27 May 1072. See *Regesta Regum Anglonormannorum*, i, Nos. 64-5.
[2] In 1086

monks (if you can call them so) in holding to a submission obtained by injustice and violence. The monks
of Canterbury wrote a charter and sealed it with the
king's seal which they obtained by fraud, saying that the
case between the two archbishops had been tried before
the king and the bishops and principal men of England,
and that it was proved and admitted that the archbishop
of York was bound to make his profession by oath to
the archbishop of Canterbury [1]; but that Lanfranc, for
love of the king, remitted the oath to Thomas, without
prejudice to his own successors. How far from the truth
this is, how fabricated, may easily be judged from the
fact that neither does an abbot make his submission to
his bishop by oath, nor a bishop to his metropolitan,
but only to the supreme pontiff by the custom of the
metropolitan church of Rome; and archbishops, when
they receive the *pallium*, swear obedience and fealty.
But the monks sent several copies of this charter to
churches and monasteries to be preserved in their
archives.

   Now it happened some years later [2] that when the
king was ready to cross to Normandy, both archbishops
followed him to the Isle of Wight. And it was told the
king that that charter had been written and sealed. The
king took it amiss, and told both archbishops that it was
no charter of his; and if archbishop Thomas had made
any concessions on account of his love or fear of the
king by way of exception, personally and for a limited
time, he did not wish the church of York to be prejudiced
thereby. But he gently prayed archbishop Thomas to
have patience, and that if God should permit him to
return, he would adjust the question lawfully and
canonically between the two archbishops. Many persons
heard this, including Ranulf, who is still living as bishop

episcopus, tunc quidem capellanus et custos sigilli regis sub Mauricio cancellario, postea Londoniensi episcopo, et Gilbertus ᵃ Crispinus monachus L[anfranci] archiepiscopi, postea abbas Westmonasterii,¹ qui ambo coram multis edixerunt, et, si quis dubitaret, iurare parati cartam sic confirmatam fuisse, et regem, sicut predictum est, inde respondisse; et quod ipse rex Gilleberto Crispino, nobili genere monacho, preceperat, ut hoc testimonium Eboracensi ecclesie perhiberet, quicquid de ipso contingeret. Rex non multo post in Normannia obiit, cui successere ᵇ filii eius, Rodbertus in ducatu ᶜ Normannia, Willelmus in regno Anglie. Sed quod intendimus prosequamur.

Hec sic extorta professio ad aures Urbani summi pontificis ² pervenit. Quod graviter accipiens T[home] archiepiscopo litteras direxit, quarum exemplum hoc est.

Urbanus episcopus, servus servorum dei, dilecto in Christo filio, T[home] Eboracensi archiepiscopo, salutem et apostolicam benediccionem. Querelam non modicam habet adversum te mater tua, sancta Romana ecclesia; cum enim Beatus Gregorius, gentis Anglorum apostolus, dicat, scilicet ut inter Cantuariensem et Eboracensem archiepiscopos ille prior habeatur ᵈ qui prior [fuerit] ordinatus, tu [post] acceptum ab apostolica sede pallium, post iuratam, sicut mos est metropolitanis, fidelitatem, inconsulto Romano pontifice Cantuariensi [archi]episcopo tuam ecclesiam indebite ᵉ subdidisti, et cartam ei professionis contra decretum beati Gregorii fecisti, quod quam graviter ferre nos convenit prudenciam tuam latere non potest. Volumus igitur, et apostolica tibi auctoritate

---

ᵃ Gillus, MS   ᵇ successe in MS   ᶜ interventu, MS
ᵈ habebatur, MS. This is compared with another copy of this letter in the *Reg. Magnum Album* at York, part i. 41.
ᵉ Om. in *R.M.A.* i. 41

of Durham, and was then a chaplain and keeper of the king's seal under Maurice the chancellor, afterwards bishop of London, and also Gilbert Crispin, a monk of archbishop Lanfranc, afterwards abbot of Westminster.[1] Both these told many other people of it, and were prepared to swear, if any one doubted, that the charter had been thus [i.e. fraudulently] confirmed, and that the king had made answer as aforesaid. Also, that the king had ordered Gilbert Crispin, a nobly born monk, to bear this testimony to the church of York, whatever might happen to himself. Not long afterwards the king died in Normandy and was succeeded by his sons, in Normandy by Robert, by William in the kingdom of England. But let us continue our story.

Pope Urban II [2] came to hear of the profession thus extorted, was seriously disturbed, and sent a letter to archbishop Thomas in the following terms:

Urban, bishop, servant of the servants of God, to his beloved in Christ, Thomas, archbishop of York, greeting and the blessing of the Apostle. Thy mother, the holy Roman church hath a serious complaint against thee. Whereas the blessed Gregory, the apostle of the English, saith that of the archbishops of Canterbury and York he who was first ordained shall have precedence; thou, after having received the *pallium* from the apostolic see, and sworn fealty, as is the manner of metropolitan bishops, didst, without consulting the bishop of Rome, unduly submit thy church to the archbishop of Canterbury, and didst make a charter of profession to him, contrary to the decree of the blessed Gregory; our grievous displeasure at which cannot escape thy prudence. We will, therefore, and bid thee to appear before us by apostolic

---

[1] Ranulf died in 1128, and Gilbert in 1117.   [2] A.D. 1088–99

precipimus, quatinus nobis usque ad pascha domini presenciam tuam super hoc satisfacturus exhibeas, nisi forte legatorum nostrorum R. diaconi, filii nostri, cardinalis, et confratris nostri Hereberti The[t]-fordensis episcopi certa permissione[a] remaneas. Prefatos autem legatos nostros, quibus in Anglie regno commisimus vices nostras, vobis plurimum commen-

F.2v damus, et ut ope,[b] consilio, / et commendacione iuvetis rogamus.

Circa idem tempus L[anfrancus] archiepiscopus defunctus est, et vacavit sedes aliquot annis.[1] Ab antiquo extitit consuetudo inter duos metropolitanos Anglie, ut altero defuncto alter in provincia defuncti archiepiscopalia faceret, utpote episcopos consecrare, regem coronare, coronato die natalis Domini, pasche et pentecostes, missam majorem cantare. Hec interim fecit T[homas] archiepiscopus, nec quisquam episcoporum erat qui hoc in sua ipsius dyocesi archiepiscopo presente presumeret. Ordinavit etiam episcopos Herbertum Norwicensem, et Radulphum Cicestrensem, et Herveum Pangornensem.

Succedente tempore dedit rex Willelmus iunior archiepiscopatum Anselmo Beccensi[c] abbati, viro merito sanctitatis celebri. Quem cum ex decreto Honorii pape T[homas] archiepiscopus, pontificalibus vestimentis indutus, consecrare paratus esset, sicut mos est, scripta peticione et lecta ut archiepiscopus eum in primatem tocius Britannie consecraret, T[homas] discessit, vestiarium introivit, et se pontificalibus exuit. Erant cum archiepiscopo de Eboracensi ecclesia Hugo decanus, Rann[ulfus] thesaurarius, Durandus archidiaconus, Gill[ebertus] cantor, et aliqui ex canonicis. Exierunt statim post eum et qui consecrari debebat et Walchelinus Wint[oniensis] episcopus, et pedibus archi-

---

[a] From *R.M.A.* i. 41 ; provisione, MS   [b] ope] *R.M.A.* ; eos ipse, MS
           [c] Bescenti, MS

authority before Easter and satisfy us on this matter ; unless thou remain, by the permission of our legates, our son R., cardinal deacon, and our brother Herbert, bishop of Thetford. We commend to thee our afore-said legates, to whom we have committed our affairs in England, and ask thee to assist them with thy help, advice, and commendation.

About the same time archbishop Lanfranc died, and the see was vacant for some years.[1] It was the ancient custom of the archbishops, that if one of them died, the other exercised the archiepiscopal functions in his place : consecrating bishops, crowning the king, singing high mass before the king when he wore his crown at Christmas, Easter, and Whitsuntide. Thomas followed the custom ; nor was there any bishop who presumed to do any of these things in his own diocese when the archbishop was present. He ordained bishops Herbert of Norwich, Ralph of Chichester, and Hervey of Bangor.

In course of time the younger King William gave the archbishopric to Anselm, abbot of Bec, a man with a deserved reputation for sanctity. When archbishop Thomas, wearing his pontifical vestments, was ready to consecrate him in the usual manner, in accordance with the decree of Pope Honorius ; on a petition having been written and read that the archbishop should consecrate him primate of all Britain, Thomas withdrew, entered the vestry and put off his pontificals. With the archbishop there were from the church of York, Hugh the dean, Ranulf the treasurer, Durand the archdeacon, Gilbert the precentor and some of the canons. The candidate for consecration and Walkelin, bishop of Winchester, at once went out after him and kneeling at

[1] A.D. 1089–93

C

episcopi affusi humiliter deprecati sunt ne moleste
acciperet. Quibus archiepiscopus : 'Cum duo tantum
sint metropolite in Britannia, alter nisi super alterum
primas esse non potest. Si timore, vel amore, et vivendi
consilio personaliter et indebite alicui me subieci, liberatus sum. In primatem neminem consecrabo.' Et illi :
'Disponite', inquiunt, 'peticionem pro vestra voluntate,
nolumus nec in peticione nec in consecracione nisi que
pacis et caritatis, et que dei sint querere'. Hiis verbis
archiepiscopus placatus, pontificalibus se reinduens, ad
altare regressus est. Quod igitur scriptum erat 'in
primatem' minime lecto, et ex toto abraso, peticione
correpta, ut in metropolitam Cantuariensem consecraretur, assistentibus fere omnibus totius provincie coepiscopis, et abbatibus plurimis, et diversi ordinis
clericis et laicis, Anselmus a T[homa] archiepiscopo
solempniter, sicut tantum virum decebat, in metropolitam consecratus est. Quod in conspectu tot et tantarum personarum actum est, mendaciter scribere vel
nequiter negare, et apud homines turpe et apud Deum
criminosum est.

In crastinum T[homas] archiepiscopus Cantuaria
recessurus, loquens cum Anselmo archiepiscopo coram
episcopis qui ibi aderant, interdixit ei ex parte dei, et
sancti Petri, et domini pape, et societate quam invicem
habere debebant, ne Robertum Bloeth, Lincolniensis
ecclesie electum, Lincolniensem ordinaret episcopum.
Non prohibebat quin eum Dorracestrensem [a] ordinaret
episcopum, sicut et antecessores sui fuerant, verum
Lincolinum oppidum, et magnam partem provincie
Lindissi dicebat fuisse et iure esse debere parochiam
Eboracensis ecclesie, et iniuria illi ereptam esse cum
tribus villis, scilicet Stou, et Ludha, [et] Niuwerca, que
proprie fuerunt sáncti Petri Eboracensis, quod et ipse

---

[a] Corracestrensem, MS

his feet humbly besought him not to take it amiss. The archbishop replied, 'Since there are only two metropolitans in Britain, one of them cannot be primate except over the other. Though I personally and unfairly submitted, whether for love, for fear, or to save my life, I am now free. I will consecrate no man primate.' They said, 'Deal with the petition as you wish : we seek nothing in the petition, or consecration, but peace and charity and the things that are God's'. The archbishop was appeased by these words, resumed his pontificals, and returned to the altar. The word 'primate' was not read, and was completely erased from the petition, which was amended to a request that Anselm should be consecrated metropolitan of Canterbury ; and he was consecrated metropolitan by archbishop Thomas, in the presence of almost all the bishops of the province, several abbots, clerks of various orders and laymen, as it was fitting such a man should. A false report and a wicked denial of what was done in the sight of so many important persons is disgraceful in men's eyes and criminal in God's.

The next day, archbishop Thomas, talking with archbishop Anselm in the presence of the bishops who were there as he was about to leave Canterbury, forbade him in the name of God, of St Peter, and of our lord the pope, and by their own mutual fellowship, to ordain Robert Bloeth, elect of Lincoln, bishop of that see. He did not forbid him to ordain him bishop of Dorchester, as his predecessors had been ; but said that the town of Lincoln and a great part of Lindsey were and rightly should be the diocese of the church of York, and had been wrongfully taken from it, together with three towns, Stow, Louth, and Newark, which belonged to St Peter of York ; as he was prepared to prove if justice

diracionare paratus erat si ei rectitudo consentiretur.[1]
Ipsi vero electo hoc calumpniabatur, qui et hoc audiebat.
Venerat autem ad consecracionem archipresulis sui, et
paucis primo diebus ab ipso Lincolie ordinandus episcopus; set propter hanc calumniam ordinacio illius
diucius dilata est donec rex Willelmus quandam concordiam fecit inter illos, T[homa] quidem archiepiscopo invito, et renitente, et coacto, nec consenciente,
nec consulto Eboracensis ecclesie capitulo.   Hoc autem
F.3 Anglia tota novit / quod propter hanc concordiam
Robertus episcopus W[illelmo] regi ter mille libras
dedit.   Iam antea Remigio episcopo [2] T[homas] archiepiscopus hanc calumpniam fecerat.   Et cum Remigius
Lincolniensem ecclesiam dedicandam parasset, T[homas]
archiepiscopus interdixit ei ne eam dedicaret; quod
nequaquam dimittere volens, nocte precedente qua
eam dedicare in crastino speravit, infirmitate correptus
ex qua et paulo post vitam finivit, nec ipse eam, nec
successor eius Robertus, dedicavit.   Licet sit a proposito
digressio, hoc tamen de Lincolia inseruisse non incongruum visum est.

Ordinato Anselmo a T[homa] archiepiscopo, multa
fuit inter eos de primatu vel subieccione questio vel
contencio.

Post aliquot annos inter regem et archiepiscopum
[Cantuariensem] discordia orta est pro eo quod archiepiscopus investituras ecclesiarum per baculum et an-
nulum fieri prohibebat;   eas enim summi pontifices
Gregorius ultimus et Urbanus regibus et principibus
sub anathemate interdixerant, unde rex iratus compulit eum de regno exire.   Exulatus itaque Romam
venit, ubi [ab] Apostolico pie memorie Paschali,[3] et
cardinalibus, et ceteris Romanis benigne et honorifice pro

were granted him.[1]   He made this claim of the bishop elect, who was among the audience.   He had come to the consecration of his archbishop, and was to have been ordained bishop of Lincoln by him within the next few days ; but his ordination was put off on account of this claim until King William arranged a concord between them against the will of archbishop Thomas, who opposed it, and without consulting the chapter of York.   All England knows that bishop Robert gave King William £3,000 for this.   Archbishop Thomas had previously made the same claim against bishop Rémy.[2] And when Rémy had prepared the church of Lincoln for dedication, archbishop Thomas forbade him to dedicate it.   He refused to put it off, but on the night before the day on which he hoped to dedicate it, he was seized with a sickness of which he shortly afterwards died.   So neither he nor his successor Robert dedicated it.   Though this Lincoln story is a digression, I thought it not inappropriate to put it in.

After Anselm's ordination by archbishop Thomas, there was much dispute or contention between them as to primacy and submission.

Some years later a quarrel arose between the king and the archbishop of Canterbury, because the archbishop forbade investitures of churches to be made with a staff and a ring ; since Pope Gregory VII and Pope Urban had by anathema forbidden kings and princes to do so ; for which the king drove him into exile.   He therefore went to Rome, where he was received by the late Pope Paschal [3] and the cardinals and the other Romans with the kindness and honour due to his

---

[1] This dispute was settled by a charter of William II (*Monasticon*, viii. 1271).
[2] Ob. A.D. 1092
[3] Paschal II (1099–1118)

sanctitate sua et exilii sui causa susceptus, aliquamdiu conversatus est. In Gallias reversus, Lugduni, que prima sedes est Galliarum, apud Hugonem reverendum archiepiscopum diucius moram fecit. Religiosus incola religioso exuli omne studium humanitatis exhibuit. Similiter et canonici metropolis illius, quibus nec magis nobiles nec nobilius liberales Gallia habet.

Dumque ibi peregrinaretur, contigit regem W[illelmum] diro infortunio interemptum esse. Henricus vero, frater eius, qui erat cum eo in Anglia, successit ei in regno. Robertus comes Normannie, qui fuerat in sancto exercitu ad expugnandam Ierusalem, non multo post in Normanniam rediit. Qualiter inter fratres convenit, et satis notum est et nostra nichil interest.

Audito T[homas] archiepiscopus, qui tunc erat in Ripun, de morte regis, accelerans versus Lundoniam, obtunc audivit Henricum regem esse consecratum; quod egre ferens Lundoniam pervenit, inventoque ibi novo rege et episcopis, conquestus est iniuriam sibi factam de regis consecracione, quam ex iure ecclesie sibi competere certum erat, cum Cantuariensis archiepiscopus non adesset. Nec auditum habebat, nec ecclesiasticae consuetudinis erat regem nisi ab aliquo regni sui archiepiscopo consecrari debere. Quod nequaquam refellere valentes, rex et episcopi humiliter deprecati sunt eum ne gravius acciperet, dicentes festinatam esse consecracionem, ne prestolando eum qui de longe erat regnum fortasse turbaretur. Quibus verbis placatus est. Erat enim satis mansueti animi, et morbo et senio tunc plurimum debilitatus. Lundonie postea concilio convocato, archiepiscopus, et episcopi, principes et proceres, et alii, factis regi hominiis, et fidelitatibus iuratis, regnum ei assecuraverunt. Archiepiscopus, a rege licencia accepta, domum regreditur, nec deinceps sese viderunt.

sanctity and his exile, and stayed there some time. He returned to Gaul and made a long stay at Lyons, the principal see of that land, with archbishop Hugh. The native churchman treated his exiled brother with zealous humanity. So did the canons, than whom there are none more noble or more nobly generous in all Gaul.

While Anselm was thus abroad, King William died by an unfortunate accident. His brother Henry, who was with him in England, succeeded him as king. Robert, count of Normandy, who had been on the crusade to capture Jerusalem, soon afterwards returned to Normandy. The terms on which they agreed are well enough known, and are not our concern.

When archbishop Thomas, who was then in Ripon, heard of the king's death, he hastened to London, and only then heard that King Henry had been consecrated. Indignant at this he reached London, and finding the new king and the bishops there, complained of the wrong done to him by the king's consecration, which was lawfully his province, since the archbishop of Canterbury was absent. He had never heard, nor was it the custom of the church, that the king should be consecrated except by one of the archbishops of his realm. The king and the bishops could not dispute this, but humbly begged him not to be unduly offended; saying that the consecration had been hastened for fear that the kingdom might be disturbed while they awaited his coming from a distance. This satisfied the archbishop, who was a mild man, and much weakened by illness and age. At a council afterwards summoned to London, the archbishop, bishops, princes, nobles and others did homage, swore fealty, and confirmed the king in his realm. The archbishop took leave of the king and went home, and the two never saw each other again.

De archiepiscopo breviter recapitulare volo. Quando archiepiscopatum suscepit,[a] cuncta hostili vastacione depopulata et vastata invenit; de septem canonicis, (non enim plures fuerant), tres in civitate et ecclesia combusta et destructa reperit. Reliqui vel mortui, vel metu et desolacione erant exulati. Ecclesie vero recooperte, et iuxta facultatem suam restructe, canonicos quos invenerat restituit; dispersos revocavit ad deo serviendum et ecclesie; aliquos addidit; refectorium refecit, et dormitorium; prepositum constituit qui ceteris preesset, et eos procuraret; villas aliquas et terras et ecclesias dedit, et ab aliis ablatas reddidit; plurima de suo proprio canonicis necessaria administrabat; archidiaconos quoque sapientes et industrios

F.3v per diocesim / divisit. Ipse vero dono regis aliquamdiu xii. villas habuit, quas Aldredum predecessorem suum de Wigornensi episcopatu sibi retinuisse supradiximus; set eas, molimine et instinctu Lanfranci archiepiscopi, idem rex ei abstulit.

Annis pluribus canonicis communiter sic vescentibus, consilio quorundam placuit archiepiscopo de terra sancti Petri, que multum adhuc vasta erat, singulis prebendas partiri; ita enim et canonicorum numerus crescere posset, et quisque,sicut per se, partem suam studiosius et edificaret et excoleret. Quod et sic factum est. Tunc enim statuit decanum, thesaurarium, cantorem, dans cuique digne, et ecclesie, et suo, et personarum honore : magistrum scolarum iam antea statuerat. Ecclesiam, que nunc est, fundavit et fecit, et eam pro posse suo clericis, libris, ornamentis ornavit, et munivit, nec tam cuiuslibet rei quam [b] bonos et honestos clericos habendi cupidus fuit.

Vixit autem in archiepiscopatu annis ferme xxx.,

[a] In margin : *Nota de Cambustione ecclesie* (?)   [b] quod, MS

To sum up the archbishop's history: when he received the archbishopric, he found everything deserted and waste; of the seven canons (there were no more), he found three in the burnt city and ruined church. The rest were dead, or driven away by fear and misery. He reroofed and to the best of his ability rebuilt the church to which he restored the canons whom he had found there; he recalled the fugitives to the service of God and the Church and added to their number; he rebuilt the refectory and dormitory. He appointed a provost to preside over the others and to manage their affairs; he gave manors, lands, and churches himself and restored those which others had taken away. He bestowed much of his own property on the canons; he assigned wise and diligent men to be archdeacons in the diocese. He had of the king's gift the twelve manors in the diocese of Worcester, which, as I said, his predecessor Aldred kept; but at the instance and on the advice of archbishop Lanfranc, the king took them away from him.

The canons had long lived in common, but the archbishop, after taking advice, determined to divide some of the lands of St Peter's which were still waste into separate prebends, to leave room for a growing number of canons, and each of them might be eager to build on and cultivate his own share for his own sake. This was done. He then appointed a dean, treasurer, and precentor, endowing each of them as befitted the church, himself, and their individual dignities. He had already established a master of the schools [i.e. a chancellor]. He founded and built the present church and adorned and furnished it to the best of his power with clerks, books and ornaments: above all else he desired to have good and reputable clerks.

He was archbishop for nearly thirty years. No other

quo nec alter episcopus tempore suo persona decencior,
nec magnis et minimis magis ^a unanimiter dilectus, quia
nec magis liberalis nec minus austerus,^b neque quibuslibet in seriis et iocis honestis magis consentaneus; postremo, in omnibus fere et amabilis, et laudabilis, et reverendus. Henrico rege nonas Augusti consecrato, et non
multo post Anselmo archiepiscopo mandato regis ab
exilio revocato, T[homas] archiepiscopus, xiiii. kalendas
proximi Decembris, die Dominica, m.c. anno, Eboraci
obiit. Cuius epitaphium est hoc.

Orba pio, viduata bono pastore, patrono,
    Urbs Eboraca dolet vix habitura parem.
Qualia vix uni persona, sciencia, vita
    Contigerit ^c T[home] nobilis, alta, bona.
Canities, hilaris facies, statura venusta,
    Angelici vultus splendor et instar erat.
Hic numero atque modo doctrine seu probitatis
    Clericus omnis erat, vel magis omnis homo.
Hec domus et clerus sub tanto presule felix,
    Pene quod est et habet muneris omne sui est.
Octavis Sancti Martini transiit ille,
    Cui pietate dei sit comes in requie !

Girardus

Sede usque ad proximam Epiphaniam vacante, translatus est in eam Girardus Herefordensis episcopus, qui
fuerat W[illelmi] primi, secundi, regum cancellarius;
clericus quidem sciencia et eloquencia tempore suo nulli
aut paucis secundus, et qui Virgilio in metro et Tullio in
prosa parum cessisset.

Monachi Cantuarienses, non bene cantantes Ebor.,
quia ab illa indebita professione liber erat, archiepiscopum suum instigaverunt et impulerunt, ut ^d a Giraudo
professionem exigeret. Eorum impulsu fortiter exegit,

bishop in his time had more personal dignity, or was more generally popular with great and small. For none was more generous or less severe, nor more agreeable in any company whether on serious business or in clean fun. In almost all matters he was lovable, praiseworthy, and reverend. After Henry had been consecrated on 5 August, and Anselm recalled from exile by the king's command, on Sunday 18 November 1100, archbishop Thomas died at York. This is his epitaph:

> A tender shepherd and a master dear
> > York widowed mourns, nor hopes to find his peer.
> Thomas was handsome, learned, good as well:
> > Seldom to one man such rich virtues fell.
> White-haired and merry, full of manly grace,
> > He shared the splendour of an angel's face.
> Such learning, with such honesty combined,
> > A perfect clerk—or rather, man—defined.
> This house of clergy, happy 'neath his sway,
> > Owes to him all it is, or has today.
> Saint Martin's octave was the day he died:
> > God grant him rest by good Saint Martin's side.

GERARD

The see remained vacant till Twelfth Day [1101], when Gerard, bishop of Hereford, was translated to it. He had been chancellor to kings William I and II, and was a clerk second to none, or few, in his time for learning and eloquence. He almost rivalled Virgil in poetry and Cicero in prose.

The monks of Canterbury, who could not well chant the praise of York, because it was free from the profession [of submission] which it did not owe, aroused their own archbishop and urged him to press for the profession. On their motion he earnestly demanded it,

et litteras suas ad dominum papam, quas ipse petebat,
pro sua dimissione, et translacione, et pallei requisicione tradere diu negavit, nisi prius professionem faceret, aut Roma reversum se professurum promitteret.
Verum Girardus, sapiens et disertus,[a] dicens hoc inhonestum esse, et non canonicum hac districcione professionem [b] vel promittere, tandem litteras illius accepit,
pollicens se reversum quicquid iuste debebat ei facturum.   Et scimus quia non exhibuit.

Ad requirendum palleum Romam profectus, aliquot
dies ibi moratus est, ubi in pluribus causarum accionibus sciencia et facundia eius laudata et approbata, a
reverendo papa Pascali et a tota curia honoratus est
et magnifice laudatus.   Abierant cum eo duo episcopi,
quos rex propter negocium suum miserat, cum quibus
et ipse reversus est.   Accepit ab apostolica sede palleum et privilegium quod subscriptum est.

Postea placuit Anselmo et Girardo archiepiscopis
F.4 concilium / celebrare.   Quo in Westmonasterio con-
gregato,[1] cum monachi archiepiscopo suo sedem singu-
lariter celsam parassent, Girardus indignatus, et dei
odium ei qui sic paraverat vulgariter orans, pede sub-
vertit, nec sedere voluit, donec sibi cum archiepiscopo
sede pari parata, liquido volens ostendere, ei nullam
subieccionem debere.

Sicut fecerat A[nselmus] archiepiscopus Willelmo
regi, sic fecit et regi Henrico, investituras prohibendo,
nec quenquam episcopum vel abbatem manu regia
investitum consecrare vel benedicere solebat.   Set licet
rex moderacius agens, odium patens in eum non exercuit,
non eum postmodum sincere dilexit.   Propter interdictum et anathema Romane ecclesie rex tandem in-

---

[a] desertus, MS　　　　　　　　　[b] promissionem, MS

[1] 29 September 1102

and for a long time refused to hand over his own letters
to the pope, which Gerard required for his release and
translation, and for his request for the *pallium,* unless
Gerard should first make his profession or promise to
make it on his return from Rome. But Gerard, wise as
well as learned, said that it was dishonourable and against
canon law even to promise profession under such
pressure, and so at last obtained Anselm's letter, promising to do whatever he was justly bound to do on his
return. And we know that he made no such profession.

He went to Rome to claim his *pallium* and stayed
some days there, winning praise and approval for his
knowledge and eloquence in several cases on trial. He
was honoured and highly praised by Pope Paschal and
the whole *curia.* Two bishops accompanied him, whom
the king had sent on his own business, and he returned
with them. He received from the pope his *pallium* and
the bull of privilege written below.

Archbishops Anselm and Gerard afterwards decided
to hold a council. When this assembled at Westminster,[1]
and the monks had prepared a seat higher than any of
the others for their archbishop, Gerard felt himself
insulted, and openly cursing the man who had done
this, kicked over the seat, and would not sit down until
his seat was made as high as the other archbishop's ;
plainly showing that he owed him no subjection.

Archbishop Anselm treated King Henry as he had
King William by forbidding investitures ; nor would he
consecrate any bishop nor bless any abbot who had
received investiture at the king's hand. But although
Henry was more moderate, and did not show open
hatred of him, he never sincerely loved him afterwards.
He did at length give up the investitures because of the
prohibition and anathema of the Roman church ; a con-

vestituras dimisit, dimissione quidem qua nichil aut
parum amisit, parum quidem regie dignitatis, nichil
prorsus potestatis quem vellet intronizandi. Credo
equidem de investituris sane sensisse venerabilem Ivo-
nem Carnotensem episcopum, quo nec alter in Gallis
tempore suo melius in divinis eruditus et exercitatus,
nec fide et doctrina magis catholicus extitit. Dicebat
parum interesse qualiter investiture fierent, sive virga,
sive anulo, sive manu, sive mica, seu quocunque modo,
dum canonica eleccio et libera consecracio ecclesiis
servarentur, nec quicquam Symoniace contagionis inesse,
cum neque dans neque accipiens intelligat sacramentum
vel rem sacramenti dare vel accipere, set villas, predia,
redditus que de munificencia regum et principum ecclesiis collata ᵃ sunt. Set, si fas est dici, adhuc habet
ecclesia decimantes mentam et anetum, et colantes
culicem, et deglutientes camelum, de manuali investi-
tura tumultuantes, de eleccione et consecracionis libertate nichil mutientes. Quibus si licet ᵇ misceri sacra
prophanis ludibrio potest dici illud Persii,¹

> Egroti veteris meditantes sompnia, gigni
> De nichilo nichil, in nichilum nil posse reverti.

Girardus archiepiscopus ecclesiam de Laxtona ecclesie nostre in prebendam dari a rege optinuit, et vi.
ecclesiarum, quas de villis suis rex ei dedit, Driffeld,
Chillum, Pochelintonam, Pichering, Broch, Sned, quinque Sancto Petro; sextam vero, Sneid ᶜ scilicet, dedit
Sancto Germano Salebi.²

Vixit G[irardus] in archiepiscopatu annis vii. et
mensibus fere quinque, et obiit xii. kalendas ᵈ Iunii.

ᵃ collate, MS   ᵇ scilicet, MS
         ᶜ Sneid vero, MS   ᵈ die, MS

cession which cost him little or nothing, a little, perhaps, of his royal dignity, but nothing of his power to enthrone anyone he pleased. I think the sound view on investitures was that of Ivo, bishop of Chartres, who was unsurpassed in all Gaul for his theory and practice in divinity and in catholicity of faith and doctrine. He said that it mattered little how investiture was given, by a staff, a ring, the hand, a loaf, or in any way, so long as the church retained canonical election and free consecration, and no simony was involved, because both the giver and the receiver of the investiture understood that what was given and received was not a sacrament or anything sacramental, but manors, farms, and rents conferred on the church by the generosity of kings and princes. But the church, if we may be permitted to say so, has men in it who tithe mint and anise and strain out the gnat and swallow the camel; who rage against investiture by [lay] hands, and are mum about election and free consecration. Indeed, if we may profane such a sacred matter with a jest, we may say with Persius : [1]

> Pondering the dreams of an old sick man's thought,
> 'Of nought nought comes, and nought returns to nought'.

Archbishop Gerard obtained from the king the gift of the church of Laughton-en-le-Morthen as a prebend. The king also gave him six churches from his manors: Driffield, Kilham, Pocklington, Pickering, Aldborough, and Snaith; the first five for St Peter [of York]; but he gave the sixth, Snaith, to St German of Selby.[2]

Gerard lived seven years and almost five months as archbishop, and died on 21 May [1108].

---

[1] *Sat.* iii. 83-4.
[2] See W. Farrer, *Early Yorkshire Charters*, i, Nos. 426-8.

[THOMAS SECUNDUS]

Septima die successit ei T[homas] regis capellanus, [ecclesie] Sancti Iohannis Beverlacensis prepositus, nepos T[home] reverendi senioris, cui rex eadem die Lundoniensem episcopatum, vel in proximo, daturus, requisicione decani Hugonis et quorundam de nostris, qui tunc erant ad curiam, consilium mutavit, et ei Eboracensem ecclesiam tradidit.

Multorum desideriis dies ille desideratus advenit, quando in metropolitem metropolis nostra illum suscepit, quibus si antea elegisse licuisset, Thome Thomas, patruo nepos, quasi iure hereditario proxime success[iss]et. Erat enim apud nos sub patruo suo, amabili et amicabili educatus, et decenter eruditus, moribus et conversacione gratus, ipseque archiepiscopus factus pro consanguinitate et nominis similitudine, et aliqua morum consuetudine patruum suum nobis in se ex parte reddidisse visus est. Licet morte L[anfranci] archiepiscopi T[homas] ab illa indebita, et personali, et violenter extorta professione liberatus esset; quod verbo, actu ostendit, Anselmum archiepiscopum in primatem, sicut petebatur, consecrare renuens, licet postea professio illa a Girardo fuisset exacta, set iuste denegata. Monachi tamen Cantuarienses, quod iniustum affectare et impudenter petere non desistunt, set vigilando cogitantes, dormiendo computantes, de perdita professione dolore F.4*v* tabescunt, neque quibus / modis eam reparent, dummodo optineant, quicquam attendunt. T[homa] igitur in archiepiscopum electo, monachi suo archiepiscopo suggerunt, monent, incitant quatinus modo de restituendo ecclesie sue quod perdiderat cogitet, et viriliter laboret, electum nostrum consecrari Cantuariam vocet, set illum nullatenus nisi facta professione consecret.

[THOMAS II]

Six days later he was succeeded by Thomas, the king's chaplain, provost of St John's, Beverley, a nephew of Thomas I. The king had intended to give him the bishopric of London that very day or the next. But at the request of Hugh the dean and some others of our people who were then at court, he changed his mind and gave him the church of York.

Many had been longing for the day in which our mother-city received as its metropolitan the man Thomas, who would have succeeded his uncle Thomas, almost by right of inheritance, if they had had the power to elect him any sooner. For he had been brought up among us under his beloved and friendly uncle, well educated, and agreeable both in morals and manners. As archbishop, his kinship, his same Christian name, and a certain likeness of character seemed in a way to have brought his uncle back again. Though Thomas had been released by Lanfranc's death from that undue, personal, and extorted profession, as he showed in word and deed when he refused to consecrate Anselm primate; the profession, however, had been demanded from Gerard and justly refused. Yet the monks of Canterbury do not cease to aim at and shamelessly demand what is unjust; they think on it while awake and dream of it in their sleep, and pine away for grief; nor do they mind by what means they recover it, as long as they succeed. So when Thomas was chosen archbishop, the monks hint to their own archbishop, advise, and urge him now to take thought how to restore to his church what it has lost. Let him be a man, let him call our archbishop elect to Canterbury to be consecrated, and refuse to consecrate him till he has made his profession.

D

Huius rei ius et iniuria electo nostro non erat ignota.
Et nos illi ad nos misso et gratanter recepto interdicentes
ne professionem faceret, consilium dedimus, ut regem
consulens voluntatem eius sentiret. Tunc ipse dixit se
iturum ad curiam ; necesse habebat loqui regi. Cumque
iam dimidium itineris peregisset, venit ad eum qui ex
nostra parte litteras istas detulit.

Dilecto patri et diligendo domino, T[home] dei
gracia Eboracensis ecclesie electo archiepiscopo, capitulum eiusdem ecclesie eleganter semper agere, et ad
id quod ᵃ possunt servicia et oracionum suffragia. Ad
curiam vadis domino regi colloquuturus. Dixisti enim
nobis. Si vero ut ad presens consecreris, istud minime,
nec consiliatus es nobiscum. Scimus quod in consecracione professio a te exigetur. Vide quid agas,
ut quidam sapiens ait, consilium velox penitentia
sequitur. Subieccio nostre ecclesie Cantuariensi insti-
tucioni prime Christianitatis huius regni non con-
cordat ; quem prioratum beatus Gregorius inter
alterutram precepit, tute nosti. Quod autem dominum nostrum T[homam] archiepiscopum Lanfranco
fecisse pretendunt, ecclesie nostre preiudicare non
debet ; iuvenis erat, deceptus fuit, gravatus fuit,
invitus fecit, coactus fecit, et id quidem absque con-
sensu et consilio ecclesie sue, nec tamen legit, set
tantum legere consensit, et id quidem mestus nimium
et lacrimans. Propter hanc qualemcunque professionem quod ab apostolico Urbano vocatus fuerit,
ipse scis, et ipsas litteras habens. Anselmo in Cantuariensem archiepiscopum recepto, cum T[homas]
archiepiscopus ante altare paratus esset ut eum con-

ᵃ qua, MS

The archbishop elect knew the rights and wrongs of the case. And we, when he had been sent to us and thankfully received, forbade him to make the profession, and advised him to consult the king and hear his pleasure in the matter. He then said he must go to court; he must speak to the king. And when he was half-way there, there came to him a man and brought him the following letter from us:

To our beloved father and dear lord, Thomas by the grace of God archbishop elect of York, from the chapter of that church, a successful life, and their best service and prayers. You are going to court, you told us, to speak with the king; but if this is with a view to your immediate consecration, you have not asked for any advice from us. We know that a profession will be asked from you at the consecration. Take heed to what you are doing; as is wisely said, 'Hasty decisions are soon regretted'. The subjection of our church to that of Canterbury is contrary to the original institution of Christianity in this realm: as you know, St Gregory ordained that the primacy should be shared. Our church should not be prejudiced by the submission which they [i.e. the monks of Canterbury] assert that our lord, archbishop Thomas made to Lanfranc. He was young, he was cheated, he was under pressure, he did it unwillingly, under compulsion; and he did it without the consent and advice of his church. He did not read; he only consented to do so, and that with great sorrow and tears. You know that he was summoned [to Rome] by Pope Urban because of this alleged profession, and you have the letters.

When Anselm was received as archbishop of Canterbury, and Thomas was before the altar ready

secraret antistitem, peticione facta ab episcopis Anglie
[ut in primatem tocius] [a] Britannie ordinaretur, sur-
rexit et di[s]cessit a choro, ac vestiarium ingrediens
se divestivit.   Set Anselmus archiepiscopus secutus
est eum cum Walchelino episcopo, et prostratus pedibus eius deprecatus est eum ne [b] moleste acciperet
quod audierat, huiusmodi peticionem per se nec
scriptam nec lectam asserens, tanquam venia postu-
lata rogavit eum humiliter ut rediret.   Redeunte
T[homa] archiepiscopo, et peticione correpta ut in
Cantuariensem archiepiscopum ordinaretur, ordinatus est.   Hoc audierunt et viderunt decanus noster,
et cantor, et alii de nostris.   Denique decanus, quando
fuit Rome cum Girardo archiepiscopo, sicut ipse
testatur, a cancellario Romane ecclesie diligenter
perscrutatus est de contencione harum ecclesiarum,
quid inde Roma sentiret, et quid in decretis sanctissimus haberet, at ille dixit, Roma[m] nec aliud sentire,
nec habere quam quod in registro beati Gregorii
scriptum est.

Respice ad Girardum archiepiscopum ! hoc probe,
hoc viriliter, hoc egit egregie !   Londonie in concilio
sedere noluit [eo] quod Anselmo archiepiscopo altior
sedes data erat, donec et illi eque digna parata est
sedes.

Diximus que tacere non debuimus ; tu vero age
quod te et ecclesiam a deo tibi commissam non dedeceat, et Roma iure arguere non possit.   Respectum
capere, vel longum vel eciam modicum, ad providen-
dum multum adiuvare potest.   Optimam partem
consilii det tibi deus eligere et sequi !

His in itinere lectis, ad regem perveniens, humiliter

---

[a] The words in brackets are inserted from p. 7, to make sense.
[b] moleste eum ne, MS

to consecrate him bishop, and the English bishops petitioned him that Anselm should be ordained primate of all Britain; he rose and left the choir, entered the vestry, and disrobed. But Anselm, with Walkelin, bishop of Winchester, followed him, and lying prostrate at his feet, begged him not to take amiss what he had listened to, saying that he had neither written nor read the petition, and begging pardon, humbly asked him to come back. When Thomas came back and the petition had been amended to a request that he should be ordained archbishop of Canterbury, he was ordained. Our dean, precentor, and others of us heard and saw this. Finally, the dean, when he was in Rome with archbishop Gerard, as he himself witnesses, diligently inquired of the chancellor of the Roman church about the contention between the two churches, what Rome thought of it, and what decisions his Holiness had about it. And the chancellor said that there was no opinion in Rome, nor had he any decisions, differing from what is written in the Register of St Gregory.

Look at archbishop Gerard! How honest, how manly, how excellent were his actions! He refused to sit in the council at London because archbishop Anselm had been given a higher seat than himself, until a seat of equal dignity was made ready for him.

It was our duty not to keep back what we have told you. Do you act worthily of yourself and the church committed by God to your charge, and so that Rome can have no complaint against you. Looking back, far or only a short way, is a great help to looking forward. God grant that you may choose and follow the best advice!

After reading this letter during his journey, he came

F.5 deprecatus, super / hac re eum consuluit. Consultus
rex benigne respondit, et parti nostre favere promisit,
et ne profiteretur prohibuit. Gavisi sumus valde. Ex
alia parte Cantuarienses regem sollicitabant, ut, sicut
pater suus fecerat, electum nostrum Cantuariam venire
faceret consecrari, et subieccionem profiteri. Bonum
regem, boni regis filium, bona facta patris sequi debere.
Rex non acquievit illis, set bene et caute stetit pro
nobis, utrum vere pro nobis, an propter hoc quod non
bene Anselmum archiepiscopum amabat quia investituras prohibuerat, tunc quidem incertum, postmodum evidens fuit, nisi forte rex propter aliud animum
suum mutavit. Plures vero quorum consilio rex plurimum utebatur dicebant ei non esse sanum consilium ut
altero alteri archiepiscopo professo totum regnum uni
subiceretur. Venit ergo H[erbertus] Norwicensis episcopus ad electum nostrum, dicens quod archiepiscopus
professionem dimitteret, [si] tantum in primatem eum
recognosceret; set noluit, de rege bene confidens.

Circa idem tempus ¹ rex in Normanniam transivit.
Exspectato aliquamdiu T[homa] electo ut veniret consecrari, et non veniente, Anselmus archiepiscopus misit
quendam clericum cum litteris quibus moram consecracionis sue redarguit, ostendens electum episcopum
ultra xl. dies non consecratum esse non debere. Man-
dabat ergo, diem statuens illi, ut Cantuariam veniret,
facere et suscipere quod debebat. Ille, causas aliquas
dilacionis pretendens, placide respondit se Cantuariam
venire quam cicius posset opportune. Auditis litteris et
responso, iteravimus interdictum ne profiteretur consecracionem accipiendo. Nec multo post tempore

---

¹ July 1108

to the king and humbly asked his advice. The king, after considering, gave him a kind answer, promised to favour our side, and forbade Thomas to make the profession, to our great joy. On the other hand, the Canterbury party besought the king to do as his father had done, and to make our archbishop elect come to Canterbury to be consecrated and make his profession. A good king, they said, the son of a good king, ought to follow his father in doing good. The king did not agree, but stood out firmly and carefully for us. But whether he was really on our side, or only because he disliked archbishop Anselm for having forbidden investitures, was then uncertain, but clear afterwards, unless the king changed his mind for any other reason. However, many of the king's usual counsellors told him it was not a good plan that one archbishop should make his profession to the other, and the whole realm be subject to one. So Herbert bishop of Norwich came to our archbishop elect, saying that the archbishop would waive his profession, if he would merely recognize him as primate; but he refused, having full confidence in the king.

About this time[1] the king crossed to Normandy. Anselm waited for some time for Thomas to come and be consecrated, and as he did not come, sent a clerk to him with a letter, in which he complained of his delay, and set forth that an elect ought not to remain unconsecrated more than forty days. He therefore ordered him to come to Canterbury to do and receive what was due, fixing a day. Thomas made some excuses for his delay, and coolly answered that he was coming to Canterbury as soon as he conveniently could. When we heard the letter and his answer, we repeated our prohibition of his making his profession on receiving consecration. And not long afterwards our archbishop

electus noster misit ad archiepiscopum dominum Ste-
phanum ¹ monachum suum cum litteris subscriptis.

    Dilecto domino et reverendo patri, A[nselmo] dei
gracia Cantuariensis archiepiscopo ecclesie, T[homas],
Eboracensis ecclesie electus archiepiscopus, licet indignus, salutem, et quecumque potest servicia. Ad vos,
venerande pater, venire disposueram, paratis iuxta facultatem meam ad iter et ad alia facienda necessariis ;
licencia vero accepta a capitulo nostre ecclesie, et
summonitis quibusdam quos mecum venire idoneum
visum erat, dixerunt se nuper perpendisse ª ex litteris,
quas benignitas vestra michi miserat, et ex aliis que
audierant, quod Cantuariensis ecclesia subieccionem
nostre requirebat, atque ideo se nolle ᵇ venire. Con-
tradixerunt autem michi ex parte dei et sancti Petri, et
ex auctoritate sancte Romane ecclesie, ne ecclesiam
michi commissam Cantuariensi indebite subicerem.
Septima vero die post dicessum meum ab illis per
unum ex archidiaconis ecclesie contradictum istud
iteraverunt. Nec id eis [satis] visum est, set litteris
suis hoc ipsum acriter interdicentibus usque ad Wire-
cestriam me persecuti sunt, asserentes se michi nullam
obedienciam exhibere, ne[c] debere, et [apud] apostolicam sedem me accusare, si subieccionem hanc facere
presumpsero. Hinc igitur et inde me coartant an-
gustie. Turpe quidem est ad consecracionem venire,
et non consecratum redire. Consecracionem autem
suscipere, et contra appellacionem Romane ecclesie,
quibus episcopus si non habere (*sic*) ᶜ presertim cum ᵈ
sacri canones dica[n]t, 'nullus invitus ordinetur episcopus', inhonestum est et formidabile.² Vestre vero

---

ª semper pendisse, MS   ᵇ velle, MS
   ᶜ A hopelessly corrupt passage, some words having been omitted. The
sense suggested is that he would not willingly be a bishop against the wishes
of his church.   ᵈ est, MS

   ¹ Presumably Stephen, first abbot of St Mary's, York (1082–1112)

elect sent his monk Dom Stephen [1] with the following letter :

To our dear lord and reverend father, Anselm, by God's grace archbishop of the church of Canterbury, Thomas, archbishop elect (though unworthy) of the church of York, greeting and all the service in his power. I had arranged to come to you, reverend father, and had made the necessary preparations for my journey and for other business. But on taking leave of the chapter of my church and summoning those whom I had thought fit to take with me, they said that from the letters which you kindly sent me and from what they had heard besides, they had lately thought that the church of Canterbury was demanding the subjection of our church, and for that reason they wished not to come. They forbade me, in the name of God and St Peter, and by the authority of the holy Roman church, improperly to subject the church committed to me to that of Canterbury. On the seventh day after my leaving them, they repeated their prohibition through one of the church's archdeacons; nor did they think this enough, but pursued me to Worcester with letters severely prohibiting this course, saying that they neither rendered nor owed me obedience and must accuse me before the apostolic see if I took upon me to make this submission. I am thus hemmed in on both sides. It is disgraceful to come to be consecrated and return unconsecrated. But to accept consecration and (in the face of an appeal to the Roman church) to have no-one to whom he is a bishop, (especially as the sacred canons say, 'Let no-one be ordained bishop against his will'), is dishonourable and dreadful.[2] Yet I fear to

[2] The Latin text is obscure, but this seems a possible conjecture.

dileccionis dulcedinem exacerbare timeo, si venire ad
vos longius differo. Propterea, serenissime domine,
inicio super vos consilium meum, ex quo maxime
pendet spes mea post deum. Beatitudinis autem et
sciencie vestre consilium omnipotenti presto est, et
benignum, et efficax. Circa personam meam sancti-

F.5v   tati vestre quantumcunque postularetis / subicere,
grande michi videtur dignitatis insigne. Optimam
partem consilii det michi deus, et bonitas vestra,
eligere et sequi !

Paucis in medium diebus, misimus et nos H[ugonem]
archidiaconem (*sic*) cum litteris infrascriptis.

Sciencia et sanctitate venerando seniori A[nselmo]
Cantuariensi archiepiscopo, capitulum Eboracensis
ecclesie, ab eo salvari, 'qui salvos facit rectos corde'.¹
Quod noster electus consecracionem suam tamdiu
distulit, cause fuerunt et alie, et quas nobis mandavit
pace vestra liceat nobis loqui. Vos mandastis illi, et
summonuisti eum nimis aspere, ut nobis ᵃ visum est,
utᵇ termino a vobis prefixo veniret ad vos facere et
suscipere quod debebat. Quid a deo sanctarum
manuum vestrarum imposicione suscipere debeat,
scimus. Quid vero facere debeat, id nescimus. Set
fortasse dicitis, aut monachi vestri, professionem.
Confidimus de sanctitate vestra vos in nullo negocio
nisi que dei sunt querere. Et certe concedimus et
volumus ut archiepiscopus noster sanctitati vestre
cedendo, assurgendo, inclinando, reverenciam et obedienciam exhibeat. Ecclesiam autem nostram vestre
subicere contra decreta illius agit qui eas fidei funda-
mento fundavit, et in eis archiepiscopos ordinavit, et
sua cuique privilegia dedit. Alia vero ab aliis apos-
tolicis de eadem re decreta ecclesia nostra habet :
Romane sedis instituciones qui rescindunt, contra

ᵃ vobis, MS   ᵇ et, MS

exasperate your good temper, if I defer coming to
you any longer.   For this reason I cast the burden of
advising me upon your serenity, in whom, after God,
is my chief hope.   Your blessed and learned counsel is
with the Almighty, kind and helpful.   I am proud to
make you any personal submission you may require.
May God, and your goodness, grant that I may choose
and follow the best of your advice.

A few days later, we also sent H[ugh] the archdeacon
with the following letter :

To the venerable, learned, and holy elder, Anselm,
archbishop of Canterbury, the chapter of the church
of York, salvation from Him 'who preserveth them
that are true of heart'.[1]   Among the reasons why our
archbishop elect has so long deferred his consecration
are some which he ordered us, with your permission,
to tell you.   You ordered him, and summoned him,
as we think rather roughly, to come to you, by a date
which you fixed, to do and receive what he should.
We know what he should receive from God by the imposition of your sacred hands : but we do not know
what he should do.   Perhaps you or your monks say,
'Make his profession'.   We are sure that your holiness seeks nothing in any matter but the things that
are God's.   And we certainly grant and will that our
archbishop show his reverence of, and obedience to
your holiness by giving way, rising, and bowing.   But
to subject our church to yours is to act contrary to the
decrees of him who established them on the foundation of the faith, ordained archbishops in them, and
gave their privileges to each.   Our church has other
decrees of subsequent popes on the same point ; and
to contravene the institutions of the Roman see is a

[1] Psalm 7 : 11

sacros canones agunt. Propterea omnes una voce indiximus electo nostro ne faciat subieccionem in recipiendo consecracionem. Nec de nobis quilibet ad hec secum veniret, nisi ut contradiceret; nec reverenti quisquam ei obviam procederet; nec ut archiepiscopo obediret. Viro sapienti et religioso in multis utile est sui iuris esse, suo ipsius uti consilio. Consiliarii autem quidam, et clerici et monachi, querunt preesse quam prodesse, tendentes et tendere instigantes ad prelacionem propter elacionem. Certo scimus nos nichil per contencionem, nec per elacionem, aut per inanem gloriam facere, set omnia in nomine domini, et recte pro bono. Dominus custodiat vos ab omni malo! Custodiat animam vestram dominus!

Mirari satis nequeo tam sancte opinionis virum si[c] obstinate petere quod nec sancti patres scriptum reliquerunt, nec ecclesiastica consuetudo tenet, cum et ipse, ut credo, bene meminerit qualiter T[homas] primus eum consecrando egerit.

Item misit archiepiscopus ad electum duos episcopos, Ricardum Londoniensem, et Radulphum Roffensem, ut quod littere et episcopi viva voce facerent, summonentes quatinus die ab illis statuta esset Cantuarie facere quod debebat et suscipere.

'Consecrando quam consecraturo [a] maior incumbit confeccionis festinacio. Et credo quod graviter illi a deo imputatur, cuius iniusta exaccione vel superba refragacione diucius retardatur. Veniam gaudenter consecrari, si vos, episcopi, michi dixeritis quod non exigar subieccionem profiteri; alioquin non audeo, pro-

[a] consecratura, MS

breach of canon law. For these reasons we have unanimously forbidden our elect to make submission when he receives consecration. Neither would any of us come with him for this except to object to it; nor would any come to meet him on his return, nor obey him as archbishop. In many matters it is profitable for a wise and pious man to be independent, and make his own decisions. But some counsellors, clerks as well as monks, seek precedence more than profit, aiming and urging others to aim at preferment for the eminence it gives. We are quite sure that we are not acting out of rivalry, ambition, or vainglory, but in the Lord's name and in a just cause. The Lord keep you from all evil! The Lord preserve your soul!

I cannot wonder enough that a man with such a reputation for sanctity should so obstinately pursue a thing for which the fathers have left no written authority, and which is not the custom of the church; since he must, I suppose, well have remembered how Thomas the first behaved at his consecration.

The archbishop also sent two bishops to the archbishop elect, Richard, of London, and Ralph, of Rochester, so that the bishops should convey the effect of the letter by word of mouth, summoning him to be at Canterbury on the day named in the letter to do and receive what he should. [Thomas replied:]

'A candidate for consecration has more reason to make haste than the consecrator. And I believe that God demands a heavy reckoning from the man by whose unjust claim or proud opposition consecration is too long deferred. I will gladly come to be consecrated, if you bishops can assure me that I shall not be required to profess subjection. Otherwise I dare not, against the

hibentibus illis quibus preesse debeo, ex parte Romane ecclesie, et paratis defendere loco opportuno et tempore Eboracensem ecclesiam quod exigitur Cantuariensi non debere.'

Persuasorie loquebantur episcopi ne turbaret regnum, ne divideret ecclesiam. Non erat melior quam patruus suus. Et ille : 'Cum sit utraque ecclesia unius regni et unius corone, non est ecclesiam dividere, suum cuique ius velle retinere. Culpa est homini cuius iniuria turbacio venit. Et patruus meus quid et quomodo Lanf[ranco] fecerit, bene audivi : quod vero Anselmo archiepiscopo egerit, melius novi. Iam tunc eram cum eo. Si quid sponte vel invitus perperam fecisset, nichil ab eo heredi/tate possideo.'

F.6

Litteris utrinque missis et remissis, nunciis utriusque euntibus et redeuntibus, aliquantum temporis processerat, cum tandem rex de Normannia litteras suas ad archiepiscopum misit, mandans amicabiliter ut ab hac summonicione et professionis exaccione desisteret, donec ipse in Angliam rediret. Tunc quidem, deo auxiliante, illi controversie finem hastivum [a] imponeret. Ita electi nostri consecracio diucius induciata est. Interea ille, litteris a capitulo de eleccione sua acceptis, propter contencionem hanc monstrandam, et palleum requirendum Roman pergeret.[1]

Favonius nobis prospere flabat, quia rex noster iusticie nostre bene favebat. Dedit ergo rex domino decano litteras suas, [quas] ipse petebat, ad dominum papam pro electo nostro commendaticias, excusatorias, deprecatorias, quod viro bene litterato, casto, et religioso, et canonice, archiepiscopatum concesserat, set quibusdam causis obstantibus, absque magna difficultate,

[a] hostium, MS

prohibition of those of whom I ought to be head, made in the name of the Roman church, and by men who are ready to prove at a fit time and place, that the church of York owes no such subjection to Canterbury.'

The bishops tried to persuade him not to disturb the realm or divide the church. He was no better, [they said] than his uncle. But he replied, 'Since both churches belong to one realm and one crown, there is no division of the church in each choosing to retain its own rights. The blame lies on the man by whose wrongdoing the disturbance arose. I know by hearsay what my uncle did to Lanfranc, and how; what he did to archbishop Anselm, I know even better, for I was with him at the time. Whatever wrong he wilfully or unwillingly did, is not my inheritance.'

Time went on. Letters were sent and returned on both sides: envoys came and went. At last the king sent a letter from Normandy to the archbishop, bidding him, in a friendly way, to give up the summons and demand for profession till he himself should return to England. Then, by God's help, he would put a speedy end to the dispute. Thus the consecration of our archbishop elect was again respited. Meanwhile, he obtained letters from the chapter as to his election, [and sent the dean] to Rome [1] to report the dispute and to ask for the *pallium*. We had a favouring wind, since the king supported the justice of our cause. So the king gave the dean the letter to the pope which he requested, commending, excusing and apologizing for our archbishop elect; saying that he had granted the archbishopric to a learned, chaste, and devout man in accordance with canon law, but that for various reasons, [the elect] could not come to Rome without great difficulty. He

---

[1] There seems to be a lacuna in the MS. as the sentence has no principal verb on which the subjunctive *pergeret* should depend.

[eum] Romam venire non posse. Quapropter paternitati sue supplicabat, ut quemlibet a latere suo virum,
iustum et discretum, in Angliam mitteret, qui electo
archiepiscopo palleum deferret, et causam inter duos
metropolitanos canonice decideret. Summus pontifex,
filii sui regis precibus annuens, contencionis causa plene
cognita, dominum Olricum, presbyterum-cardinalem,
ortu Remensem, clericum bonum et prudentem, cum
decano misit cum palleo et litteris de contencionis
diffinicione, sicut visum fuerat domino pape et curie
Romane.

Antequam in Normaniam venisset, Anselmus archiepiscopus a seculo migraverat.[1] Cardinalis secum
adduxerat quendam monachum, nomine Gaufridum,
Dunonensis monasterii priorem, clericum bonum et
sapientem. Venientes autem rex benigne suscepit, et
diebus aliquot ibi moratos misit eos in Angliam precedere eum, paulo post secuturum. Fecerunt[a] ita,
neque rex post eos diu moratus est. De causa nostra
adhuc bonam spem dabat.

Nos quidem iam audieramus quod defuncto A[nselmo] archiepiscopo regis animus mutatus erat et magis
tepide parti nostre favebat. O imprudens prelacionis ambicio! O iniqua falsitatis excogitacio! Cogitaverunt[b]
quidam et que nequiter confi[n]xerunt, et 'iniquitatem in
excelso locuti sunt',[2] quod A[nselmus] archiepiscopus, in
infirmitate qua vitam finivit, T[homam] Eboracensem
electum excommunicaverat, et omnes ei communicantes,
nisi Cantuarie professionem faceret.[3] Quod si, maligno
consilio seductus, graviter excedens fecisset, occultasse
debuerant. Sin autem, quod verius est, nec unquam in

---

[a] This sentence, which is repeated two or three lines later, after the
word 'favebat', seems properly to come here.
[b] Castigaverunt, MS

[1] 21 April 1109   [2] Psalm 72 : 8 (Vulgate)

accordingly besought the holy Father to send to England
a just and discreet legate *a latere* to bring the *pallium* to
the archbishop elect, and to decide the cause between
the two metropolitans by canon law. The pope, granting
the prayer of his royal son, and having fully realized the
cause of the dispute, sent with the dean the cardinal-
priest Ulric, a native of Rheims, a good and prudent
clerk, with the *pallium* and with letters about the settle-
ment of the dispute, as seemed good to the pope and the
Roman court.

Before Ulric reached Normandy, archbishop Anselm
had departed this life.[1] The cardinal had brought with
him a monk named Geoffrey, prior of Dunois, a good
and wise clerk. The king received them graciously
when they came, and after they had stayed a few days,
sent them before him on to England, intending to follow
shortly. They did as they were bid, and the king did
not stay much longer. He still gave good hope of our
cause.

Now we had already heard that since the death of
Anselm the king had changed his mind and was cooling
in his zeal on our behalf. How foolish is the ambition
to be first! How wicked it is to devise a falsehood!
'They have devised' a malignant falsehood, and 'spoken
iniquity on high'[2] [saying] that archbishop Anselm in
his last illness, had excommunicated Thomas archbishop elect of York and all communicating with him,
unless he made his profession at Canterbury.[3] If he did
so, misled by evil counsel, it was an outrage, and they
ought to have concealed it. But if, which is nearer the
truth, he never meant to do anything of the kind, to

[3] The letter to Thomas, of which copies are said to have been sent to
all the bishops, is printed in Eadmer, *Hist. Nov.* p. 118.

E

cor eius ascendit, patri suo sacerdoti tantum crimen
imposuisse apud homines, ignominia est apud deum.

Rege in Angliam regresso, multi de Cantuariensibus
obviam illi veniunt, magna offerentes, maiora pollicentes, obnixe precantes ne Cantuariensis ecclesie dignitatem imminui pateretur; quibus rex ad proximam
Pentecosten exspectare precepit.

In Pentecoste ad curiam congregati sunt electus
noster, episcopi, et abbates, principes et proceres, clerici
et monachi, et multi alii. Cardinalis quoque mandato
regis ibi venerat prima die et secunda Pentecostes. Rex
electo nostro et quibuslibet de nostris loquebatur, bene
promittebat. Deinde conveniunt ad regem episcopi et
abbates, et monachi Cantuarienses, multa offerentes, /
F.6v plura quam facile quis credere velit promittentes, archiepiscopatum quoque, quamdiu vellet, in propria manu
tenere sine querela eorum concedentes, ut Cantuariensem ecclesiam stare faceret sicut pater eius reliquerat.

Coartatus rex aliquantum : 'Nescio,' inquit, 'quomodo id facere possim, cum electo archiepiscopo et
omnibus Eboracensibus bene semper promiserim non
eos cogere, nec a iusticia declinare, set saltem utrique
ecclesie ex equo me habere. Vos autem s[c]itis quod
dominus papa propter huius cause descisionem, me
mandante, legatum suum ᵃ legaverit. Qui si causam
hanc suppressam viderit, forsitan me in corde suo de
fraude vel levitate redarguet, et se delusum reputabit.'
'Bene,' inquiunt, 'domine, potestis facere, nec erit
inhonestum nec difficile, quoniam quod pater vester,
rex bonus et sapiens, in regno suo stabilivit, et carta et
sigillo suo firmavit, stabile et firmum servare debetis,
nec Cantuariensem ecclesiam in discrepacionem trahere,
unde sub regibus, patre vestro et fratre, investita fuit.

ᵃ suum] After this in the MS come the words 'datum longe', which are
inexplicable and no doubt corrupt.

have published such a charge against their father in God amongst men, is disgraceful in God's eyes.

When the king returned to England, many of the Canterbury clergy came to meet him, making great offers, and greater promises, urgently beseeching him not to suffer the dignity of the church of Canterbury to be impaired. The king told them to wait till Whitsun.

At Whitsuntide there assembled at court our archbishop elect, bishops and abbots, princes and lords, clerks and monks, and many others. The cardinal also had come there at the king's command on the first two days of Whitsun. The king talked to our elect and to some of us; he promised well. Then came to the king the bishops and abbots, and the monks of Canterbury, making great offers, and promising more than anyone could easily believe; even granting that he might keep the archbishopric in his own hands as long as he liked without any complaint from them, if only he would let the church of Canterbury stay as his father had left it.

The king was somewhat embarrassed. 'I do not know how I can do that', he said, 'since I have always promised the archbishop elect and all those of York not to force them, nor to act unjustly, but at all events to be impartial to both churches. But you know that our lord the pope has sent his legate at my request to decide this case. If he sees this cause quashed, he will perhaps in his heart charge me with deceit or fickleness, and consider himself cheated.' 'Well, my lord,' they said, 'you can do it: it will neither be dishonourable nor difficult; since what the king your father, a good and wise king, established in his realm, and confirmed by his charter and seal, you ought to keep stable and firm; and not to divest the church of Canterbury of the rights with which it was endowed by two kings, your father

Et carta quidem presto est. Quando vobis placebit, in medium proferetur. Legato dicetis rem diligencius perscrutatam et melius conditam aliter esse quam putaveratis, neque, ut speramus, voluntati vestre contraire conabitur. Postremo Anselmus archiepiscopus noster, in infirmitate qua defunctus est, nobis prohibendo mandavit, ne Eboracensi electo communicaremus nisi Cantuariensi ecclesie profiteretur; cui, ac si superstes esset, in hoc volumus obedire.'

Hiis itaque suggestionibus, persuasionibus, instigacionibus, magis autem muneribus magnis, et pollicitacionibus maioribus et multimodis, rege distracto, ex occasione carte et communicacionis prohibicione, Favonius noster in[a] procellosum Aquilonem conversus est. Cartam vero illam rex antea multum improbaverat, de surrepcione eius veritate per nos accepta. In crastino mandavit rex electo nostro per episcopos et per comitem de Mellent, primo blandiens, demulcens, deprecans ut ab episcopis consecracionem suscipiens ecclesie Cantuariensi professionem faceret, sine preiudicio ecclesie sue et successoribus suis, propter amorem suum et pacem regni, et propter illam, sive prohibicionem, sive excommunicacionem, quam Anselmus archiepiscopus fecisse dicebatur.

Mirati sumus vehementer de tam subita et inopina mutacione. Hesterno enim bene promiserat. Audito regis mandato misit electus ad eum S[tephanum], venerabilem Eboracensis monasterii abbatem, mandans, supplicans, obsecrans, ut dominum regem suum, quatinus, sicut promiserat et inceperat, sic staret, dicens de professione illa in presencia eius et legati in causam velle venire, et iudicium canonicum subire. Aliter profiteri nec velle nec debere, nec ipse rex et patronus

---

[a] MS repeats 'noster in'.

and brother. We have the charter to support us. When-
ever you please it shall be produced. You may tell the
legate that on more careful examination and better
reflection, the case is not as you had thought; and we
may hope that he will not try to oppose you. Last of
all, archbishop Anselm, in his last illness, forbade us to
communicate with the elect of York unless he should
make his profession; and on this point, we will obey
him as if he were still living.'

These suggestions, arguments, and pressure, or rather
the great gifts and even greater promises of all kinds
which accompanied them, so shook the king, that by
occasion of the charter and the excommunication, our
favouring breeze was turned into a stormy tempest. The
king had previously scouted the charter, when he had
heard from us the truth about its repudiation. The
next day the king sent orders to our elect by the bishops
and the count of Meulan, beginning with flattery, coaxing, and apology, that he should accept consecration by
the bishops, and make his profession to the church of
Canterbury, without prejudice to his own church or to
his successors, for love of the king, for the peace of the
realm, and on account of the prohibition or excommunication, which archbishop Anselm was said to have
made.

We were astonished at such a sudden and unexpected
change. For yesterday, the king had made fair promises.
On hearing the king's orders, the archbishop elect sent
to him Stephen, abbot of York, to bid, beseech, and
adjure his lord the king to stand by his promises and go
on as he had begun; saying that he wished to proceed
to trial before the king and the legate and be judged
by canon law. He neither wished nor was bound to
make his profession on any other terms, nor ought the

ecclesie sue debeat eum cogere. Istud vero interdictum,
seu anathema, Anselmum archiepiscopum fecisse ficticium erat, et magis tacendum quam eloquendum.
Quod si verum, nemini nocivum, quia irracionabiliter
factum. 'De carta illa patris vestri vere scimus quod
sine consciencia et assensu regis et T[home] archiepiscopi facta fuit. Et si placet dignitati vestre, inquirat
a Rann[ulfo] Dunelmensi episcopo, et a Gilberto Westmonasterii abbate (ibi tunc erat curia), et firmiter
precipiat, et adiuret ut veritatem inde dicant. Sciunt
enim bene; et iste tunc temporis Lanfranci archiepis-
F.7 copi monachus et familiaris erat; et ille / sigillum patris
vestri sub Mauricio cancellario custodiebat.' Ad quod
rex indignanter respondit non esse homines istos quibus
de hoc credi deberet, preter sibi iniuncta. Abbas et alia
addidit, quantum ausus est, et illi visum est oportere.

Paulatim fautores regi dicebant quod [non] esset
bonus heres si patris statuta destitui sineret. Et
quidam de episcopis,[1] turpiter assentator, se vidisse
testatus est quod nec ipse, nec alius, nec simile huic
usquam viderat; scilicet quod quando T[homas] Anselmum consecravit, consecrato professionem fecit; de
quo magis ridendum est quam respondendum estimo.
Set tantum regi dictum est a nobis quod quicunque hoc
dixerat, in caput suum mentitus fuerat. Misit iterum
rex ad nos qui dicerent quod de statutis patris sui in
disceptacionem non veniret, neque quenquam duceret,
set si [a] professionem faceret, amorem eius haberet; si
non, in finem perderet, et ipsum et omnes sibi genere
propinquos de tota terra sua exterminaret. Ac si de

[a] per *ins.* MS

king, the patron of his church, to compel him. It was a
lie, that Anselm had made that interdict or anathema;
and one that it was better to suppress than to publish.
And if it were true, the curse could hurt nobody,
because it was unreasonable. 'As to that charter of
your father's, we know that it was made without the
knowledge and consent of the king and of archbishop
Thomas. May it please your majesty to inquire of
Ranulf, bishop of Durham, and of Gilbert, abbot of Westminster (where the court then was), and firmly order
and adjure them to speak the truth. For they know
well: the latter being at the time one of archbishop
Lanfranc's monks and a member of his household, while
the former kept your father's seal under Maurice, the
chancellor.' To which the king indignantly replied that
these were not credible witnesses to this, beyond orders
to themselves. The abbot added as much as he dared
and thought necessary.

Step by step, the king's flatterers told him that he
would not be a good heir if he suffered his father's
statutes to be repealed. And one of the bishops,[1] with
disgusting subservience, bore witness to having seen what
(or the like of which) neither he nor anyone else had
ever seen; namely that when Thomas consecrated
Anselm, he made his profession: a story deserving
laughter rather than refutation. But all that we said to
the king was, that whoever had said that lied in his
teeth. The king again sent messengers to us to say that
he would not discuss his father's statutes nor produce
any witness; but that if [Thomas] would make his
profession he should have the king's love; if not, [the
king] would eventually ruin him, and banish him and
all his kinsmen from all his lands. Just as though the

---

[1] Samson, bishop of Worcester, Thomas's father (Eadmer, *Hist. Nov.* 208)

industria rex cogitasset, sicut pater fecit patruo, filius
faciet nepoti. Inducie ad hoc respondendi [a] usque
mane indulte sunt.

Nobis visum est nobis decere consilium cardinali[s]
requirere. Missi sunt ad eum duo ex nobis, set quasi
furtim; et dixerunt ei: 'Si noster electus ad beatum
Petrum vel ad dominum papam pertingere posset,
pedibus eorum provolutus, consilium et auxilium et
misericordiam precaretur; quia vero non potest,[b] quod
per se non audet propter regem, et nos quidem latenter
venimus, vos, qui vices apostolicas hic habetis, per nos,
vestris, tanquam beati Petri vel domini pape, pedibus
prostratus suppliciter et lacrimabiliter requirit. Rex
subito et inopinate transversus est. Hesterno sperabamus eundem habere, hodie perdidimus. Sic et sic
mandavit, talibus et talibus minarum tonitribus exterret.
Ipse vero nichil ignorabat. Excellenciam vestram consilium postulat quod Romanam ecclesiam suam non
dedeceat. Et scitote quod (nec) amore nec timore
quominus, nec in quo modo, nec alterius consilio vestrum
derelinquet.'

Tunc paululum meditatus, satis humiliter et religiose
respondit. 'Ego', inquit, 'modo debeo missam cantare,
ubi spiritum sanctum invocabo quatinus michi dignetur
inspirare quale melius et honestius consilium possim
dare. Ite modo, et cras revertimini.'

Nimirum de bono homine bene promittere bona
spes haberi solet. In crastinum revertentibus, nulla
usus ambage, locutus est. 'Ego quidem non veni
consilium dare, set contencionem unam inter duas
ecclesias precepto domini pape definire. Que si in
causam veniret, facerem propter quod missus sum.
Deus det vobis bonum consilium.' Cepit quoque narrare
suas comminaciones illi factas, de separacione eciam

[a] quas *ins*. MS. The MS also reads 'inducias'.
[b] MS repeats 'quia . . . potest'.

king had deliberately thought 'As the father did to the uncle, so shall the son do to the nephew'. We were granted respite till next morning for our reply.

We thought the proper course was to ask the cardinal's advice. Two of us were sent, almost by stealth, and said to him, 'If our archbishop elect could make his way to St Peter, or to our lord the pope, he would prostrate himself at their feet and implore their counsel, help, and mercy. But because he cannot come in person, for fear of the king (and even we have come secretly) he, through us, humbly and with tears, casts himself at your feet, as representing St Peter and the pope, with the same request. The king has suddenly and unexpectedly changed sides. We hoped yesterday to find him as he had been; today we have lost him. He gave such and such orders: he terrifies us with such and such thunderous threats. But he was not misinformed. [The archbishop elect] asks your Excellency for counsel worthy of your own Roman church. And you may be sure that neither for love or for fear of what may or may not happen, nor on any other man's advice will he depart from yours.'

The cardinal thought for a moment, and answered humbly and piously, 'I must now', he said, 'sing a mass in which I shall call upon the Holy Ghost to inspire me to give the best and most honourable counsel I can. Go now, and return tomorrow.'

There is usually good hope that a good man makes a good promise. We returned on the morrow, and he spoke plainly. 'I did not come to give advice, but by the pope's orders to settle a dispute between two churches. If the case should come into court, I should fulfil my mission. God give you good counsel.' He then began to tell of the threats which had been made to him of the

huius regni ab ecclesia Romana, si litteras domini pape
quas attulerat ostenderet, si in hoc regi contradiceret.
'Et scio', inquid, 'modo, sive in Anglia quando deo placebit egressurus,ᵃ habeo mecum fratrem et nepotes,
quibus, etsi non modo, contumeliam et iniuriam inferri
timeo, si regi contradixero.' [1]

Imputabat decano nostro quod sepius inquirenti ab
eo de voluntate regis Eboracensem electum benevolenciam eius habere dicebat, quod nunc in contrarium
relapsum erat.   Et tamen ex litteris quas rex misit
domino pape, et ipse cardinalis vidit, perpendere potuit
decanum nichil aliud quam quod credebat dixisse.
F.7v Quicquid legatus dicebat Prior Dunonensis attes/ta-
batur.   Hiis aliis fortasse legato ligamentis ligato, nichil
consilii ab eo elicere potuerunt; nichil electo nostro
reportaverunt.

Quid ergo faceret?   Quo se verteret? in angustiis
erat.   Consilium defecerat a quo speravit habere et
debebat.   Qui cum illo prius erant amodo adversus
illum.   Cum torrente omnes currebant; nullus obluc-
tabatur.   Sampson Wigornensis episcopus, et Ricardus
Baiocensis, pater et frater illius, hic fratrem, ille filium
carnaliter amantes, et regem timentes, illum archiepiscopatu ᵇ carere nolebant, regem exasperare non aude-
bant; sicque movendo, consulendo ut regis voluntatem
faceret, quasi vim inferebant.   De parentela eius aliquanti probi viri, qui illic aderant nobis, qui cum eo [ex]
ecclesia nostra, tres aut quatuor, et tristes et timidi,
aderamus, improperabant modicum curare si archiepiscopatum perderet.   Mutabantur, quibus equidem, dum
possessiones retinerent, professus aut liber tantidem ᶜ

ᵃ A corrupt passage. It should perhaps read 'modo in Anglia, sive . . .
egressurus'.
    ᵇ archiepiscopo, MS   ᶜ tandem, MS
    [1] The text is uncertain ; but this seems to be the sense.

separation of this realm from the Roman church if he should show the letters he had brought from the pope, or if he opposed the king. 'And I know', said he, 'that now in England, or when I quit it, as it pleases God, I have my brother and nephews, who may, I fear, be subjected to contempt and wrong, though not now, if I oppose the king.' [1]

He blamed the dean for having told him, in answer to his frequent inquiries as to what the king wished, that the archbishop elect of York was in favour, of which the opposite was now the case. And yet, from the letter which the king sent to the pope, which the cardinal saw, he might have reflected that the dean had said nothing but what he believed to be true. Whatever the legate said, the prior of Dunois confirmed. There may have been other bonds which tied the legate's hands; and our envoys could get no advice from him, and brought no message back to our archbishop elect.

What was he to do? Whither to turn? He was cornered. The counsel he had hoped for and should have had failed him. Those who had been with him were now against him. Everyone went with the stream : no one resisted it. Samson, bishop of Worcester, and Richard, bishop of Bayeux, his father and brother, from their natural affection to a brother and a son, and for fear of the king, were unwilling that he should lose the archbishopric, and dared not enrage the king. So by urging and advising him to do what the king wished, they practically forced him to comply. Some respectable kinsmen of his, who were present, reproached the three or four of us, sad and frightened, who were with him from the church, with not caring much if he lost his archbishopric. All those were changing sides, to whom it was the same whether he professed or remained

erat. A rege quoque nobis tanquam maiestatis reis mine contumeliarum et exilii nunciabantur, ideo quod dolere vel minimum obloqui videbamur. Temptavit et Dunelmensis episcopus ex sua parte si posset regis animum pecunia revocare, pollicens ei mille marcas argenti et centum regine pro eo ut iusticiam et iudicium canonicum Eboracensi ecclesie consentiret. Set non audivit rex bene callidus quid inter pondus et pondus numerum et numerum distaret.[1]

Sic ergo angariatus et districtus, mestus et gemens, nobis nec concedentibus nec contradicentibus, demencia enim esset, tandem facere consensit quod, ut verum estimo, nullatenus fecisset si exilii, et fatigacionis, et ceterarum incommoditatum corpus paciens haberet; set corpulentus erat, et pinguior quam oporteret. Proxima die dominica[2] a Lundonensi episcopo et coepiscopis in ecclesia beati Pauli consecratus est, professione facta nova et barbara, personali, set nulli persone (quis enim Cantuariensis futurus esset archiepiscopus soli deo notum erat), salva obediencia et fidelitate domini pape et regis Anglie, et salvo iure Eboracensis ecclesie professio determinata est, que non habuit exemplum, nec puto habituram exemplar. Set qualiscunque fuit, Cantuarie pro maximo erat. Nil mirum si torta, que extorta.

Proclamatum autem fuit a Herberto Norwicensi episcopo in plena ecclesia, precepto regis, quod hoc quod, T[homas] Eboracensis hic faciebat, non iudicio, set iussu regis et voluntate erat. Quod Dunelmensis episcopus, altius ascendens, melius supplevit, dicens: 'Eboracensis electus Cantuarie aut Eboraci consecrari debet; quod modo hic consecratur et profitetur, non

---

[1] Literally 'knowing the difference between weight and weight, and between tale and tale'

[2] 27 June 1109

free, so long as they kept their possessions. We were told of the king's threats against us of disgrace and exile as traitors, because we seemed to grieve and object even a little. The bishop of Durham, for his part, tried to recall the king's intention by a bribe, promising him a thousand marks of silver and a hundred to the queen, if they would consent to justice and a judgment by canon law for the church of York. But the king would not listen, well knowing which side could bid the higher.[1]

Under such compulsion and duress, with sighs and groans, without either our consent or refusal (for it would have been madness to refuse), Thomas at length consented to do what I really think he would never have done, if his body could have borne exile, weariness, and the discomforts they involved. But he was full-bodied and fatter than he should have been. On the next Sunday[2] he was consecrated by the bishop of London and his brother bishops in St Paul's church. He made a strange and uncouth profession, personal, but to no person (for God alone knew who would be the next archbishop of Canterbury), saving his obedience and fealty to the pope and the king of England, and saving the rights of the church of York. It was limited, without precedent and, I imagine, not likely to be repeated. But such as it was, the Canterbury people made much of it. No wonder that an extorted profession should be misshapen.

But it was proclaimed by Herbert, bishop of Norwich, by the king's order, that what Thomas of York was here doing, was not a judicial sentence, but was by the order and will of the king. The bishop of Durham, speaking from a pulpit, was more explicit, and said, 'The archbishop of York ought to be consecrated at Canterbury or at York. That he is consecrated and makes his

iudicamento, set voluntate regis et imperio quadam dispensacione factum est, nec vult rex Eboracensi ecclesie, nec successoribus T[home], hoc esse in preiudicium, nec Cantuariensi in exemplum. De hoc appello vos omnes qui auditis in testimonium.'

In huius rei testimonium rex litteras istas fieri et sigillo suo sigillari precepit.

Henricus dei gracia rex Anglorum, episcopis et baronibus tocius regni Anglie salutem. Sciatis quod professio illa, quam T[homas] secundus Eboracensis archiepiscopus fecit Cantuariensi ecclesie, defuncto Anselmo, hoc modo facta est. Voluntas mea et consilium quorundam meorum fidelium fuit propter quasdam necessitates, quamquam ipse T[homas] Eboracensis archiepiscopus et Eboracensis ecclesia per privilegia sua parati essent diracionare quod facere non deberet. Effecit igitur eam de sola persona sua, precepto meo coactus, salva prius obediencia Romani / pontificis et fidelitate mea, eo videlicet tenore, ut Eboracensis ecclesia libertatem aliquam vel privilegia, que ipsa iuste habere debeat, per hoc scriptum meum vel ipsius factum nullo tempore perdat. Et si aliquando de eadem re inter illas ecclesias vel archiepiscopos earum placitum fuerit, quod, illa vice, mea voluntate et precepto factum fuit, Eboracensi ecclesie vel archiepiscopis eius ad disracionandam libertatem suam nullo modo noceret. Valete.

F.8

Et ne professio illa propter presenciam nostram plus auctoritatis habere videretur, interesse noluimus. Set quidam amici [a] discedentes Eboracam venerunt, capitulo, ut gestum erat, nunciantes; qui audientes de mutacione regis mirati sunt, de professione doluerunt,

[a] amia, MS

profession here is not done by virtue of a judgment, but by the king's will and command, by way of dispensation, nor does the king wish it to prejudice the church of York, or the successors of Thomas, or to be a precedent in favour of the church of Canterbury. Of this I call upon all of my hearers to bear witness.'

In witness of this the king ordered the following letters to be made and sealed :—

Henry, by the grace of God king of the English, to the bishops and barons of all the realm of England, greeting. Know ye that that profession which Thomas II, archbishop of York, made to the church of Canterbury after the death of Anselm, was made in the following manner. It was my will and the counsel of some of my lieges, for certain necessary reasons, although Thomas archbishop of York and the church of York were prepared to prove by their privileges that he was not bound to make it. He made it therefore in his own person only, compelled by my order, saving beforehand his obedience to the pope and his fealty to me, expressly stipulating that the church of York shall not lose any liberty or privileges to which it is justly entitled by this my letter or by his own act. And that if, at any future time this matter should be brought to trial between these churches and their archbishops, what has on this occasion been done by my will and command should not prejudice the church of York and its archbishops in claiming their liberty. Farewell.

And lest this profession should seem to have more authority because of our presence, we declined any concern in it. But some of our friends went off to York and related what had happened to the chapter, who were astonished at the king's change of front, regretted

set propter angariam et districcionem minus ei imputave-
runt.

Consecratus archiepiscopus recessit Eboracam, adducens secum cardinalem palleum deferentem, quibus qua
decuit honorificencia susceptis, archiepiscopus accepto
palleo missam celebravit, et tunc Turgotum, qui fuerat
prior Dunelmensis ecclesie, episcopum Sancti Andree
de Scocia presente cardinali consecravit. Foderoc [a]
vero, predecessor eius, quia fuerat a Scotis ordinatus,
consilio et imperio regis Malcon et regine Margarete
venit ad primum T[homam] satisfacere et reconsiliari,
atque Eboracensi ecclesie et T[home] archiepiscopo et
successoribus suis canonicam subieccionem professus est,
et in Eboraca, iubente archiepiscopo, ecclesias dedicavit.
Quod fortasse cum de primo Thoma agerem dixisse
debueram.

Post pallei suscepcionem, factis ibi tribus diebus,
archiepiscopus cardinalem magnifice donatum iuxta
facultatem suam, honorifice et accurate reduxit usque
ultra flumen Treentam. Cumque digredi deberent,
cardinalis precepit archiepiscopo ex auctoritate sancte
Romane ecclesie, diem illi statuens quatinus domino
pape presenciam suam exhiberet, super hoc satisfacturus quod contra statutum beati Gregorii et contra
sentenciam curie Romane professus erat. Quod ille
egre ferens, cum regem id se mandare dixisset, cardinalis precibus eorum qui aderant, et regis amore sive
timore, tandem invitacionem illam remisit, sicque
valedicentes amicabiliter digrediuntur, scilicet archiepiscopus ad sua, ille ad regem, ut ab eo licencia et
benedicione quam desiderabat accepta inde Romam
regrederetur.

[a] Eod hoc, MS

the profession, but blamed the archbishop less because of the pressure and duress.

When the archbishop had been consecrated, he retired to York accompanied by the cardinal with the *pallium*. They were received with becoming deference, and the archbishop, having received the *pallium*, celebrated mass, and then, in the cardinal's presence, consecrated Turgot, formerly prior of Durham, as bishop of St Andrews in Scotland. His predecessor, Foderoc, because he had been ordained by the Scots, on the advice and command of King Malcolm and Queen Margaret, came to Thomas I to make satisfaction and be reconciled, and made profession of his canonical subjection to the church of York and to archbishop Thomas and his successors, and dedicated churches in York by the archbishop's orders; a fact which I ought perhaps to have mentioned when dealing with Thomas I.

After receiving the *pallium* and spending three days at York, the archbishop conducted the cardinal, to whom he had given as handsome a present as his means permitted, with all honour and due ceremony, across the Trent. As they were about to part, the cardinal, by the authority of the Roman church, ordered the archbishop, naming a day, to present himself before the pope to answer for having made his profession, contrary to the statute of Saint Gregory and the sentence of the Roman court. On his resenting this and saying that the king had ordered him to do so, the cardinal, at the prayer of the persons present and out of love (or fear) of the king, at length revoked the summons. So they parted friends and went their ways, the archbishop to his own place, the cardinal to the king, to receive from him the leave and blessing which he wished for, and return to Rome.

F

T[homas] iste Michaelem, hominem sanctum, Glesguensi ecclesie ordinavit episcopum, qui Eboracensi
ecclesie et T[home] archiepiscopo, et successoribus suis
canonicam obedienciam profitendo scriptam tradidit.
Hic aliquamdiu cum archiepiscopo conversatus, iussu
illius in diecesi nostra ecclesias dedicavit, et ordines
fecit; in ecclesia de Morlund, in qua felici fine ad deum
migrans, sepultus requiescit. Huius antecessores Mag-
suen et Iohannem Kinsinus Eboracensis archiepiscopus
consecravit, sicut a viris veracibus accepimus qui se
hoc vidisse testabantur; set propter hostilem impug-
nacionem, et desolacionem, et barbariem terre, diu
ecclesia sine pastore fuit, donec David comes, postea
rex Scocie, predictum Michaelem episcopum constituit,
[et] T[home] archiepiscopo consecrandum transmisit.

Radulphum vero, urbis Eboracensis presbiterum, in
ecclesia sancti Petri ab Orcadensibus electum T[homas]
Orcadum insularum ordinavit episcopum, cuius predecessores ab archiepiscopis nostris ordinati fuerant, a
primo T[homa] Radulfus; a Girardo, Rogerus Wite-
biensis monasterii monachus.

Ecclesie sancti Petri duas prebendas fecit. Hagul-
F.8v staldensem ecclesiam / constituendis ibi canonicis re-
gularibus tradidit, et aliquas circum terrulas dedit.
Prebendis canonicorum sancte Marie de Sutwella eandem libertatem a rege Henrico obtinuit, quam nostre,
et sancti Iohannis Beverlacensis et sancti Wilfridi de
Ripon prebende habent; et, quod ad ipsum pertinebat,
ab episcopali consuetudine et exaccione in ecclesiis et
terris liberas eas et quietas concessit et confirmavit.
Aldredus bone memorie, ultimus Angligena archiepiscopus, prebendas illas de terra exempticia fecit, set
regias consuetudines vel exacciones ab illis emere non
potuit, quibus vendere non licebat.

This Thomas ordained a holy man, Michael, bishop of Glasgow, who professed canonical obedience in writing to the church of York and to archbishop Thomas and his successors. He stayed some time with the archbishop, dedicated churches on his authority in our diocese, and held an ordination. He is buried in Morland church where he happily departed to God. Archbishop Cynsige consecrated his predecessors, Magnus and John, as we have been told by truthful men, who bore witness that they saw this. But owing to the attacks of enemies, and the desolation and barbarism of the land, that church was long without a shepherd, until earl David, afterwards king of Scotland, appointed the said Michael bishop, and sent him to archbishop Thomas to be consecrated.

Thomas also, in St Peter's church, ordained Ralph, a priest of the city of York, elected by the men of the Orkneys, as bishop; whose predecessors were ordained by our archbishops, Ralph by Thomas I, Roger, a monk of Whitby, by Gerard.

He made two prebends in the church of St Peter. He gave the church of Hexham to the regular canons to be established there, and some small lands thereabouts; he obtained from King Henry the same liberty for the prebends of the canons of St Mary's, Southwell, as our prebends have, and those of St John of Beverley and St Wilfrid of Ripon; and granted and confirmed that, so far as he was concerned, they should be free and quit of all episcopal custom and exaction in their churches and lands. Aldred of happy memory, the last English-born archbishop, made those prebends of land free of geld, but could not buy the king's customs or taxes from those who had no power to sell them.

Vixit T[homas] iunior in archiepiscopatu annos v. et menses fere ix., et obiit xi. kalendas Marcii, iuvenis adhuc etate, mundus carne, quem nemo cognovit feminam cognovisse.

Post decessum Anselmi archiepiscopi non fuit usque tunc archiepiscopus Cantuarie. Ad proximas Roga- ciones [1] translatus est in eam Radulphus Rofensis epi- scopus, ante Sagiensis monasterii abbas, qui si tantum sanctitate profectus est quantum dignitate, novit ille quem nichil potest latere. Ecclesia nostra usque ad Assumpcionem sancte Marie [2] vacavit. Dixit quidam,

O multum ante alias infelix littera theta.[a]

Solebant enim Gentiles frontibus damnatorum, ad notam infamie, figuram Θ littere calido [b] ferro imprimere, unde et Persius :

Et potis es nigrum [c] vicio prefigere theta.[3]

Apud Grecos Θ, apud Latinos elementum illud T. nuncupatur. De primo in secundum, de secundo in tercium, quorum nomina per T. litteram incipiunt, propter professionem hanc tempestatis grando grandis graviter grassata est, hoc est de Thoma in Thomam, de illo in Thurstinum. Girardus enim archiepiscopus, licet in eum huius grandinis aliquis horror intonuit, quia episcopus translatus per consecracionem coartari non potuit, facilius et sine lesione evasit, auxilio quoque regis qui Anselmo archiepiscopo contrarius erat, et prelacionem eius amplius extendi non curabat.

THURSTINUS

In crastino Assumpcionis Sancte Sanctarum suscepit ecclesiam nostram Turstinus regis capellanus, Lundoni- ensis ecclesie sancti Pauli canonicus, clericus litteris

[a] teta, MS   [b] caligo, MS   [c] morum, MS

Thomas the younger lived five years and almost nine months as archbishop, and died 21 February [1114], still young in years, chaste, not known by any man to have known a woman.

After the death of archbishop Anselm there was not till that time any archbishop of Canterbury. At the following Rogationtide [1] Ralph, bishop of Rochester, formerly abbot of Séez, was translated to be archbishop there, but whether he was as much advanced in holiness as he was in dignity, only he knows from whom nothing is hidden. Our church was void until the Assumption.[2]

Someone has said, 'Most hapless of all letters T'. For the Gentiles used to brand with a hot iron the letter Theta on the foreheads of condemned criminals as a mark of infamy. And Persius says, 'And a black Theta you can brand on vice'.[3] The letter is called Θ in Greek and T in Latin. Of those archbishops whose names began with T, on account of this profession, the heavy storm of hail has swept from the first to the second, from the second to the third : from Thomas to Thomas, and from him to Thurstan. For archbishop Gerard (though some of the horror of this hailstorm thundered against him) who, being translated as a bishop, could not be coerced by refusal of consecration, escaped more easily and unhurt; being also helped by the king, who was opposed to archbishop Anselm, and not anxious that his superiority should be enlarged.

THURSTAN

On the morrow of the Assumption of the most holy Virgin, the king's chaplain, Thurstan, canon of St Paul's, London, took upon him our church, a learned

---

[1] 3–6 May 1114   [2] 15 August   [3] *Sat.* iv. 13

admodum eruditus, in secularibus prudens et indus-
trius, in providendis, et apparandis, et agendis domi et
milicie, et peregre necessariis solvendis [a] strenuus et
curialiter efficax. Propter que regi W[illelmo] Iuniori
domesticus et carus fuerat, regi Henrico familiaris et
acceptus et secretarius erat, et apud ipsum plurimum
poterat. Per illum rex, bene credens illi, presens et
absens, in Anglia et Normannia plurima disponebat,
distribuebat, et efficiebat; que prudenter et liberaliter
agendo, infra et circum principibus et ceteris notus et
dilectus habebatur. In deferendo et faciendo honorem
advenis et ignotis, religiosis et secularibus, largus et
hilliaris, et benigne serviens et decenter. Et hec quidem
fuerunt illi et honori et commodo in locis pluribus, et
tempore opportuno. Dimissione facta ab episcopo cuius
erat canonicus, in nostrum illum suscepimus.

Cogitans vero ex his que audierat et viderat de
predecessoribus suis quod professio ab eo exigeretur,
locutus est regi, dicens incongruum esse metropolitanum
duas professiones facere, alteram Romano pontifici,
quam denegare non poterat, alteram alteri metropolitano, quod beati Gregorii statutis adversatur, et in
aliis regnis nusquam erat; et si contencio aliqua inter
regem et Cantuariensem episcopum oriretur, illi magis
F.9 eum obedire / oporteret cui professione obligatus esset.
Iisdem verbis cum comite de Mellent, qui erat
consiliarius regis, habitis, ita rem esse, sicut dicebat,
intellexit. Rex primo se non eum cogere profiteri
respondit.

Subdiaconus erat, et in proximo Decembre a Willelmo Wintoniensi episcopo diaconus ordinatus est.

[a] solverunt, MS

clerk, prudent and diligent in worldly affairs, energetic
and courteously efficient in providing, preparing, and
acting in domestic and military matters, and in necessary
payments abroad. For these reasons he was a favourite
member of the household of William II, and a trusted
servant of King Henry, with whom he had great influ-
ence. The king, having full confidence in him, whether
present in England or absent in Normandy, used him
to make arrangements and payments, and do business
of all kinds. His prudence and free-handedness in this
made him known and beloved by gentle and simple in
and around [the court]. In welcoming and doing
honour to foreigners and strangers, religious and secular,
he was lavish and cheerful, serving them kindly and
becomingly. This too added to his honour and advantage in many places and at the right time. He was
released by the bishop whose canon he was, and we took
him to be ours.

But thinking, from what he had heard and seen of
his predecessors, that a profession would be demanded
from him, he spoke to the king, saying that it was
inconsistent that a metropolitan should make two pro-
fessions, one to the pope, which he could not refuse, the
other to the other metropolitan, contrary to the statutes
of Saint Gregory, and nowhere existing in other realms;
and that if any dispute should arise between the king
and the archbishop of Canterbury, he ought rather to
obey that one to whom he was bound by his profession.
He used the same words to the count of Meulan, who
was the king's counsellor, and was told that the case was
as he had stated. The king at first answered that he
was not compelling him to make the profession.

Thurstan was a subdeacon, and was ordained
deacon the following December by William, bishop of

Eodem mense rex in Normanniam transivit. Diaconus
ab archiepiscopo vel a suffraganeis suis in sacerdotem
ordinari refugit, ne ideo plus iuris in eo posset reclamare.

Veniens Eboracam, sicut dignitatis huius mos exigit,
in nostrum susceptus, a Roberto Cestrensi episcopo
intronizatus est.   Deinde placuit ei Dunelmensem episcopum et Haugustaldensem ecclesiam visitare.   Eo
pergens, cum predicto episcopo et ceteris probis viris,
invenit Dunelmi Turgotum, episcopum sancti Andree
de Scocia, in infirmitate iacentem, de qua non con-
valuit; qui de eius provectu atque adventu non modice
gavisus, tradidit se in manus eius, eum patrem et
metropolitanum suum recognoscens, et, si deus eum
sospitati restitueret, se ei devote obediturum promit-
tens.   Diebus aliquot apud Hestoldesham factis, Ebo-
racum reversus est, et episcopo Cestrensi ad propria
regresso, in parochia sua aliquantulum conversatus.

Quadam [die] in capitulo congregatis, quesivit a
nobis consilium de professione quam ab eo exigendam
non dubitabat.   Habito inter nos seorsum consilio
contulimus, et visum est nobis nos illi profitendi vel
minime nullum dare consilium.   Alterum experti era-
mus esse contra regem et fere totam Angliam; alterum
erat contra decretum beati Gregorii et consuetudinem
ecclesiasticam.   Alterum erat tranquillitatis et pacis;
alterum erat timoris et socordie et prevaricacionis.
Utrum horum ei suaderemus quorum uterque in dubio
nobis erat?   Animum eius ex ᵃ modica conversacione
nondum cognosse poteramus.   Ex consulto igitur illi
respondimus a nobis de hac re nullum habere consilium.   Litteratus erat; decreta legerat; canones sciebat; que cui persona profiteri debeat, non ignorabat:
set si quid ᵇ honestius et iustius agens ab archiepiscopo

ᵃ est, MS   ᵇ quod, MS

Winchester. In the same month the king went over to Normandy. As a deacon, he refused to be ordained priest by the archbishop or his suffragans, lest the former should be able to claim more right over him on that account. He came to York, was received by us with due regard to his dignity, and was enthroned by Robert, bishop of Chester. He then chose to visit the bishop of Durham and the church of Hexham. On his way there, with the bishop and other worthy men, he found at Durham Turgot, bishop of St Andrews in Scotland, lying in what proved to be his last illness. He rejoiced extremely at Thurstan's promotion and his visit, put himself in his hands, recognizing him as his father and metropolitan, and promising, if God restore him to safety, his devout obedience. After a few days at Hexham, he returned to York, and when the bishop of Chester had gone home, occupied himself in diocesan affairs.

One day, as we were assembled in chapter, he asked our advice about the profession which he felt sure would be required of him. We retired to discuss the matter among ourselves, and decided to give him no advice whether to make his profession or not. We knew from experience that one course meant opposing the king and almost all England; the other was contrary to the decree of Saint Gregory and the custom of the church. One meant peace and quiet; the other, fear, cowardice, and transgression. Which of them should we advise him, when we were ourselves in doubt about both? The little acquaintance we had with him was not enough for us to know his mind. We therefore deliberately answered him that we had no advice to give him about it. He was an educated man, he had read the decrees, he knew the canons; he knew who should make his profession to whom. But if for any just or honourable action

violenter eiceretur, id ei pollicebamur, nos alium nec
metu, nec dampno, neque quo modo, nisi precepto
summi pontificis, recipere. Quod audiens, consilium
suum aperuit, nolle profiteri, set velle Romam proficisci,
et domini pape consilium et preceptum sequi. Et nos
igitur, ut de nostra pollicitacione cercior esset, et ad
bene agendum magis animaretur, illi, licet nondum
episcopo, nondum sacerdoti, subiecctionem et obedienciam canonicam ultro promisimus. Nec multo post,
electis quos de nostris secum ducere placuit, et de
eleccione sua litteris ad dominum papam acceptis, ad
mare tendit.

Radulphus [archi]episcopus iam antea illi mandaverat, et in profeccione hac citra mare ei colloquens
dixerat quatenus Cantuariam veniret et sacerdos ordinari,
et archiepiscopus consecrari. Cui, quod iustum et
decens videbatur, respondens, neutrum voluit. Primo
Natali domini, quod prope erat, in Normanniam transivit, licencia regis inde Romam profecturus; set
archiepiscopus misit post eum ad regem recia aurea et
obices argenteas, quibus retento Romam properanti via
obstru[er]etur. Prohibitus est igitur Romam ire.

Eo tempore Cono Prenestinus episcopus, vir venerabilis, verax, et iustus, et constans, in Francia et
Normannia sedis Apostolice legacione fungebatur. Huic
vero rex mandavit consilium dari sibi quid de Ebora-
F.9v censi / electo eum agere oporteat, quem Cantuariensis
archiepiscopus absque subieccionis professione consecrare nolebat, et ipse modo cum eo erat necdum
quidem sacerdos ordinatus. Regi legatus remandavit
ut ab aliquo suffraganeo suo, si quis illic adesset, eum
presbyterum ordinari faceret, ordinatum ad ipsum mitteret, et ipse eum ad dominum papam cum litteris suis,

of his own he should be forcibly deposed by the archbishop, we promised him not to accept any other for fear,
or through loss, or for any other reason except a direct
command from the pope. On hearing this, he told us
his plan : he would make no profession, but go to
Rome and follow the pope's advice and orders. And
we, to confirm our promise and encourage him to do
this, freely promised him our submission and canonical
obedience, though he was not a bishop or even a priest.
Soon afterwards he chose those of us whom he wished
to take with him, received letters to the pope about his
election, and took his way to the sea.

Archbishop Ralph had previously ordered him, and
had personally told him, before he crossed the sea on
his journey, to come to Canterbury to be ordained
priest and consecrated archbishop. He made a just
and proper reply, but would do neither. First, on
Christmas day, which was near, he crossed to Normandy,
intending, with the king's leave, to proceed thence to
Rome. But the archbishop sent after him to the king
golden nets and silver bolts to catch him and block his
way to Rome. So he was forbidden to go there.

At that time Cuno, bishop of Palestrina, a venerable,
just, and steadfast man, was acting as legate of the
apostolic see in France and Normandy. The king sent
to him to get advice what he should do about the elect
of York, whom the archbishop of Canterbury would
not consecrate without his making his profession of
submission. He was now with the king, and had not
yet even been ordained priest. The legate sent back
word to the king to have him ordained priest by one of
the archbishop's suffragans, if one were there, and send
him after ordination to himself. He would then send
him to the pope with a letter, so that the pope might

ut eum consecraret, et consecratus palleum acceptum deferret. Quorum alterum fecit, alterum vero non consensit. Erat cum rege Ranulphus Dunelmensis episcopus; ab illo precepto regis in Pentecoste...[1] dicens se haut longe post venturum pacem inter archiepiscopum et ipsum componere, et de eius consecracione, deo adiuvante, bene disponere. Post Pentecosten reversus est, et rex ad proximum festum sancti Iohannis. Quia vero inter archiepiscopum et electum [de] consecracione non erat concordia, qui episcopale officium non poterat, sacerdotale devote faciebat, et iuxta scienciam et facultatem suam interiora et exteriora strenue gerebat, dolens quod plene non poterat ad quod destinatus erat.

Circa festum sancti Michaelis convocavit rex apud Londoniam episcopos et abbates, principes et primores regni sui, cum eis de pace, de statu regni, de negociis acturus. Inter quos diversi ordinis plurimi affuerunt. Ibi rex electo nostro de dilacione consecracionis sue conquerenti, adstante comite de Mellent, et Nigello de Albaneio, consilium dedit quatinus proborum virorum testimonio archiepiscopum conveniret, et ab eo consecrari humiliter requireret. Quod si antequam faceret, aliquid quod iniustum videatur exigeret, in sentenciam et voluntatem domini [pape] inde se ponere diceret.

Letus de consilio, et secum adhibitis Gaufrido Rotomagensi archiepiscopo, Iohanne Lexoviensi episcopo, Rannulfo Dunelmensi, et multis clericis et monachis, et quibusdam laicis, archiepiscopum coram pluribus de suo numero cuiusque ordinis suppliciter requisivit ut eum consecraret. Cui ille: 'Libenter', inquit, 'faciam, si feceritis quod debetis'. Et Eboracensis: 'Ex iure

---

[1] There seems to be a gap in the MS, but it is clear Thurstan was ordained at this stage.

consecrate him, and he might then take home his
pallium.   One of these things he did ; but did not consent
to the other.   Ranulf, bishop of Durham, was with the
king ;   by him, at the king's command, [Thurstan was
ordained priest] ¹ at Whitsuntide.   [The bishop then
encouraged him] he would come back to compose the
difference between him and the archbishop, and, with
God's help, to arrange for his consecration.   He returned
after Whitsuntide, and the king at Midsummer following.
But because the archbishop and the elect were not
agreed about the consecration, the latter not being able
to do duty as a bishop, devoutly did it as a priest, and
worked hard to the best of his knowledge and power
inwardly and outwardly, grieving that he could not
fulfil the work for which he was appointed.

About Michaelmas, the king summoned to London
the bishops and abbots, princes and nobles of his realm,
to treat with them of peace, of the state of the realm,
and of other business.   Many of different ranks were
present.   There, with the assistance of the count of
Meulan and Nigel d'Aubigny, the king advised our
elect, who complained of the delay in his consecration,
to confront the archbishop, with proper witnesses, and
humbly desire to be consecrated by him.   But if the
archbishop, before doing so, should make any apparently
unjust demand, he should say that he appealed to the
sentence and will of our lord [the pope].

Rejoicing in this advice, he took with him Geoffrey
archbishop of Rouen, John bishop of Lisieux, Ranulf
bishop of Durham, many clerks and monks, and some
laymen, and in the presence of many of all ranks,
humbly begged the archbishop to consecrate him.   The
archbishop replied 'Willingly, if you will do what you
ought'.   The elect of York answered, 'I demand to be

ecclesiarum nostrarum, quarum archiepiscopi sese de-
bent invicem consecrare, a vobis consecrari postulo.
Si quid deinde ecclesie vestre, vel persone me debere,
vel canonice monstrare poteritis, exhibere non recuso.'
Tunc Rotomagensis archiepiscopus : 'Non est', inquit,
'tantarum personarum uti duplicitate verborum. Quid
ab alterutro exigat, vel alterutro deneget, aperte uterque
denunciet.' 'Non loquar ambicione', ait Cantuariensis ;
'nisi professione prius tradita nequaquam illi manus
imponam.' Ad quod electus : 'De hoc in sentenciam
et consilium domini pape paratus sum me ponere'.
Et ille : 'Non ita iuvenis, non sum adeo levis, nec sic
agilis, nec sic apparatus, ut modo tantum iter agrediar'.
Et addidit :[a] 'Si dominus papa michi ore ad os preciperet, ut vos, seposita professione, consecrarem, de hoc
minime obedirem'. Quod multi qui aderant pensantes,
nec canonice nec sapienter dictum reputaverunt.

Electus apud archiepiscopum nichil assecutus, peticionem suam et responsum eius, et excessum in matrem suam, sanctam Romanam ecclesiam, regi retulit.
Quod ille indecenter dixisse cognoscens, tamen nec
grave nimium, nec bene multum accepit. Noster electus, per se et per quoscunque poterat, regi insistebat,
deprecans, supplicans, obsecrans, ut dominum et regem
F.10 suum, ut ei Romam ire permitteret, / ostendens ecclesie
sibi commisse et persone sue in bonorum et detrimentum esse, et in periculum magnum anime fructus
archiepiscopi recipere, et officium episcopale non facere,
et quod appellabatur non esse. De tanta vero dilacione, et propter quid minime mandata, apud apostolicam sedem accusari, et ex iusticia redargui et graviter
iudicari posse, nec regem nec regnum hoc decere.

[a] adierunt, MS

consecrated by you in the right of our churches, whose
archbishops ought to take turns in consecrating each
other. I do not refuse to perform anything which you
can then show to be due therefor to your church or yourself by canon law.' The archbishop of Rouen then said,
'It does not become persons of such dignity to be
ambiguous. Let each openly state what he demands of,
or refuses to the other.' 'To be quite plain,' said the
archbishop of Canterbury, 'I will not lay hands on this
man, unless he hands over his profession.' The elect
replied, 'On this point I am ready to put myself on the
sentence and counsel of our lord the pope'. The other
said, 'I am not young enough, light enough, supple
enough, nor am I prepared to make such a journey
now'. And he added, 'If our lord the pope were to
order me by word of mouth to consecrate you without
having your profession, I should not obey him'. Many
who were there, on reflection, thought that neither
good law nor good sense.

The elect, having got nothing from the archbishop,
reported to the king his petition and its answer, and the
insult to his mother the holy Roman church. The king
admitted that the archbishop had spoken unbecomingly,
but took the matter neither too seriously nor very well.
Our elect both in person and by anyone else he could,
pressed the king by prayer, supplication, and conjura-
tion, as his lord and king, to let him go to Rome, showing
that it was both a material damage to the church
committed to his charge and to himself and a great
danger to his soul to receive an archbishop's income
without doing a bishop's duties, and not to be what he
was called. He might justly be charged and severely
judged at the apostolic see for so long a delay and for
not sending to explain the reason, and this did not become

Quapropter exorabat ut eum ire,[a] vel saltem mittere, benevole concederet, ut quid regi, quid sibi super hoc agendum esset a domino papa acciperet. Set rex neutrum hac vice concessit, set nec pro utraque ecclesia se missurum promisit. Sic oportune et importune electus regi insistebat; archiepiscopus vero regem interpellare et insimulare omnimodis non desistebat, nec eum abire vel mittere sineret, set ut ad profitendum cogeret, accusans quoque eum quod rege inconsulto ad apostolicam sedem illum invitaverat, quod huius regni consuetudo[b] non extitit, rem sic aggerando super fratrem suum, et coepiscopum designatum aggravare desiderans. Et ipse quidem ignorabat quod consilio regis hoc fecerat, quamquam et ipse rex postmodum, fortasse non recolens, illis eciam quibus presentibus sic consiliatus erat negavit. Set, si opus fuisset, testimonium illi non defuisset.

Littere vero quas supradiximus a nobis eum de eleccione sua accepisse, non statim, set transacto et eo amplius toto anno ad proximum Natale tandem summo pontifici et pio patri Paschali perlate sunt, paternitatem et misericordiam eius deprecantes, quatinus eleccionem nostram apostolica auctoritate confirmaret, ostendentes quoque conquerendo quod Cantuariensis archiepiscopus a consecrando eum manum retrahebat pro eo quod ei professionem exhibere recusat, quia hoc et beati Gregorii et Honorii decretis obviat, et id a metropolitanis soli Romano pontifici deberi non ignorat. Id eciam apud regem optinuit ut apostolicam sedem adire non permittat, et sic consecracio eius diutius iusto differebatur.

[a] irem, MS   [b] consueto, MS

the king or the kingdom. He therefore prayed that the king would permit him to go, or at least to send, so that he might hear from the pope what the king, and he himself, ought to do. But the king granted neither of his requests on this occasion, nor did he promise himself to send on behalf of both the churches. The archbishop elect thus pressed the king both in and out of season. But the archbishop did not cease to harass the king and make all sorts of false accusations. He should not [said he] let him either go or send, but compel him to make his profession. He also accused him of having summoned him to appear before the apostolic see without consulting the king, contrary to the custom of the realm ; piling up the charge against his brother with the intention of injuring his fellow-bishop designate. He did not know that it was by the king's advice that the elect had done this, though the king himself afterwards denied having done so (perhaps he had forgotten), to the persons in whose presence he had given the advice. But, had it been necessary, there would have been no lack of witnesses.

But the letter, which, as we said before, he received from us about his election, was not transmitted to our holy father Pope Paschal at once, but more than a year later, at Christmas. It besought him, as a merciful father, to confirm our election by apostolic authority, and also complained that the archbishop of Canterbury held back his hand from consecrating him, because he refuses to make his profession to him, since this is contrary to the decrees of Saint Gregory and of Honorius, and he well knows it is due from metropolitans to the bishop of Rome only. The archbishop has also got the king not to allow [our elect] to approach the apostolic see, and so his consecration has been unduly long

G

Auditis reverendus papa peticione et querimonia, illi
benigne annuens, hunc pie condolens, pro utraque
scripsit quibus debuit, et, sicut decuit, clero scilicet
Eboracensi de eleccionis confirmacione, Radulpho archiepiscopo mandando precipiens ut electum consecraret
absque professionis exaccione. Que littere in Quadragesima in Angliam pervenerunt. Quas misit clero, hee
sunt:

P[aschalis] episcopus, servus servorum dei, dilectis
filiis Eboracensis ecclesie clericis, salutem et apostolicam benediccionem. A beato Gregorio, qui [a] per
ampliorem dei graciam gentis vestre apostolus factus
est, novimus institutum, ut post Augustini obitum
ipse inter metropolitanos Anglie primus haberi de-
buisset qui prius consecrari meruisset. Si qui [b] ergo
hanc institucionem conantur evertere, dominica sunt
increpacione redarguendi. 'Quare', inquit, 'transgre-
dimini precepta domini propter tradicionem [c] homi-
num?' [1] Nos igitur eleccionem quidem electi vestri
actam canonice, ut a vobis accepimus, confirmamus.
Ceterum subieccionis professionem que soli Romane
debetur ecclesie, aut exigi ab eo aut reddi omnimodis
prohibemus. Quod autem a Thoma quondam archiepiscopo presumptum sive surreptum, quam graviter
predecessor noster, sancte memorie Urbanus papa,
pertulerit, ex ipsius litteris quas ad eum misit potest
evidenter agnosci. Nos igitur ad ipsum ratum habentes electum vestrum, si Cantuariensis episcopus
pro consuetudine ecclesiarum ipsarum noluerit consecrare, ab ecclesie vestre suffraganeis precipimus /
F.10v   consecrari. Porro cum ad nos venerit, nos ei per
dei graciam affeccione debita quod nostri est officii
conferemus, set cercius noverit nichil a nobis per

---

[a] quod, MS   [b] quod, MS   [c] traditiones, A

delayed. The pope heard our petition and complaint, graciously granting the former and sympathizing with the latter, and in both cases wrote to the proper persons, viz. to the clergy of York, confirming the election, and to archbishop Ralph, ordering him to consecrate the elect without exacting any profession. The letters reached England in Lent. This is that to the clergy:

Bishop Paschal, servant of the servants of God, to his beloved sons the clergy of the church of York, greeting and apostolic blessing. We know that the blessed Gregory, who by the more abundant grace of God was made the apostle of your nation, ordained that after the death of Augustine that one of the metropolitans should be the first, who had first received consecration. Whosoever therefore attempts to break this ordinance, must be refuted by the reproof of our Lord. 'Why' (said he) 'do ye also transgress the commandment of God by your tradition?'[1] We therefore confirm the election of your elect, which as you assure us, was canonical. But we altogether forbid the profession of subjection, which is due to the church of Rome only, to be exacted from or given by him. How seriously our predecessor Pope Urban of holy memory regarded what was obtained by threats or by trickery from the late archbishop Thomas, can be plainly seen from the letter which he sent to him. We therefore, confirming your elect, order him to be consecrated by the suffragans of your church, if the [arch]bishop of Canterbury refuses to consecrate him in accordance with the custom of the churches. Furthermore, when he comes to us, we shall by God's grace bestow on him with due affection that which pertains to our office. But he may be

[1] Matt. 15 : 3

intermissas personas nisi presens affuerit impetrandum. Datum Laterani, nonis Ianuarii.[a]

In ea Quadragesima, rex apud Salesbiriam de cuius-[vis] dignitatis et ordinis hominibus concilium magnum convocavit. Ad quod cum electus noster et quidam ex nobis pergeremus, obviam venit qui predictas litteras attulit. Dominica qua cantatur, 'Iudica me, Deus, et d[iscerne] c[ausam] m[eam] de [gente] n[on] s[ancta]',[1] que dicitur prima Dominice Passionis,[2] concilium sedit. Ibi de electo nostro iudicium conciliatum est. Tercia die Passio[nis] eius fuit in qua audierat introitum[b] ad missam 'Exspecta Dominum, viriliter age et c[on-fortetur] c[or] t[uum], et s[ustine] d[ominum]'.[3] Que secuta est Prophetica lectio, 'Convenerunt Babilonii ad regem'.[4] Sicut in Proverbiis habetur, 'Vir malevolus fodit',[5] tantum archiepiscopus antea foderat, tantum ibi fodit, tanta dedit, tanta promisit, quod regem adversus eum aperte insurgere fecit. Mandavit ergo illi, non per ecclesiasticas personas, ut conveniens esset, set per duos consules et duos proceres, Robertum comitem de Mellent, Willelmum comitem de Warrenna, Willelmum archi-camerarium[6] suum, et Nigellum de Albeneio, primo pretendens ei quod frater suus et ipse eum educaverat, plurimum dilexerat, privatum sibi fecerat, ad quod erat exaltaverat; fidelitatem in[c] usus suos et consuetudines iuraverat; ne turbaret regnum nec ecclesiam scandali-zaret; set, sicut antecessores sui fecerant, subieccionem profitens consecracionem susciperet.

Quibus ille ait: 'Beneficia que enumeratis cuncta recognosco, et domino meo regi gracias habeo. Fide-

---

[a] Compared with another copy in the *Reg. Magnum Album* at York, i. 48   [b] introivit, MS   [c] et, MS

[1] Ps. 43 : 1   [2] 19 March 1116   [3] Ps. 27 : 18
[4] Bel and the Dragon 29. The portion appointed for the Epistle on Tuesday in Passion week   [5] Prov. 16 : 27

sure that nothing can be obtained from us through an intermediary unless he is himself present. Given at the Lateran, 6 January [1116].

In Lent of that year, the king called a great council at Salisbury of certain of the clergy and laity. As our elect and we were on our way there, there met us a man bringing the above letters. The council sat on the Sunday on which is sung: 'Give sentence with me, O God, and defend my cause against the ungodly people',[1] which is called the first of our Lord's Passion.[2] In it judgment was considered about our elect. It was on Tuesday in Passion week, when the Introit is 'O tarry thou the Lord's leisure: be strong and he shall comfort thine heart; and put thou thy trust in the Lord'[3]; there followed the lesson from the prophets, 'The men of Babylon assembled before the king'.[4] As it is written in the Proverbs, 'An ungodly man diggeth up evil'[5]; the archbishop had dug so much beforehand, so much now, gave so much, promised so much, that he made the king openly attack Thurstan. He sent to him, not as would have been proper, by clergy, but by two earls and two nobles, Robert, count of Meulan, William, earl of Warenne, William his chamberlain,[6] and Nigel d'Aubigny. He represented, first, that his brother and himself had brought Thurstan up, had shown much affection for him, had made him his confidant, and raised him to the position he now held; he had sworn fealty to the king's use and customs; let him not then disturb the realm and disgrace the church; but make his profession and receive consecration as his predecessors had done.

Thurstan's reply was: 'I acknowledge all the benefits which you recount and am grateful to my lord the king.

---

[6] This is presumably William de Tancarville, chamberlain of Normandy.

litatem quam feci, dei auxilio, bene servabo; usus
et consuetudines suas non iuravi, nec quicquam nisi
salvo ordine meo feci. Non est regni turbacio, non
est ecclesie scandalum, ecclesie cui me preesse voluit,
[supra] quam nulla in regno esse debet et regii diadematis dimidium est, suum ius defendere; quod ipsius
regis agere esset, vel saltem, ut bonum et iustum ad-
vocatum, equaliter se tenere. Qui scandalum iniuste
movet et facit, attendat quis est qui dicit, "Ve homini
illi per quem scandalum venit".[1] Profiteri vero nec
debeo nec audeo, quia hoc decreto beati Gregorii et
Honorii et Urbani paparum redargucionem adversari
non ignoro. Si quid predecessores mei inconsulte vel
coacti fecerunt, hereditate non possideo sanctuarium
Dei.[2] Set suppliciter deprecor dominum meum regem
meum, ut ecclesie, cui me vel quam michi tradidit,
rectitudinem et iudicium iustum consenciat.'

Ad regem redeunt, sic ordine rem referentes. Inimici iudices [a] nostri erant. Archiepiscopus enim et
complices sui erant cum rege. Noster in capella quadam cum paucis remanserat, nec quemlibet de nostris
adesse voluit, ne, si regi contradiceret, ipse illis impu-
taret. Premunitus fuerat ab aliquo amico talem as-
sultum [b] illi fieri. Qui prius venerant redeunt verbum
regis adbreviatum nunciantes, et ipsi quidem testes,
quoniam illum diligebant. 'Rex', inquiunt, 'de professione causam non ingredietur, nec ingredi consenciet,
set alterum erit e duobus; aut vos professionem facere,
aut regis odium incurrere; nec quenquam vobiscum
[con]sanguinitate propinquum in tota terra sua remanere.'

<table>
<tr><td>[a] iudici, MS</td><td>[b] assubeum, MS</td></tr>
<tr><td>[1] Matt. 18 : 7</td><td>[2] Ps. 83 : 13</td></tr>
</table>

The fealty which I swore I will, God helping me, honestly keep. I never swore to "use and customs" and did nothing without "saving my order". It is no disturbance of the realm or disgrace to the church for me to defend the rights of the church of which he made me the head, of which no church in the realm ought to take precedence, and which is the half of the king's crown; a task which should be the king's, or else he should at least hold the balance even, as a good and just patron. Let him who provokes and causes an offence consider who said, "Woe to the man by whom the offence cometh".[1] But I neither ought or dare to make my profession, knowing well that this is contrary to the decree of St Gregory and to the confutations of Honorius and Urban. Whatever my predecessors may have done in ignorance or under compulsion, I do not "take to" myself "the houses of God in possession".[2] But I humbly beseech my lord the king to consent to a righteous and just judgment for the church to which he gave me, or which he gave to me.'

The messengers returned to the king and reported the proceedings. Our enemies were our judges; for the archbishop and his fellow-plotters were with the king. Our elect had remained in a chapel with few attendants: he would not have any of us present, lest, if he opposed the king, he should lay the blame on them. He had been warned by one of his friends that such an attack would be made. The first messengers came back with a shorter message from the king, and were themselves witnesses, since they loved him. 'The king,' they said, 'will not open the question about the profession, nor allow it to be opened. It must be one of two things. You must make your profession or incur the king's hatred; nor may any of your kindred remain in all his lands.'

In arcto res sita erat. Pauca premeditatus, a deo consilio accepto, sic ait: 'Grave quidem michi est regis odium sempiternum habere, gravius / autem deum et Romanam ecclesiam scienter offendere; ut vero neutrum faciam, quod rex michi dedit, eligo potius dimittere. Ite, si vobis placet, et regi sic nunciate.' Euntes renunciaverunt. Archiepiscopus et quidam de assistentibus non credebant. Quibus comes de Mellent ait: 'Si bene novi hominem, non dixit quod facere nolit; set, ut audiatur a pluribus ex ore ipsius, coram veniat'. Mandatus ᵃ ad regem venit, et relato ab internunciis quod detulerant, plene concessit. Manum igitur porrigenti, et ipse, manu in manum, quod ei donaverat regi dimisit. Omnes fere qui viderunt lacrimati sunt. Rex eciam, quamvis crimen faceret, suspiravit et flevit. Solus archiepiscopus non plorasse dicitur. Credo cor eius religione ᵇ induratum fuisse, set Eboracensem clerum cepit coram rege insimulare quod per eos archiepiscopatum dimiserat. E contra noster electus, nunc vero eiectus, illos excusare, et de sciencia, et honestate, et probitate satis laudare. Et adiciens: 'Nichil', inquit, 'habeo modo in Eboracensi ecclesia preter fraternitatis amorem, et nunc quidem, dei auxilio et eorum, paratus essem causam illam pro defensione canonice defendere contra quicunque inde vellent canonice agere'. Ad quod nemo fuit qui responderet.

Qui cum eo de nostris venerant, quid et qualiter actum esset necdum sciebant. Scientibus vero meror, pietas, gaudium simul oborta sunt. De amisso pastore meror; de angaria in quam fuerat pietas; de vigore et constancia gaudium; et dolore, et pietate, et gaudio

F.11

ᵃ Mandatis, MS   ᵇ relig'e, MS

There was no escape. He thought a little, took counsel with God, and replied, 'It is a dreadful thing for me to have the king's everlasting hatred, but even more dreadful knowingly to offend God and the church of Rome. To avoid doing either, I prefer to resign what the king gave me. Pray go to the king and tell him so.' They did so. The archbishop and some of those present were incredulous. The count of Meulan told them, 'If I know my man, he means what he said; but let him come, so that more may hear it from his own mouth'. At the king's order, he came to him, and when the messengers had reported the result of their mission, admitted it entirely. The king offered his hand, and the elect, grasping it, resigned what the king had given him. Almost all the spectators were in tears. The king too, though it was his own wrong-doing, sighed and wept. Only the archbishop is said to have refrained. I believe his heart to have been hardened by his being a monk; but he began falsely to accuse the clergy of York before the king, of having caused the elect to resign the arch-bishopric. On the other hand, our elect, but now rejected, excused them and spoke in praise of their learning, honour, and uprightness. He added, 'I have now no share in the church of York except the love of the brotherhood. And now I would be ready, by God's help and theirs, to defend their cause at canon law against all who might choose to plead the same.' There was no reply.

Those of us who had come with him did not yet know what had happened, or how. When we knew, we were overcome by grief, pity, and joy, all at once: grief at the loss of our shepherd, pity for the distress in which he had been, and joy at his energy and stead-fastness. And by grief, pity, and joy [we came to] love

amare.[1]   Nec gestu tristicie signum dedit, set more
solito [a] iocunde et iocose agebat, ac si nichil contrarii
contigisset ; quod omnes suos modice consolabatur.

Verbum hoc per Angliam et Normanniam cito di-
vulgatum est.   Quod plerique pensantes vehementer
admirati sunt, clericum scilicet curialem, et de mensa
regia nutritum, et sic familiarem, tantum illi restitisse ;
quia indebitum poscebatur, tanto honori renunciasse.
Quibus vero bonitas et vigor mentis inerat, eum viriliter
egisse testabantur ei, et magnifice in laudem ascribebant.

Litteras domini pape, quas supradictum est eum
paulo ante suscepisse, Radulpho archiepiscopo, cui mit-
tebantur, non tradidit ; non enim modo habebat cui
consecraretur.   He tamen hic subscripte sunt:

Carta prememorati domini pape Paschalis [b]

[Paschalis] episcopus,[c] servus servorum dei, venerabili fratri, R[adulpho] Cantuariensi archiepiscopo,
salutem et apostolicam benediccionem.   Inter Cantuariensem et Eboracensem episcopos consuetudinem
a beato Honorio novimus institutam, ut alter con-
secretur ab altero.   Ceterum professionis exaccio nec
a beato Gregorio instituta est, nec iusticie racione
conceditur, unde et a predecessoribus nostris eam
prohibitam novimus.   Nos quoque te, frater karissime, ne ab Eboracensi archiepiscopo in consecracione
professionem exigas prohibemus, et illi ne faciat
interdicimus.[d]   Quod si propter hoc te ab eius consecracione subtraxeris, nos aliis ut eum consecrent

---

[a] subito, MS   [b] Pelagii, MS
[c] Collated with another copy in the *Reg. Magnum Album* at York,
i. 42
    [d] interdiximus, A

   [1] There appears to be a break in the text, but the meaning can be
guessed.

[him].¹ Nor did he show any sign of sadness, but was as merry and jocose as usual, as though nothing had happened to him; which was some poor consolation to us all.

The story was quickly spread far and wide throughout England and Normandy. Most people who thought over it were astonished that a clerk of the court, fed at the king's table, and so near a member of his household, should have offered such resistance, should have renounced so great an honour because more than was due was demanded from him. But those with good and stout hearts protested that he had shown himself a man, and praised him highly.

He did not present the pope's letter, the receipt of which was mentioned above, to archbishop Ralph, the addressee, for there was now nothing for him to be consecrated to. However, here it is:

Letter of the aforesaid Pope Paschal

Paschal, bishop, servant of the servants of God, to his venerable brother, Ralph, archbishop of Canterbury, greeting and apostolic blessing. We know that there is a custom established by the blessed Honorius between the bishops of Canterbury and of York, that each should be consecrated by the other. But the exaction of a profession was neither instituted by the blessed Gregory, nor is it permitted on the score of justice; wherefore we know it forbidden by our predecessors. We also therefore, dearest brother, forbid you to exact a profession from the archbishop of York at his consecration; and command him not to make it. But if you, on this account, refuse to consecrate him, we shall order another person to do

precipiemus. Etsi enim prioris locum obtineas, non tamen aut ecclesie tue suffraganeus est, aut tibi obedienciam debet.

Qui de nostris cum electo archiepiscopo venerant, abiecto, licencia accepta, domum tristes regrediuntur, quomodo actum sit nunciantes. Qualiter inde nobis visum fuerit ex subiectis litteris quas paulo ante [a] illi misimus agnosci potest.

Littere capituli Eboracensis ad suum electum quasi repulsum per regem [b]

F.110   Eborace metropolis archiepiscopo electo / et dilecto, et nunc quoque dilectissimo, T[urstino], capitulum eiusdem ecclesie salutem et amiciciam, et devote subieccionis obedienciam. Egregia probitatis tue magnificencia tibi gloriam, amicis tuis leticiam, adversantibus contulit confusionem,[c] et nostrum copiosius erga te accendit amorem. Omnibus fere de providencia vestra communis est sentencia in te benediccionis et laudacionis. Colloquentes de te invicem gratulantur ; plerique pre gaudio, alii pietate tue destitucionis lacrimantur ; et si qua adversus eos, quod nequaquam fecisti, non facienda fecisses, pro huius facti tui honestate de cordibus eorum diluta et penitus deleta forent. Gloriari potes, set in domino gloriare. Etenim si non est in deo gloriacio, vanitas est et elacio, et quidam sapiens ait : 'Aurum magna inflacio'. Qui vero de se humiliter senciens, divine efficacie ascribit quod facit, et facilius proficit quod intendit, et a deo premium recipit, set non aliunde requirit. Hec autem superflue dixisse videmur, modesciam et humilitatem tuam cognoscentes. Quia ergo pro ecclesie libertate tuenda, vel magis pro

---

[a] vero, MS
[b] This rubric is placed in the MS immediately after Pope Paschal's letter.   [c] confessionem, MS

it. For even though you are the senior, he is not
a suffragan of your church, nor owes you any obedience.

Those of us who had come with the archbishop elect
took leave of the archbishop rejected, and went home in
sorrow, with news of what had passed. What we
thought of it may be seen from the letter, which we sent
him a little before.

*Letter of the chapter of York to its archbishop
elect because of his rejection by the king*

To its best loved Thurstan, elect and beloved archbishop of the metropolitan city of York, the chapter
of the same church, greeting and friendship, and
the obedience of devout submission. The unusual
splendour of your uprightness has brought glory to
yourself, joy to your friends, confusion to your enemies, and kindled our love towards you in fuller
measure. The general feeling is one of blessing and
praise for your foresight. Those who speak of you
rejoice together: most weep for joy, but others in
pity for your displacement. And if you had acted
unfitly to them (which you never did), that would
have been washed away and erased from their hearts
by your honourable conduct now. You may well
boast, but do so in the Lord. For if your boast be
not in the Lord, it is vanity and pride; 'Gold puffeth
up', saith the wise. But he who is humble of heart,
and ascribeth his deeds to God, both succeeds better
in his aims and receives his reward from God, but
does not look for it from any other giver. But to us,
who know your modesty and humility, it seems need-
less to say this. Therefore, because you have fought

eiecta dignitate restituenda, constanter decertasti, nichil nos separabit a tua obediencia, et spirituali, quam super nos suscepimus, paternitate. Et quidem non essemus ecclesie filii, set privigni, si aliqua persuasione vel comminacione alium te vivente super nos pateremur induci, nisi forte iudicio aut precepto cui iure non liceat refragari. Ex hoc enim tua prelacio, vel si dici debet dominacio, nobis est amabilis et desiderabilis. Viriliter egisti. Confortetur cor tuum, et nostrum quidem bene confortatum est. Spem enim habemus per regem Anglorum nobis cum honore et gaudio tue restitucionis.

Archiepiscopus archiepiscopatum nostrum diucius vacare nolens, ne mora aliqua destitutus restitueretur, regi suggessit ut alteri daret qui patri suo et suis usibus et consuetudinibus contumaciter non refragaretur. Scriptum habebat in corde suo cui dare volebat, iuste et religiose de restitucione cogitans. Cui non erecta petenti rex recte respondit: 'Non sic estimo archiepiscopatum liberum esse. Pro amore meo quod potuit michi dimissum fecit. Aut cicius aut serius aliud forsitan quam putetis audiemus.'

Post modicum rex mare transiens in Normanniam, quinque annos fere continuavit. Exul noster cum eo transivit, quem satis honorifice secum habebat, nec volebat quod quilibet eum nisi archiepiscopum[a] vocaret, dissimiliter faciens et dicens, et contra quod fecerat alios dicere nolens. Cumque ibi moraretur, recogitans se regi dimittere non potuisse nisi quod a

[a] archiepiscopatum, MS

for the liberties of the church, or rather for the restoration of its dignity, nothing shall separate us from your obedience and the spiritual fatherhood which you have assumed over us. And indeed we should not be children, but step-children of the church, if through persuasion or threats we should allow another to be set over us, while you live, except by a judgment or command which we could not lawfully resist. After this, your presidency, or perhaps better, your lordship, is loved and desired by us. You have played the man. Let your heart be strong, and ours is of good comfort. For we hope that you may be restored to us with honour and joy by the king of England.

The archbishop was unwilling that our archbishopric should any longer be void, lest the displaced elect should be restored after a short delay. So he suggested to the king that he should give it to another who would not obstinately oppose his [spiritual] father and his uses and customs. He had it written in his heart to whom he wished to give it, with just and pious thoughts of restitution. But the king gave the right answer to his unrighteous request, 'I do not consider the archbishopric free to that extent. The elect, for love of me, resigned to me what was in his power to resign. Sooner or later we shall perhaps hear something you are not thinking of.'

A little later the king crossed to Normandy and stayed nearly five years. Our exile crossed with him, and the king treated him with sufficient honour, and refused to let anyone call him anything but archbishop, contradicting his own acts by his words, and unwilling that others should blame what he had done. And while Thurstan stayed there, he recollected that he had had no power to resign to the king any more than he had received

rege acceperat, neque regem recepisse nisi quod de-
derat, et dominus papa eleccionem eius litteris suprascriptis confirmaverat, Romam eundi [licenciam] a rege
quesivit, cui sepe per se et alios instanti rex non aquievit.
Ab Anglia longa cathena retentus in Normannia quasi
sub custodia detinebatur. Ille nec de itinere suo fur-
tum facere, nec regem adhuc exasperare volebat. Exoniensis episcopus,[1] a rege contra nos Romam trans-
missus, iam redierat; qui, nichil adeptus, Cantuariensi
archiepiscopo consilium dando mandaverat, ut ipsemet
sine dilacione dominum papam requireret. Cui adqui-
escens sic se facere dixit et paravit.

Transacto trium mensium spacio, communicato
nostro comproborum virorum de provincia nostra consilio, idoneum, et factu opportunum visum est, regem /
F.12 [de] archiepiscopo ab illo nobis tradito et suscepto
requirere. Duobus archidiaconis de ecclesia nostra, et
uni canonico Beverlacensis ecclesie, et monacho uni
Eboracensis monasterii obediencia hec iniuncta est.
Paratis commeatibus, mari transito, pervenerunt ubi rex
erat, adventu, et quod ei volebant loqui, prius per quendam de suis [nunciatis]. Eos accusatus est quod sine
licencia sua illuc transierant. At illis respondentibus
non estimare se esse huius momenti quod de hac re
licenciam querere deberent, ille subiunxit: 'Rex ad
presens non potest loqui vobis, set iubet ut exspectetis [a]
eum', usque tunc et illic, diem et locum designans. Sic
ter et quater de termino in terminum, de loco in locum
protrahens, audire nos protelavit. Prestolabatur eum
cuius adventum presto esse audierat, Cantuariensem
archiepiscopum, de quo que verba aut que alia afferret
scire volebat [ante]quam illos audiret. Interim cum

[a] expectatis, MS

[1] William de Warelwast, 11 Aug. 1107–27 Sept. 1137

from him, nor the king to have received more than he
had himself given; and the pope had confirmed his
election by the letter above written. So he asked leave
to go to Rome; but though he pressed his request in
person and through others, the king would not agree.
He was kept in Normandy, away from England, as if on
a long chain, under guard. He would not 'steal away',
or further exasperate the king. The bishop of Exeter,[1]
who had been sent to Rome by the king to plead against
us, had now returned without success, and had advised
the archbishop of Canterbury to seek the pope in person
without delay. The archbishop agreed, said he was
ready, and made his preparations.

After three months, having taken counsel with other
worthy men of our province, we thought it right, and a
suitable occasion, to demand of the king the archbishop
whom he had given us and we had received. The task
was enjoined on two archdeacons of our church, a canon
of Beverley, and a monk of the monastery of York. They
made their preparations, crossed the sea, and came to
where the king was, having previously announced their
arrival and their wish to speak with the king by one of
his courtiers. The king accused them of having come
without his leave. But when they answered that they
did not consider themselves of sufficient importance to
need to ask leave, he replied, 'The king cannot speak
with you now, but bids you wait for him', until such
and such a place and time, which he named. He thus
put off hearing us three or four times, adjourning it from
time to time and from place to place. He was waiting
for the coming of the archbishop of Canterbury, which
he had heard was near, wanting to know what message
or what else he brought, before giving our messengers a
hearing. Meantime all, or two, or one of them stayed

H

illo propter quem venerant morabantur omnes, vel duo, vel unus, quibus eque liberaliter impendebat, ac si archiepiscopi redditus ei detulissent, vel sibi servari sperasset.

Adveniente archiepiscopo, et cum rege locuto, tunc demum et nostris cum rege loquendi dies certus et locus prefixus est. Ad quem venientes, premissa salutacione ex parte nostra et benigne reddita, sic aiunt, 'Eboracensis ecclesia vos, dominum et regem suum, humiliter requirit, quatinus restituatis illi archiepiscopum quem dedistis. Nos illum suscipimus : sicut de eo nobis bene promisistis, quantulum inter nos conversatus est, et nos invenimus. Precepto nostro ecclesie diaconus et sacerdos ordinatus est ; obedienciam et subieccionem, sicut animarum nostrarum preposito, illi promisimus ; si inconsulte vel coactus ecclesiam dimisit, quanti ponderis esse debeat prudenciam vestram nosse non ambigimus. Potuit autem potestati vestre dimisisse que de libertate regum et principum et ceterorum ecclesie donata sunt ; alia non potuit. Nemo est preter summum pontificem qui nos a iugo subieccionis sue absolvere queat. Nisi per illum non possumus alium recipere, utpote deinceps honore carituri et infamia notandi.'

Adhibuerant secum Ranulphum Dunelmensem episcopum et quosdam ecclesie nostre amicos. Respondenti regi quod bene consuleret ecclesie nostre et pro quo petebant, et illi subdiderunt : 'Oporteret, domine rex, et bene et celeriter, etenim nec parochia, nec diocesis, nedum provincia sine gravi periculo diu vacare potest. Et quia in regno vestro ad nutum vestrum [a] cuncta procedunt, ac [b] cor regis in manu dei est,[1] et vobis

---

       [a] in *ins.* MS   [b] ad, MS

with the man for whose sake they had come ; and he treated them as liberally as if they had brought him the revenues of an archbishop, or he had hoped they were being saved up for him.

When the archbishop came and had spoken with the king, our messengers were at last given a day and place for their interview. They came with our greeting, which was politely returned, and said, 'The church of York humbly requests you, her lord and king, to restore to her the archbishop whom you gave. We accept him. In the short time that he has been with us we have found him to fulfil the good promise which you made to us of him. At our bidding he has been ordained deacon and priest of the church. We have promised him obedience and submission as to one set over our souls. We have no doubt you know, in your wisdom, what weight should be given to his having resigned the church unadvisedly and under compulsion. He had the power to resign into your hands whatever was given to the church by the generosity of kings, princes, and others ; but nothing more. There is no one but the pope who can release us from the yoke of submission to him. Except by his means we cannot receive another, since henceforth we must lose our honour and bear a black mark.'

They had called to their aid Ranulf, bishop of Durham, and some other friends of our church. When the king replied that he would take good counsel for the church and for him on whose behalf they prayed, our friends added : 'That should be done well and quickly ; for neither a parish nor a diocese, not to speak of a province, can be void for long without grave danger. And because in your kingdom all things obey your nod, and because "The king's heart is in the hand of the Lord" [1] ;

---

[1] Prov. 21 : 1

magis incumbit melius providere.' Bene et celeriter se
provisurum pollicitante, licencia accepta discesserunt,
et cum exule nostro locuti, quamcicius repatriantes ad
propria reversi sunt.

Preter emulos nostros nemo fuit qui requisicionem
hanc iusticie et honestati nobis non annumerasset.
Quem Cantuariensis ^a eici fecerat, faciebat adhuc et
detineri ne Romam iret. Ipse vero paratus venerat
illuc ire. Expoliatus noster ad regem veniens dixit se
nolle longius remanere, set de statu suo et de consilio
anime sue apostolicum consulere. Rex vero, isto constanter et diu negante et renitente, precibus, blandiciis,
promissis vix optinere potuit ut remaneret quousque
archiepiscopus redisset, firmiter ei verbo paciscens quod

F.12v quicquid ipse / detulisset, ad nichil eum cogeret, donec
et ille Romam pergens ex ore domini pape audisset.
Dixit quoque noster se audisse a familiaribus suis illum,
non impetrato quod querebat, nuncquam redditurum,
set Ierosolimam adire. Cui rex ait : 'Etsi ipse ierit
Ierosolimam, et ego vos Romam ire permittam'.

Romam proficiscens, iuste oracionis causa Apostolorum limina visitare desiderans, dixit se euntem cornua emere, quoniam Rome omnia venalia erant. Utrum
propter cornua, vel alia, emenda, scimus quod cum
sit Cantuariensis possessio opulens ^b et redditibus fe-
cunda, archiepiscopus professionis huius adipiscende
causa de thesauro ecclesie aliquantum venundedit ; de
terris vero aliquas dedit, aliquas in vadimonium posuit.
Paupertatem de paupere loco propter resistendum in-

<hr>

^a Cantuariensem, MS   ^b optilens, MS

it is the more your duty to make better provision.' As
the king promised that he would provide well and
quickly, they took their leave, and departed, and after
speaking with our exile, went home as quickly as they
could.

Everybody but our rivals gave us credit for a just
and honourable petition. The archbishop of Canterbury
managed to have the man whom he had displaced still
further hindered from going to Rome. He had, however, come prepared to make the journey himself. The
victim came to the king and said that he would stay no
longer, but consult the pope about his position and his
soul's health. But the king, despite his steadfast and
prolonged refusal and resistance, only just succeeded by
prayers, coaxing, and promises, in persuading him to
stay till the archbishop should return; making a definite
bargain that whatever answer the archbishop brought
back, he would not compel him to anything until he
also had gone to Rome and had his answer from the
pope's mouth. Our elect also said that he had heard
from those about him that the archbishop, if he failed
in his request, would never come back, but go to
Jerusalem. And the king replied, 'Even if he does go
to Jerusalem, I shall allow you to go to Rome'.

As the archbishop set out, desiring to visit the
threshold of the Apostles for his duty of prayer there, he
said that he was going to Rome to buy horns, since at
Rome everything was for sale. Whether he really meant
to buy horns or something else, we know that though
the temporalities of Canterbury are rich, and bring in
a good income, he sold some of the treasure of the
church for the sake of obtaining Thurstan's profession.
He sold some of the lands and gave others in pledge.
He was not a man in poor circumstances giving or selling

iurie nec dedit nec vendidit. Invadiavit deo ei necessaria adminiculante.

Erant cum archiepiscopo in profeccione hac Herbertus Norwicensis episcopus, et Hugo Certesiensis
abbas et medicus, et Willelmus de Corbolio Dorover-
nensis canonicus, postea regularis canonicus et prior
sancte Oside, qui et Radulfo in archiepiscopatum
successit. Moventibus illis interim nec adhuc multum
progressis,[a] archiepiscopus morbo graviter tactus in
Francia in lectum decidit, unde post longum, et vix,
nec bene convalescens, ceptum iter cum suis arripuit.
Transcensis Alpedibus in Lumbardia Herbertus episcopus, egritudine valida percussus, ulterius tunc ire
non valuit. Fortasse de ambobus ideo deo sic placuit,
quod ambo sic cornua empturos superbe dixerant, et
erecto collo, nec ignoranter, adversus iusticiam esse
currebant. Abbas medicus, [qua]si deo illos pro mag-
niloquio suo castigante, salutem servare nequivit. Deo
postea miserente, de restituenda forsitan adiuvit.

Episcopo diebus aliquot exspectato, nec convales-
cente, archiepiscopus cum reliquis suis Romam venit.
Cornuum venditorem nullum ibi invenit. Beneventi
tunc degebat sanctus et verus pater apostolicus, Symonis
Petri vicarius, Symonis Magi adversarius. Versus Bene-
ventum non habens archiepiscopus bonum ventum, non
exhibuit suum adventum, neque quem querebat invenit
eventum. Quo si venisset, cornua venalia nulla illic
invenisset. Loquens igitur ad dominum papam per
internuncios sepe missos et remissos, et temptata curia
et retemptata, nec prece, nec precio, neque quolibet
modo optinere potuit quod petebat : responsumque est
illi quod pro camera sua auro et argento plena professionem ecclesie nostre illi non concederet. Set ne nichilo

---

[a] progressus, MS

his poor means to resist a wrong. God had given him
enough, but yet he went into debt.

The archbishop's companions in this journey were
Herbert, bishop of Norwich, Hugh, abbot of Chertsey,
a physician, and William of Corbeuil, canon of Canterbury, afterwards a Canon Regular and prior of St
Osyth's, who succeeded to Ralph's archbishopric. On
their way, before they had gone very far, the archbishop
fell seriously ill in France and took to his bed. It was a
long time before he could resume his journey, only just
recovered and not too well. They crossed the Alps, but
in Lombardy bishop Herbert fell sick and could go no
further. Perhaps God so willed in both cases, because
both had proudly said they would buy horns, and were
stiff-neckedly, and knowingly hastening to commit
injustice. The abbot, their physician, was unable to
keep them well, as though God were punishing both of
them for boasting; he may possibly have helped them
to recover, when God afterwards took pity on them.

They waited some days for the bishop; but, as he
got no better, the archbishop and the others came on to
Rome. He found no seller of horns there. The holy
and true apostolic father, the vicar of Simon Peter, the
adversary of Simon Magus, was then staying at Benevento. The archbishop having no 'good wind' for
Benevento, made no 'advent' there, nor did he find the
'event' what he expected. Had he got there, he would
have found no horns for sale. He conversed with the
pope by means of go-betweens passing backward and
forward, he tried the papal court again and again, but
neither by prayer nor for a price could he obtain what
he sought. The answer was that the pope would not
grant him the profession of our church for his room full
of gold and silver. But lest he go away ashamed at

effecto pudibunde rediret, dedit ei dominus papa
litteras, quibus mandando precipiebat, quatinus haberet
quicquid iuste et canonice predecessores sui possedisse
dinoscebantur; quod nullus contraibat nec calumpniabatur.

Redeunte in Normanniam, facies eius, sicut Moisi,
non apparuit cornuta,[1] nec multi videntes eum exterriti sunt. Set sepe recogitavi que cornua empturum
se iactavit. Sunt cornua dei de quibus Abacuc dicit,
'Splendor eius, ut lux erit; Co[rnua] in m[anibus]
eius'.[2] Sunt cornua diaboli, de quibus in Apocalipsi, bes-
tia habebat 'decem cornua, et cauda eius trahebat ter-
ciam partem stellarum celi'.[3] Sunt et cornua iustorum
F.13 et cornua reproborum de / quibus Psalmista in eodem
versu, 'Et omnia cornua peccatorum con[fringam], et ex-
[altabuntur] c[ornua] i[usti]'.[4] Horum alia cornua
desideranda sunt, et precio multo, si venalia essent, com-
paranda; alia viriliter confringenda, vel studiose cavenda.
Cornua duorum [sic] mala expugnant; cornua bona im-
pugnant.

Litteris domini pape quas archiepiscopus detulerat,
regi, et quibus utrique placuit expositis, dictum est ei
quod in Anglia vel Normannia remansisse melius et
honestius fuerat. Ipse vero [pro]posuit necdum in
Angliam reverti. Vetus proverbium est, 'Quod rex
loquitur stabile debet esse'. Turstinus presbyter venit
ad regem dicens: 'Domine, archiepiscopus rediit. Quantum vobis placuit exspectavi. Tempus est modo et me
Romam ire.' At illi nondum volenti, et [ut] adhuc
aliquantum exspectaret exhortanti,[a] respondit: 'Vos
scitis, domine, salva reverencia vestra loquor, quid

---

^a exornanti, MS

¹ Exod. 34 : 29-30 (Vulgate)   ² Hab. 3 : 4
     ³ Rev. 12 : 3-4   ⁴ Ps. 75 : 12

having gained nothing, the pope gave him a letter in which he gave command that he should have whatever his predecessors were known to have possessed; things which nobody opposed or claimed.

When he returned to Normandy, his face did not appear to have horns, like that of Moses,[1] nor were many afraid when they saw him. But I have often thought over the question, what were the horns which he said he was going to buy. There are the horns of God, of which Habakkuk says, 'And his brightness was as the light: he had horns coming out of his hand'.[2] There are the devil's horns, of which, in the Revelation, the beast had 'ten horns . . . and his tail drew the third part of the stars of heaven'.[3] There are also the horns of the just and the horns of the wicked, of which the Psalmist speaks in the same verse, 'All the horns of the ungodly also will I break: and the horns of the righteous shall be exalted'.[4] Some of these horns are to be desired and bought at a great price, if they were for sale; others to be manfully broken and diligently avoided. The horns of the two former overcome evil: those [of the last] attack good.

When the pope's letter which the archbishop had brought was shown to the king and to such as both of them wished, the archbishop was told that it would have been better and more honourable for him to have stayed in England or in Normandy. But he was not minded to return to England even now. It is an old proverb, 'The king's word must be sure'. Thurstan the priest came to the king and said, 'My lord, the archbishop has come back. I have waited the time you fixed. Now, it is time for me to go to Rome.' But when the king was unwilling and exhorted him to wait a little longer, he replied, 'You know, my lord, saving your

michi pepigistis'. Nescio qua pocione oblivionis vel contradiccionis archiepiscopus regem potaverat, set prorsus et hac vice licenciam eundi denegavit. Putabat enim facile eum a papa consecrandum, quod et rex nolebat, et archiepiscopus nimium metuebat, nec ille adhuc voluit regem offendere, exspectans tempus miserendi eius. De qua re consilium a nobis requirenti litteris istis mandavimus illi.

Secunde littere eiusdem capituli ad eundem electum

Dilecto et electo domino et patri suo T[urstino] canonici sancti Petri et sui de bono incepto medium, continuum ad honestum finem. Hoc vobis, venerande sacerdos, suggerere,[a] persuadere et deprecari volumus ut, quantum potestis, salva fidelitate Jesu Christi, et sancte ecclesie libertate et vestro honore, vel eundo vel huc redeundo, vel quicquid faciendo, studeatis regis benevolenciam retinere. Qua retenta si Romam ieritis, quem vel quos de nobis vobis placebit mandabitis: si vero aliter, tamen sit in consilio vestro, quo semper in hac re sapiencius et utilius usi[b] estis quam alieno. Hoc ideo vobis dicimus quia sicut ira regis discesseritis et aliqui de nobis vobiscum, levius erit euntibus quam remanentibus, si non possent defendere, eos non misisse. Scimus vere quod quando Willelmus de Beverlie Romam ivit, rex magno scrutinio scrutatus est si nostra missione vel consilio isset.

Misimus et illi alias litteras, set occulte, quas deferret domino pape, si Romam iret, et de eius eieccione, et per quos, [et de qua] causa diu retentus fuerat; que et hic subscripte sunt.

[a] surgere, MS   [b] usus, MS

reverence, what bargain you made with me'. I know
not with what draught of forgetfulness or contradiction
the archbishop had drugged the king ; but this time too
he refused leave to go. For he thought that Thurstan
might easily be consecrated by the pope, which the king
did not wish and the archbishop dreaded exceedingly ;
nor did Thurstan yet wish to offend the king, but waited
the time when he would take pity on him. He asked our
advice about this, and we sent him the following letter:

Second letter of the chapter to the archbishop-elect

To their beloved and elect lord and father,
Thurstan, St Peter's and his canons, may his good
beginning lead on to an honourable conclusion. We
wish to suggest to you, persuade and pray you, our
reverend priest, in going, or returning here, or whatever you do, to do your best to keep on good terms with
the king, saving your faith in Jesus Christ, the freedom
of holy church, and your own honour. If you can
do so and go to Rome, you may send for one or more
of us as you please. But if not, act on your own
judgment, which we have found, in this business,
wiser and more profitable than anyone else's. We
say this to you, because, as you and some of us with
you left under the king's displeasure, it will be easier
for those who go than for those who stay, unless they
can protest that they did not send them. We are
assured that when William of Beverley went to Rome,
the king made a strict inquiry whether he had gone
as our envoy or on our advice.

We sent him another letter, but secretly, to take to
the pope, if he went to Rome, both about his displacement and by whom, and why, he had been kept so long
from coming. This also is annexed.

Littere eiusdem capituli pro eodem electo eidem
domino pape transmisse

Patri beato et reverendo domino pape, Dei gracia
summo pontifici, clerus Eboracensis salutem et debite
ac devote subieccionis obsequium. Eboracensis ecclesia pari dignitate Cantuariensi ecclesie a beato
Gregorio gentis Anglorum apostolo instituta, nova
institucione exigitur illi subiacere et cartam professionis tradere. Que quidem exacio contra apostolicam sedem est invasio; et, si recipitur, usurpacio
facienti quoque non sine periculo. Soli etenim
Romane ecclesie metropolitanorum debetur professio.
Hanc vero professionem quia electus noster, beati
pape instituta, et apostolice sedis dignitatem, [et]
suam, servare volens, facere timuit, consilio, persuasionibus, actu Cantuariensis archiepiscopi et suffra-
ganeorum suorum, ab ecclesia, ad quam est electus,

F.13v iniuste quasi / eiectus, sicque per annum et dimidium
in exilio multas passus est molestias et tribulaciones;
et nos, populus eius, sumus quasi oves disperse et
errantes. Propter quod cum Romam adire, et a
paternitate vestra consilium vellet requirere, supra-
dictorum callida machinacione quasi sub custodia
detentus est, donec Roma redisset qui contra Romam
ire parabat, arbitrans ipse et sui electi nostri professionem, licet indebitam, a summo pontifice pecunia
se posse emere, aperiens os suum in blasphemias
contra Romam, affirmantes omnia esse venalia Rome;
set a sanctitate vestra nil nisi iustum et canonicum
impetrare valuit. Pro hac igitur integritate veritatis
et iusticie, Francia, Normannia, Anglia nomen vestrum

*Letter of the same chapter sent to our lord the pope on
behalf of the said elect*

To our blessed and reverend lord the pope, by the
grace of God supreme pontiff, the clergy of York,
greeting and the obedience of due and devout submission. The church of York, which was founded by
St Gregory, the apostle of the English, of equal
dignity with the church of Canterbury, is now by a
new constitution required to be subject to that church
and to deliver it a charter of profession. This demand
is a trespass against the apostolic see, and if it is
admitted, a usurpation not without danger to the
aggressor. For the profession of metropolitans is only
due to the church of Rome. But because our elect,
in his wish to observe the institutions of the pope, the
dignity of the apostolic see, and his own, has been
afraid to make this profession, he has by the advice,
persuasion, and action of the archbishops of Canterbury and their suffragans, been virtually ejected from
the church to which he was elected, and thus for a
year and a half has endured in exile many discomforts
and tribulations ; and we, his people, are like sheep
scattered and strayed. For this reason when he wished
to come to Rome, and ask the counsel of your fatherhood, by the cunning contrivance of those men he was
detained as though under guard until the return of
him who was preparing to go against Rome, he and
his party thinking that he could buy from the pope
the profession of our elect, though none was owed ;
uttering blasphemies against Rome, and saying that
everything there was for sale. But he could obtain
nothing from your Holiness but what was just and
lawful. For this integrity of truth and justice France,

predicant et benedicunt, et statutis illius deinceps magis contraire verebuntur. Nos vero inter alios et super alios beatitudini vestre gracias agimus, et in bonitate sanctitatis et iusticie vestre certam spem habemus. Hunc ergo dilectum nostrum T[urstinum', virum venerabilem, religiose conversacionis,[a] de cuius concordi eleccione audistis et litteris vestris confirmastis, ad vos ut ad dominum et patrem dirigimus, et quasi pedibus pietatis vestre prostrati lacrimabiliter supplicamus ut tali viro sic electo et recepto, et hac occasione eiecto, quod dignum est excellencie vestre faciatis. Elegimus potius exilium pati quam super hunc nobis alium introduci.

Comperto Rome electum nostrum sic esse eiectum, et ne Romam veniret retemptum, dominus papa tota et curia graviter tulerunt. Erat tunc in Normannia Anselmus nepos Anselmi archiepiscopi, qui modo est abbas sancti Eadmundi, missus ab apostolica sede ut in Anglia legacione fungeretur. Set rex donec et ipse rediret secum detinuit, blandiciis et beneficiis in Normannia sic ligatum quod Anglia non vidit eum legatum. Huic itaque dominus papa litteras misit, quarum unam regi traderet de eiecti restitucione, alteras Radulpho archiepiscopo de restituti consecracione. Utrarumque exempla hic inserta sunt.

Littere domini pape Paschalis [b] *ad regem H. misse*
pro eodem electo

Paschalis [b] episcopus, servus servorum dei, dilecto filio H., illustri Anglorum regi, salutem et apostolicam benediccionem. Nos auctoritate dei [c] de

---

[a] conversacioni, MS   [b] Pascasii, Pascasius, MS
[c] auctore Deo, A

Normandy, and England proclaim and bless your name, and will henceforth be the more afraid to transgress its statutes. Among others, indeed more than others, we give thanks to your beatitude, and have a sure hope in the goodness of your holiness and justice. We therefore send our beloved Thurstan, a reverend and religious man, of whose unanimous election you have heard, and have confirmed it by your letter, to you as our lord and father. And, as though prostrate at the feet of your pity, we beseech you with tears to deal as befits your excellency with such a man, so elected and accepted and on this account displaced. We would rather suffer exile than have another brought in over him.

When it became known at Rome that our elect had thus been cast out and prevented from coming to Rome, the pope and his whole court took it very ill. Anselm, nephew of archbishop Anselm, now abbot of St Edmund's, was then in Normandy, sent by the apostolic see to be legate in England. But the king kept him with him until he should go back, so bound by flattery and gifts that England never saw him as legate. The pope accordingly sent him letters, one to be given to the king, about the restoration of the displaced archbishop, the other to archbishop Ralph about his consecration when he should have been restored. Copies of both are annexed.

Letter of Pope Paschal to King Henry
on behalf of the said elect

Paschal, bishop, servant of the servants of God, to Henry, illustrious king of the English, greeting and apostolic blessing. We, by God's authority, trust not

probitate tua non tantum bona, set eciam meliora, confidimus. Idcirco monemus excellenciam tuam ut, divine gracie memor semper existas, que tibi et regni pacem et iusticie noticiam ^a tribuit. Honorem igitur dei et ecclesiarum eius in regno tuo diligenter observa et iusticiam diligenter ^b exequere, quia per honorem dei tuus profecto honor augebitur. Audivimus electum Eboracensis ecclesie, virum quidem sapientem et strenuum, sine iudicio ab Eboracensi ecclesia sequestratum, quod nimirum iusticie divine et sanctorum patrum institucionibus adversatur. Nos quidem, neque Cantuariensem ecclesiam minui, nec ^c Eboracensem volumus preiudicium pati, set eam constitutionem que a beato Gregorio, Anglice gentis apostolo, inter easdem ecclesias constituta est, firmam censemus illibatamque servari. Idem igitur electus, ut iusticia exigit, ad suam ecclesiam omnimodis revocetur. Si quid autem questionis inter easdem ecclesias agitur, presentibus utriusque partibus in nostra presencia pertractetur, ut, patrocinante deo, utraque ecclesia finem sue iusticie consequatur.^d

F.14   [Paschalis] / episcopus, servus servorum dei, venerabili fratri R[adulpho] Cantuariensi episcopo salutem et apostolicam benediccionem. Quanto amplius de vestre ^e dileccionis sinceritate confidimus, tanto amplius ammiramur quod ea videaris exigere que Romane solum competere videtur ecclesie. Nosti enim, frater karissime, beati Gregorii ad Augustinum verba ita in eius epistola de Eboracensi episcopo esse disposita : 'Post obitum tuum episcopis quos ordinav[er]it presit, ut Londoniensis episcopi nullo modo dicioni subiaceat.

^a normam, A
^b observa . . . . diligenter] *ins.* from A   ^c nec] vel, A
^d Collated with another copy in the *Reg. Magnum Album* at York, i. 48a
^e sue, A

merely in good, but even in better things from your
righteousness. We therefore admonish your excellency
always to remember the divine grace which bestows
on you peace in your realm and the knowledge of
justice. Take heed, then, of the honour of God and
of His churches in your realm, and diligently execute
justice, because by honouring God your own honour
will be increased. We have heard that the elect of
the church of York, a wise and active man, has been
deprived of the church of York without judgment,
contrary to divine justice and the constitutions of the
holy Fathers. Now we neither wish the church of
Canterbury to be made less, nor that of York to be
prejudiced; but we rule that the decision made by
St Gregory, the apostle of the English, between the
two churches be kept firm and unbroken. Let the
elect, therefore, by all means be recalled to his church,
as justice demands. And let any question pending
betwixt the churches be dealt with in our presence
and that of the parties, that by God's help, both
churches may receive full justice.

[*The pope's letter to the archbishop of Canterbury*]

Paschal, bishop, servant of the servants of God, to
his venerable brother, Ralph, [arch]bishop of Canterbury, greeting and apostolic blessing. The more
fully we trust in the sincerity of your love, the more
we marvel that you should appear to demand what is
only appropriate to the church of Rome. For you
know, dearest brother, that the words of St Gregory
to Augustine in his letter about the bishop of York
run as follows : 'After your death let him be the head of
the bishops whom he has ordained, and be in no way

I

Sit vero inter Londonie et Eborace civitatis [episcopos] in posterum ista honoris distinccio, ut ipse prior habeatur qui prius fuerit ordinatus.' Quo igitur modo, qua racione ab electo Eboracensis ecclesie professionem exigitis,[a] et propter hoc ei manum imponere detractatis,[b] cum, secundum prescriptam[c] beati Gregorii constitucionem, nullo modo dicioni tue debeat subiacere? Precipimus ergo ut pro vestrarum ecclesiarum consuetudine eum secundum sanctorum scita canonum consecretis omni subieccionis exaccione deposita. Alioquin nos eum iuxta communem ecclesiarum morem ab Eboracensis ecclesie suffraganeis precipimus consecrari. Etsi enim prioris locum optineas, nec ecclesie tue suffraganeus est, nec tibi obedienciam debet.[d]

Litteris domini pape a rege acceptis, et consilio ab hiis qui cum eo erant episcopis et ceteris quesito, et ab illis quoque qui in Anglia erant, utrorumque consilio accepto domino pape de hac revocacione obedire, (deo gracias et domino pape!), restitutus est. Ipse vero habebat litteras supradictas de eius consecracione Radulpho archiepiscopo directas. Set non fuit ei consilium eas illi in Normanniam tradere, bene scienti quod non[e] [eum] consecraret donec ad ecclesiam rediret. Credebat quod ei dictum fuerat archiepiscopum in Angliam indilate transiturum. Set credo quod plus ideo differebat quod nostrum litteras illas habere et eas illi traditurum premunitus erat. Revocatus noster ad nos regreditur, et cum gaudio magno suscipitur, et multo campliore quam prius honore et reverencia dignus iudicatur.

Evoluto aliquot mensium circulo, et Radulpho archiepiscopo ex industria morante ne precepto pape electum

---

[a] exigis, A   [b] detractas, A
[c] prescriptam, A, scripta, MS
[d] Collated with another copy of the letter in the *Reg. Magnum Album* at York, i. 48   [e] non non, MS

subject to the bishop of London. But let this distinction of honour afterwards be between the bishops of the cities of London and York, that whichever was first ordained be regarded as first.' How then, and with what reason, do you demand a profession from the elect of York, and refuse to lay your hand on him on this account, when, according to the constitution of St Gregory, he is in no way subject to your jurisdiction? We therefore order that, in accordance with the custom of your churches, you consecrate him as directed in the holy canons, without any demand for submission. Otherwise, we order him to be consecrated according to the common custom of churches by the suffragans of the church of York. For, although you hold the first place, he is neither a suffragan of your church nor owes you any obedience.

When the king had received the pope's letter, and had asked the advice both of the bishops and others who were with him and of those in England, and had been advised by both to follow the pope's advice about recalling Thurstan; thanks to God and the pope, he was restored. He had, however, the aforesaid letter about his consecration addressed to archbishop Ralph. But he thought it better not to present it to him in Normandy, knowing well that he would not consecrate him until he returned to his church. He had been told, and believed that the archbishop would return to England without delay. But I believe that he delayed all the longer, because he had been warned that our elect had that letter and would present it to him. Our elect on his recall came back to us and was received with great joy, and thought worthy of much more honour and reverence than before.

After some months, while Ralph deliberately delayed, lest he should obey the pope's orders and consecrate

nostrum consecraret, venit ad nos qui diceret papam
P[aschalem] obiisse, et Iohannem cancellarium, in papam Gelasium creatum, iam in Galliam pervenisse.
Quo audito, electus noster et nos omnes de tam bono
patre et iusto patrono graviter in iure quidem contristati
sumus, set de novo spem bonam et confidenciam in deo
habebamus. Ipse enim causam nostram multum iuverat
adversariis nostris adversatus: multis vero credibile
erat quod R[adulphus] archiepiscopus et sui nec illum
doluerunt decessisse, nec istum letati sunt successisse.

Secundum rerum mutaciones et consilia [mutare]
oportet. Consiliatum est electo nostro transmarinis et
citra, et sibi quidem hoc potissimum videbatur, in
Normannia[m] regredi, deinde et novum papam tendere. Id quidem occulte fieri decebat. Comperto rex
forsitan inhiberet. Consilio paucis revelato, cum litteris nostris et quos elegit, quasi propter alia facienda,
Londoniam venit. Ibi divisione facta, ipse viliter
indutus, et equitans non cognoscendus cum parte [a]
suorum Dorovernum, quam cito potuit transfretavit.
Reliqui apud Hestingas transierunt. Deus autem sic
disposuit quod qui primi in Normanniam venirent, ad
locum designatum exspectare iussi, non amplius una
nocte exspectantes adunati sunt. Fuit qui regi diceret
Eboracensem electum Anglia latenter egressum per
F.14v exteras regiones ad papam / perrexisse, set rex minime
credens, illo post modicum ad eum veniente, verum
non dubitabile habuit. Et iam quidam benevolus noster
ad papam pergens apud urbem Ianuam ei occurrerat.
Per quem, si quid erat de statu nostro quod non cogno-
visset, edoctus, scripsit regi et archiepiscopo, nostro
quoque electo, sicut prudencie sue visum est cuique
convenire. Que littere subscripte sunt.

a patre *ins.* MS

our elect, a messenger arrived and told us that Pope
Paschal was dead, and that John the chancellor, now
Pope Gelasius, had already arrived in France. On
hearing this, our elect and all of us, sorry as we rightly
were to lose so good a father and just patron, had good
hope of the new pope and trusted in God. For John
had been of great help to our cause in opposing our
adversaries. Many of us thought that archbishop
Ralph and his friends had not mourned the late pope
or rejoiced at the accession of the new one.

A change of circumstances involves a change of plan.
Our elect was advised, both from abroad and at home,
and himself thought it best to go back to Normandy,
and then go on to the pope. But that had to be done
secretly: if the king heard it, he might perhaps forbid
it. Few people were told: with our letter and those of
us whom he chose, he came to London as though on
other business. There we separated. He put on
common clothes, rode in disguise with a few friends to
Dover, and crossed as quickly as he could. The others
crossed at Hastings. But God so disposed that those
who got to Normandy first and were ordered to await
the others at the place appointed, did not have to wait
more than one night to be joined by the others. Someone told the king that the elect of York had secretly left
England and gone abroad to the pope. The king did
not believe it; but when the elect soon afterwards came
to him, knew the certain truth. By this time a certain
friend of ours on his way to the pope met him at Genoa
and the pope, having been told by him whatever he did
not know of our position, wrote to the king and the
archbishop and to our elect as seemed wisest to him in
each case. The letters follow.

Littere Gelasii ad eundem regem pro eodem electo

Gelasius episcopus, servus servorum dei, dilecto filio H[enrico] illustri Anglorum regi salutem et apostolicam benediccionem. Et persone vestre et regno vestro non parum detrimenti esse cognoscitur quod ecclesie tamdiu manent solacio destitute. Quod Eboracensi ecclesie accidisse perpendimus et dolemus; unde nobilitati vestre precipimus ut si Cantuariensis episcopus Eboracensem electum, secundum domini predecessoris nostri sancte memorie P[aschalis] pape preceptum, et litterarum nostrarum mandatum, consecrare noluerit, utrumque simul ad nostram presenciam dirigatis, quatinus que inter eos causa iactatur, ante nos, auctore deo, apostolice sedis iudicio decidatur.

Littere eiusdem Gelasii pape ad eundem archi-
episcopum Cantuariensem pro eodem electo

Gelasius episcopus, servus servorum dei, R[adulpho] Cantuariensi archiepiscopo salutem et apostolicam benediccionem. Pro tue religionis specimine quod filii nostri abbatis relacio apud nos maxime commendavit, predecessor noster sancte memorie P[aschalis] papa, me potissimum suggerente, in promocione seu translacione tua a rigore iusticie declinavit. Ceterum que de ᵃ te concepta est spes, nos decepisse et confudisse perspicitur. Vere siquidem religionis est Christi vestigia imitari, de quo scriptum est, 'Humiliavit seipsum, factus obediens usque ad mortem'.[1] Et de seipso ipsemet dicit: 'Discite a me quia mitis sum et humilis corde'.[2] Hanc humilitatis ᵇ for-

---

ᵃ om. MS   ᵇ quia mitis sum et humilitatis forma, A

Letter of Gelasius to the king for the same elect

Gelasius, bishop, servant of the servant of God, to his beloved son, Henry, illustrious king of the English, greeting and apostolic blessing. It is known to be damaging to your person and your realm that churches remain so long disconsolate. We have considered and lament what has happened to the church of York. Wherefore we direct your nobleness that if the [arch]bishop of Canterbury will not consecrate the elect of York, according to the order of our predecessor, Pope Paschal, of blessed memory, and the command of our letters, you shall send both of them to our presence, that whatever cause is pending between them may be decided before us, by God's authority, by the judgment of the apostolic see.

Letter of Pope Gelasius to the archbishop of Canterbury for the same elect

Gelasius, bishop, servant of the servants of God, to Ralph, archbishop of Canterbury, greeting and apostolic blessing. On account of the excellence of your religion, which was highly commended to us by the report of our son the abbot, our predecessor, Pope Paschal, of holy memory, largely at my suggestion, departed somewhat from strict justice in your promotion or translation. But it is clear that the hope we had of you deceived and confounded us. True religion indeed is to follow Christ's footsteps, of whom it is written, 'He humbled himself, and became obedient unto death'.[1] And He saith of Himself, 'Learn of me; for I am meek and lowly in heart'.[2] We grieve, dearest

[1] Phil. 2 : 8   [2] Matt. 11 : 29

mam in religione tua non inveniri, frater karissime, condolemus. Cum enim predictus dominus noster suis te litteris monuisset ut Eboracensem electum, illa indecenti professione deposita, consecrares, ecce! iam triennio contempsisti, humilitatis et obediencie oblitus, in eadem adhuc pertinacia perseveras. Unde nos fraternitatem tuam iteratis apostolice sedis litteris commonemus, ut ab hac tandem duritia desinas, et Eboracensis electi consecracionem secundum communis iusticie institucionem et apostolice sedis mandatum, Domino largiente, perficias. Quod etsi nunc contemptor extiteris, nos tibi ex apostolice sedis auctoritate precipimus [a] ut cum electo eodem nostro te conspectui representes, quatinus que inter vos causa iactatur, ante nos, auctore deo, apostolice sedis auctoritate decidatur.

Littere eiusdem ad eundem electum

Gelasius episcopus, servus servorum dei, dilecto filio T[urstino] Eboracensi electo salutem et apostolicam benediccionem. Questionem de professione illa inter te et Cantuariensem archiepiscopum tamdiu durare miramur, quia iusticia [b] manifesta est. Idcirco fraternitatem tuam litteris presentibus visitantes precipimus, ut si archiepiscopus Cantuariensis in eiusdem professionis adhuc exaccione persistit, tu ab ea omnino desistas, et [c] vel cum ipso vel sine ipso ad nostram presenciam [venias].[d]

Electus noster interrogatus a rege, licet rem bene arbitrante, cur venisset, respondit: 'Nec dignitati nostre, nec metropoli nostre utile est neque decorum,

---

[a] litteris . . . precipimus om. MS. Collated with another copy in the *Reg. Magnum Album*, i. 42   [b] institia] A; iusticie, MS   [c] om. A
[d] presenciam venias] presencias, MS. Collated with another copy of this letter in the *Reg. Magnum Album* at York, i. 48*b*

brother, that this form of humility is not found in
your religion. For though our said lord had admonished you in his letter to consecrate the elect of
York without exacting that unfit profession; lo!
forgetful of humility and obedience, you have disdained to do so for these three years and still persist in
your obstinacy. We therefore repeat to you, brother,
by a letter of the apostolic see, the admonition to
cease at last from your hardness of heart and complete
the consecration of the elect of York by God's grace,
according to the demands of justice and the order of
the apostolic see. Though you are now contumacious, we command you by apostolic authority to
appear before us with the said elect, in order that the
cause pending between you may be decided, as God
wills, by the authority of the apostolic see.

[*Letter of Pope Gelasius to the elect of York*]

Gelasius, bishop, servant of the servants of God,
to our beloved son, Thurstan, elect of York, greeting
and apostolic blessing. We are surprised that the question between you and the archbishop of Canterbury
lasts so long, since the justice is obvious. We therefore, as visitor, direct you, if the archbishop of Canterbury still persists in exacting the profession, to take no
steps in the matter, but to come into our presence
either with him or without him.

Our elect was asked by the king (who knew the
answer quite well), why he had come. He replied, 'It
is neither profitable nor becoming to our dignity nor to
our metropolitan church, and it is extremely disgraceful

persone vero mee valde inhonestum est, ibi manere,
ubi archiepiscopus esse debeo et nominor, nec quicquam episcopale facio. Nec clam me est dominum
Cantuariensem ideo retardasse, quod sciebat me pape
P[aschalis] litteras habere, precipientes ei de mea consecracione. Duo bona facit, et suam ecclesiam et
nostram archiepiscopi re[gi]mine destitutam. Equale
F.15 est pene ac reg/num vestrum nullum haberet archiepiscopum. Itcirco veni novo pape presenciam meam
exhibiturus, ut saltem de hac cura me absolvat, set id
sine consciencia et licencia vestra nolui.' Rex exspectare iussit eum in proximo quid inde vellet illi dicturus.
Prope erat Natale Domini. Litteras domini pape
G[elasii] rex acceperat.

Infra Natale electus noster, adductis secum bonis
viris, venit ad archiepiscopum in hospicium suum,
et ipse tunc aliquantum paciebatur, et litteras pape
G[elasii] illi tradidit. Quibus acceptis : 'En,' ait (por-
rexit et alias), 'He sunt littere pape P[aschalis], quas
debui vobis tradidisse, si, sicut debuistis, in Angliam
venissetis.' 'De litteris', inquid, 'defuncti pape nichil
modo habeo facere', nec suscepit eas. 'Istas videbo et
crastina vobis respondebo'. Quibusdam verborum in-
terieccionibus hinc et inde eiaculatis, noster cum suis
dicessit. Commonefactus ab aliquo archiepiscopus non
bene fecisse quod litteras pape P[aschalis] accipere neg-
lexerat, ad nostrum remisit ut eas illi remitteret, quas
remisisse plerisque molestum fuit. Postea archiepiscopus respondit, quando in provincia sua esset, si quis eum
requireret, facturum quod deberet. Proposuerat in animo
usque in longum tempus Angliam non intrare.

to me personally, for me to stay where I ought to be, and am called an archbishop, and can exercise no episcopal functions. And it does not escape me that the archbishop of Canterbury has purposely delayed [his return] because he knew that I have Pope Paschal's letter giving him orders as to my consecration. He has killed two birds with one stone : he has deprived both his own church and ours of archiepiscopal government. It is almost the same as if your kingdom were without an archbishop. I have accordingly come to present myself before the pope, that he may at all events release me from this cure ; but I would not do so without your knowledge and permission.' The king ordered him to wait for the answer he would shortly give him. It was near Christmas. The king had received Pope Gelasius's letter.

At Christmas time our elect, with some friends, called on the archbishop at his lodging (the archbishop was somewhat indisposed), and gave him the letter of Pope Gelasius. When he had received this, 'See', said he (producing another), 'this is Pope Paschal's letter, which I should have given you, if you had come to England, as you ought to have done'. 'With a letter of a dead pope', said the archbishop, 'I have nothing to do', and he refused it. 'This letter I will look at, and answer you to-morrow.' After a few remarks from either side, our elect and his friends left. The archbishop was warned by someone that he had been wrong in refusing Pope Paschal's letter, so he sent to our elect to have it sent back. Most people regretted that he sent it. The archbishop afterwards replied that when he should be in his province, he would do his part, if anyone required it of him. He had made up his mind to be a long time in returning to England.

Post Epiphaniam audito papam Turonis regi Francorum mandasse, ut illic die designato ei occurreret,
sacerdos noster obnixe[a] regi supplicabat quatinus eum
illuc ire dimitteret, set nullatenus voluit. Utrum archiepiscopus noluit, vel non potuit, nec ipse ivit. Utrique
rex concessit quos vellent mittere. Rex Francie regaliter
cum archiepiscopis, episcopis et nobili clero et procerum comitatu summo pontifici obviam ibat, et cum
eo legati nostri, quia electum nostrum satis diligebat.
Cum autem venissent ad castrum Nanthonis, nunciatum
est regi papam G[elasium] defunctum esse, et Cluniaci
sepultum; et ab episcopis et cardinalibus, qui cum eo venerant, Guidonem Viennensem archiepiscopum, invitum
et renitentem, in papam raptum, et Calixtum appellatum.
Quod audientes rex et plurimi reversi sunt. Quidam
ad eum transierunt. Ipse vero, deappellatus officio, parum agere voluit donec ab illis qui Rome erant quod isti
fecerant confirmatum accepit. De cuius translacione
quidam sic ait:

> [Sponsum] sponsa[1] suum dimisit, filia matri,
>   Mater eum rapiens fecit eam viduam.
> Alter habebit eam forsan vivente priore,
>   Nec de quatuor hiis ullus[b] adulter erit.

Confirmatus papa perambulabat Burgundiam et
Aquitaniam versus Hispanias, et Narbone concilium
tenuit.

Cognita Apostolicus multorum relacione nostre ha-
bitudinis qualitate, videlicet professionis exaccione,
consecracionis denegacione, eieccione, revocacione in
Normanniam, reditu, et per quem, et quamobrem ad
predecessores suos veniendi retinaculis, misit litteras

---

[a] obimple, MS   [b] nullus, MS

After Epiphany, hearing that the pope was at Tours and had sent to the king of the French asking him to meet him there on the day appointed, our priest earnestly besought the king to let him go there, but the king would have none of it.   Whether the archbishop would not or could not, he did not go either.   The king allowed each of them to send representatives.   The king of France went to meet the pope in royal state with archbishops, bishops, the superior clergy, and nobles, and with him our envoys, because he loved our elect well.   But when they came to the castle of Nantes, news came to the king that Pope Gelasius was dead and buried at Cluny; and that Guy, archbishop of Vienne, had been seized upon by the archbishops and cardinals who came with him, made pope in spite of his refusal and resistance, and called Calixtus.   Hearing this, the king and most of his company returned home.   Some went on to the pope.   But he, having been called away from his office [as archbishop], would do but little, until what these men had done was confirmed by those who were at Rome.   Here is an epigram on the translation :—

> She [1] yields her husband to her mother
> And must her widowhood begin ;
> If, while he lives, she wed another,
> None of the four commits a sin.

After confirmation, the pope went through Burgundy and Aquitaine towards Spain, and held a council at Narbonne.

When the pope had learned from many informants the nature of our predicament, viz. the demand of a profession, the refusal of consecration, the dismissal, the recall to Normandy, the return, and the author and reason of the restraints from approaching his predecessors,

[1] Vienne

R[adulpho] archiepiscopo, in quibus eum superbum
vocat, et de contemptu preceptorum predecessorum
P[aschalis et] G[elasii] acriter redarguit; ideo quod
de consecracione Eboracensis electi nichil eis obedientie
vel reverencie detulerat.[a] Intelligens ergo apud papam
et curiam se nichil gracie habere, set plurimum exo-
sum esse, licenciam a rege quesitam ut se excusatum
iret facile habuit; et ire voluit, set non potuit, a rege
Francorum et comite Andegavensi illi suisque conductu
denegato et adventu prohibito. 'Qui fodit foveam,
incidet in eam; et qui volvit lapidem, revertetur ad
eum.'[1] Quia igitur ipse venire, vel idoneos legatos
mittere non potuit, occulte modicum vernulam has
appologeticas deferentem transmisit.

Littere eiusdem archiepiscopi Cantuariensis ad eundem
papam /

F.15*v*   Calixto Dei gracia summo pontifici frater R[adul-
phus], indignus sancte Cantuariensis ecclesie sacerdos,
debitam subieccionem, et fidelia pro posse, si dignetur,
servicia. Per condicionem, domine pater, visum est
michi vobis offerre servicia, quia venit ad aures nostras prevaluisse super me verba iniquorum apud
Christianitatem vestram. Vocatus enim sum litteris
vestre sanctitatis sigillo signatis superbus, et anteces-
sorum vestrorum P[aschalis et] G[elasii] contemptor
preceptorum, de consecrando videlicet Eborace civitatis electo, cum nullus illorum, nec verbo, nec
scripto, nec legato, hoc vel semel in tota vita sua michi
precepit. Quod si forte ab aliquo malevolo estimetur
quod legatum deferentem consecracionis preceptum

[a] detulerant, MS
[1] Prov. 26 : 27

he sent a letter to archbishop Ralph, calling him proud, and bitterly reproaching him for flouting the orders of his predecessors, Paschal and Gelasius; because he had shown neither obedience nor respect to them in the matter of the consecration of the elect of York. So, gathering that he was out of favour with the pope and his court and thoroughly hated, he asked and easily obtained leave from the king to go and excuse himself. He wished to go, but could not, because the king of the French and the count of Anjou refused him and his men a safe conduct and forbade their coming. 'Whoso diggeth a pit shall fall therein; and he that rolleth a stone, it will return upon him.'¹ So, because he could not come himself or send suitable envoys, he secretly sent an underservant bearing the following apology:

Letter of the archbishop of Canterbury to the pope

To Calixtus, by the grace of God supreme pontiff, Ralph, unworthy priest of the holy church of Canterbury, due submission and faithful services to the best of his power, if he be thought worthy. I have thought fit, my lord and father, to offer you my services thus conditionally, because it has come to my ears that the words of the wicked have prevailed against me with your Christianity. For in letters under the seal of your holiness I have been called proud and a despiser of the commands of your predecessors Paschal and Gelasius, namely in the matter of the consecration of the elect of York, though neither of them in all his life commanded it, even once, by word, writing, or by his legate. But if any of my ill-wishers considers that I would not receive a legate bringing an order to

non receperim, aut litteras precipientes videre con-
tempserim, novit [a] Deus et novit [a] anima mea, quia
prorsus immunis est ab hoc transgressionis nevo tota
consciencia mea. Itcirco, quia priusquam divine
dignacionis miseracio vos communi ecclesie sue pre-
fecerit patrem, ego, per illius pietatis clemenciam,
considerata vestre sublimitatis humilitate, ac utili [b]
dulcis consilii delectacione, meipsum coram deo
sanctitati vestre totum effuderam, et omnes infirmi-
tates tam corporis quam anime in te, sicut preelecto
patri et sapienti medico, consulendas et refovendas
ostenderam. Commune faciendum duxi,[1] non arguendo quidem, set humiliter, ut servus domino, suggerendo miram quam in vobis credidi clemencie
sublimitatem scripture illius que dicit, 'Priusquam
interroges, ne vituperes quemquam'.[2] Mirum forsitan
videbitur quod tanto patri per tantillum famulum ex-
cusacionis mee litteras mitto, set teste deo, prohibente
multarum enormitate infirmitatum, nec per me, quod
multum desideravi, et iam bis facere temptavi, ad
vos venire, nec idoneos legatos mittere valui propter
prohibicionem regis Francie et comitis Andegavensis.
Porro quia dominus Angliacensis abbas, quem ad nos
conducendos misistis, usque ad breve tempus ad vos
redditurus est, si interim, quod semper optavi, vester
esse potero, aut nos aut legatos nostros ad [vos], deo
sanitatem et potestatem michi concedente, perducet.
Precarer sane, nisi temerarium videri timerem, ut per
hunc puerulum, quem michi notum et familiarem
esse novistis, quousque alciores et secrecioris consilii
ad vos viros mitterem, litteris vestris certificaretis
quantum de dulcedine miseracionis vestre confidere
possim.

[a] vivit, MS   [b] utilis, MS

consecrate, or disdained to look at letters conveying such an order, God knows, and my soul knows that my conscience is entirely clear of the spot of such a trespass. Now, before God in his mercy made you the father of the church universal, through His pitiful kindness, considering your humility in your lofty position and the pleasure and profit of your sweet counsel, I poured out my soul before you in God's presence, and revealed all my infirmities both of body and soul for you as my chosen father and wise physician for your advice and treatment. I therefore thought I should share [1] [my thoughts with you], making no accusations, but suggesting, as a servant to his master, the excellence of kindness (which I believe you to have) of the text 'Blame not till thou hast examined'.[2] It will perhaps seem strange that I should send my excuses to so great a father by so mean a servant; but owing to my many serious infirmities, I have neither been able to come myself to you, which I longed to do, and twice attempted, nor yet to send suitable messengers because of the ban of the king of France and the count of Anjou. Moreover since the abbot of Saint-Jean-d'Angely, whom you sent to bring me, will be returning to you shortly—if, in the meantime I can be with you, as I have always wished, God giving me health and strength—, he will bring with him either me or my messengers. I should beg, if I did not fear to be overbold, that until I am able to send more important and confidential envoys, you would let me know by letter, by the hand of this fellow whom you know to be my known and trusty servant, how far I may confide in the sweetness of your compassion.

---

[1] The text seems corrupt here.   [2] Ecclus. 11 : 7

K

Credibile est virum religiosum et sic iurantem verum dixisse estimare, set scio aliquos pro vero credere
quod litteras pape G[elasii], adhuc, eo vivente, sus-
ceperit. Cur autem litteras pape P[aschalis] in vita sua
non viderit, cause subscripte sunt.[1] Sane nec multum
mirandum est eum vel litteras videre neglexisse, vel
visis non obedisse, cum in audiencia magne dignitatis
personarum et aliorum multorum se domino pape non
obediturum edixerit, si ei ore ad os preciperet, ut
Eboracensem electum absque professione consecraret.
Rescriptum domini pape Calixti litteris suprascriptis.

Littere eiusdem pape ad eundem archiepiscopum

Calixtus episcopus, servus servorum dei, venerabili
fratri R[adulpho] Cantuariensi archiepiscopo, salutem et apostolicam benediccionem. Per condicionem
scripsisti Christianitati nostre, per condicionem tibi
sicut per dei graciam Christiano breviter respondemus.

Si, quemadmodum a tuis predecessoribus factum
est, in nostra et Romane ecclesie obediencia et fidelitate permanseris, nos te, sicut predecessores nostri
fecisse noscuntur, diligere / ac, patrocinante deo,
curabimus honorare. Alioquin 'pax nostra revertetur
ad nos'.[1]

Quod nobis suggerere voluisti, nos iam fecisse credimus, videlicet ne ante interrogacionem quenquam
vituperemus, cum tamen neminem vituperasse creda-
mus. Interrogavimus enim, et diligenter quesivimus,
et tandem [quod] de consecrando Eboracensis ecclesie
electo domini predecessores nostri, sancte memorie
P[aschalis] papa et G[elasius] scripserant ad plenum
invenimus, et scriptum fraternitati tue mandamus.

F.16

---

[1] *subscripte* must be a mistake for *superscripte*.

It might be thought that a devout man thus swearing was telling the truth ; but I know that some people are assured that he received the letter of Pope Gelasius in that pope's lifetime. The reasons why he did not see the letter of Pope Paschal in his lifetime have already been given.[1] It is surely no great wonder that he either omitted to look at the letters, or to obey them when he had looked, since he gave out in the hearing of very distinguished persons, and of many others, that he would not obey the pope, even if he met him face to face and ordered him to consecrate the elect of York without receiving his profession. The reply of Pope Calixtus to the above letter :

Letter of the pope to the archbishop

Calixtus, bishop, servant of the servants of God, to his venerable brother Ralph, archbishop of Canterbury, greeting and apostolic blessing. You wrote to our Christianity 'conditionally' ; we reply to you also conditionally, as to one by God's grace a Christian.

If you remain, as your predecessors did, in obedience and fealty to us and the church of Rome, we shall be careful, as our predecessors are known to have been, to love, and, under God's protection, to honour you. But if not, 'Let our peace return to us'.[2]

We believe that we have already done the thing which you wished to suggest to us, not to blame any one till we have examined ; though we believe we have blamed nobody. We did examine and diligently inquire, and have at last found, and send to you, our brother, in full, what our predecessors, Paschal and Gelasius, wrote about consecrating the elect of the

[2] Matt. 10 : 13

Signa ergo, frater karissime, signa cor tuum, et ad teipsum redi, neque in celum os tuum ponas aut transgrediaris terminos a patribus constitutos. 'Non est discipulus super magistrum, nec servus maior domino suo.'[1] Nos quidem, quia de affeccione tua confidenciam habebamus, super causa illa fraternitati tue scripsimus ne inde a dileccione sedis apostolice declinares : tu vero nichil pene nobis reverentie reservasti. Certe si rem grandem dixisset tibi propheta,[2] facere debuisti.

Sicut electo nostro ad papam P[aschalem] et G[elasium] ire non licuit, sic et ad Calixtum eundi licenciam a rege sepius quesitam et suppliciter postulatam nequaquam optinuit, per quem prius et nunc retentus. Et quidem rex Francie et comes Andegavensis benigne eum tum direxissent, quia et eum diligebant et super adversitate eius misericordia movebantur. Quanto papa propius Franciam accedebat, tanto ne noster electus ipsum adiret R[adulphus] archiepiscopus plus timebat. Institit ergo regi monitis et precibus ut eum faceret in Angliam reverti. Quadragesima tunc erat. Istud vero summopere conanti ante Pascha se non regressurum, respondit, dicens : 'Non est,' inquid, 'domine, honestum ecclesie cui preesse debeo, nec persone mee illic adesse quando chrisma, [ad] quod tempus imminet, non potero consecrare, nec sanctum Pascha, sicut decet metropolim et metropoliten, sollempiter facere. Et in aliquo forsitan profore potero, si quousque et vos redeatis ipse remansero.' Mandavit ergo ei rex quatinus eum veritatis assercione assecuraret se post Pascha iturum. Et ille : 'In dei consilio et regis inde me ponam'. Cui aliquis de internunciis episcopus quidem satis urbane et episcopaliter reddidit : 'De dei consilio dimissum facite, set absolute in regis consilio vos positum dicite'. Ad

---

[1] Matt. 10 : 24   [2] 2 Kings 5 : 15

church of York. Cross your heart, cross it dearest
brother, and return to yourself, nor set your mouth
against heaven, or transgress the bounds set by the
fathers. 'The disciple is not above his master, nor
the servant above his lord.' ¹ We, trusting in your
affection, have written to you, brother, not therein to
depart from the love of the apostolic see: but you
have scarcely any reverence left for us. Surely, 'if the
prophet had bid thee do some great thing',² thou
shouldst have done it.

Just as our elect was not allowed to go to Popes
Paschal and Gelasius, he never got leave to go to Pope
Calixtus, though he begged and prayed for it, being
held back by the same person as before. And the king
of France and the count of Anjou would have given him
kindly guidance, for they both loved him and were
moved to pity at his wretchedness. The nearer the
pope came to France, the more did archbishop Ralph
fear lest our elect should approach him. He therefore
more earnestly advised and prayed the king to make
him return to England. It was Lent. Though the king
made every effort, he replied that he would not return
before Easter, saying, 'It does not become the church
over which I ought to preside or myself that I should be
there at a time, now very near, when I shall be unable
to consecrate the chrism, or to celebrate the holy feast
of Easter as befits a mother church and its metropolitan.
And I may be able to be of some use if I stay until you
also return.' The king sent word to him that he must
give his solemn assurance that he would go after Easter.
He replied, 'I shall abide by the counsel of God and the
king'. One of the messengers, a bishop, made a witty
and episcopal retort, 'Let God's counsel be, but say that
you abide absolutely by the king's'. He smiled at that,

quod, sicut alii qui aderant, ipse subridens, 'Semper', ait, 'communi consilio dei proponam'.

Hiis ita regi relatis, nec multo post sicut dominus papa archiepiscopis Francie, Germanie, Burgundie, Aquitanie, Provincie, sic et in Normanniam Rotomagensi archiepiscopo, Cantuariensi archiepiscopo, Eboracensi electo litteras singulis singulas misit, mandando precipiens quatinus cum suffraganeis suis episcopis et abbatibus, omni occasione reiecta, concilio generali interessent, quod in proxima sancti Luce festivitate Remis celebrare disposuerat.   Apud Clarum-montem, que civitas est in Arvernia, diem Pentecostes sollempiter celebrans, sicut Romana consuetudo exigit, coronatus est. Inde pluribus personis pro regimine ecclesiarum scribens, et regi nostro et Cantuariensi archiepiscopo pro electo nostro litteras subiectas direxit.

Littere eiusdem pape ad eundem regem

Calixtus episcopus, servus servorum dei, karissimo in Christo filio H[enrico] illustri regi Anglie salutem et apostolicam benediccionem.   Questio que tamdiu de professione illa inter Cantuariensem archiepiscopum et Eboracensem / electum agitatur, et sedi apostolice gravis est, et Eboracensi ecclesie non modicum ingerit detrimentum.   Eapropter nobilitatem tuam rogamus ut eosdem fratres nostros ad concilium pro quo eos vocavimus, sicut aliis iam litteris rogavimus, venire permittas, quatinus, auctore deo, in nostra et fratrum nostrorum presencia diutina illa [a] questio finem debitum sorciatur.   Si quis eciam eorum antea nos visitare voluerit, eandem ei tribuas facultatem.[b]

F.16v

[a] illa] *ins.* from A
[b] Collated with another copy of the same letter in the *Reg. Magnum Album* at York, i. 48*b*

as did others who were present, and said, 'I shall always put God's counsel before the world's'.

After this had been told to the king, but only a little later, the pope sent to Normandy a letter each to the archbishop of Rouen, the archbishop of Canterbury and the elect of York, as he had done to the archbishops of France, Germany, Burgundy, Guienne, and Provence, ordering them with their suffragan bishops and abbots to take part without fail in the General Council which he had arranged to celebrate at Rheims on St Luke's day next. He was crowned at Clermont, a city in Auvergne, while celebrating Whit-Sunday, as the Roman custom demands. He wrote thence to a number of persons on ecclesiastical business, and sent to the king and the archbishop of Canterbury the following letters on behalf of our elect:

Letter of the pope to the king

Calixtus, bishop, servant of the servants of God, to his dearest son in Christ, Henry, illustrious king of England, greeting and apostolic blessing. The question which has so long been in dispute betwixt the archbishop of Canterbury and the elect of York is grievous to the apostolic see and causes serious injury to the church of York. For this reason we ask your majesty, as we have done in other letters, to allow these our brethren to come to the council for which we have summoned them, so that, by God's help, that lengthy dispute may attain its due end in the presence of ourselves and our brethren. Also, if either of them wishes to visit us before, pray give them the same leave.

Littere eiusdem pape ad eundem archiepiscopum

Calixtus episcopus, servus servorum dei, venerabili fratri R[adulpho] Cantuariensi archiepiscopo salutem et apostolicam benediccionem. Super sapiencia et religione tua non parum, frater karissime, mater tua sancta Romana miratur ecclesia, quod Eboracensem ecclesiam tanto facias tempore sine pastoris regimine permanere. Si non tibi hoc fraterne [a] caritatis compassio suaderet, frequens tamen apostolice sedis commonicio et preceptum dileccionem tuam debuit compulisse, ut, beati Gregorii distinccione contentus, eiusdem electum ecclesie consecrares. Tuam itaque fraternitatem, repetita sedis apostolice precepcione, monemus, ut, omni [b] iam tandem professionis exaccione seposita, eidem electo, patrocinante deo, manum consecracionis imponas.[c] Si quid autem aliud in eius causa tibi estimas vendicandum, concilii generalis tempore, quod in proxima beati Luce festivitate Remis per dei graciam celebrare disposuimus, auditis diligenter utriusque racionibus terminetur. Cui nimirum consilio personam tuam, sicut aliis quoque litteris preceptum est, omni remota occasione, interesse precipimus.

Quibus vero ad electum nostrum scripsit, et hic subscripte sunt.

Littere [d] eiusdem pape ad eundem archiepiscopum

Calixtus episcopus, servus servorum dei, venerabili fratri T[urstino] Eboracensi electo salutem et apostolicam benediccionem. Et tibi et Eboracensi ecclesie, ad cuius regimen per dei graciam electus es, debita

---

[a] fraterne] A ; superne, MS   [b] omnia, MS, omni, A

[c] Here the copy of this letter, in the *Reg. Magnum Album* at York, i. 49*a*, ends.

[d] Collated with a copy of this letter in the *Reg. Magnum Album* at York

Letter of the pope to the archbishop

Calixtus, bishop, servant of the servants of God, to his venerable brother, Ralph, archbishop of Canterbury, greeting and apostolic blessing. Thy mother, the holy Roman church, greatly marvels that, with thy wisdom and piety, thou causest the church of York to abide so long without a shepherd. If thy brotherly charity did not move thee, the repeated monitions and orders of the apostolic see should have forced thee to consecrate the elect of that church, satisfied with the distinction given by St Gregory. We therefore repeat to thee, brother, the order of the apostolic see that, at length refraining from exacting a profession, thou, under God, lay the hand of consecration on the said elect. But if thou deemest thou hast any other claim to make in this cause, let it be determined at the time of the General Council, which we have planned to celebrate, by the grace of God, on St Luke's day next at Rheims, after carefully hearing the arguments on both sides. We accordingly order thee, as we did by other letters, to be present in person, without fail.

The letter which he wrote to our elect is as follows :

Letter of the pope to the archbishop of York

Calixtus, bishop, servant of the servants of God, to his venerable brother, Thurstan, elect of York, greeting and apostolic blessing. We grieve, as is due, with thee and with the church of York, to the government of which thou wast by God's grace chosen, that

affeccione compatimur, quod tamdiu pro illius professionis exaccione tam grandia incommoda sustinetis.
Unde confratri vestro, R[adulpho] Cantuariensi archiepiscopo, scripsimus, precipientes ut iam tandem
resipiscere debeat, et tibi ᵃ professionis exaccione ᵇ seposita, manum consecracionis imponat. Si nos audie-
rit, deo gracias referemus. Sin autem, fraternitati tue
omnino per presencia scripta precipimus, ut ei nullam
professionem exhibeas, set sicut aliis tibi litteris
mandatum est, ad concilium venias, quod per dei
graciam in proxima beati Luce festivitate Remis
celebrare disposuimus, quatinus, auctore deo, questio
hec mediante iusticia terminetur. Datum apud
Clarum Montem, xvi. kalendas Iunii.ᶜ

Misit et dominus rex legatos suos ad apostolicum,
quibus etsi fuit iniuncta contra Eboracensem electum
petere et impetrare voluntas, non est data impetrandi
facultas; et si aliquis aliquid se impetrasse sperans
gavisus est, de quo postmodum deceptum fuisse com-
periens, egre tulit. Idem vero electus in animo diem
prefixerat, ante quam contra benevolenciam regis Normannia ad papam non egrederetur, ulterius autem
tardare nolle nisi capcione vel infirmitate detineretur.
Hoc precogitans de sociis suis unum post unum, et
de suis rebus in Franciam premisit, quam cicius posset oportune securus. Licencia tanquam de integro
quesita, et rex ab eo mandando exegit sibi potissime ᵈ
[ne] ab apostolico consecracionem susciperet. 'De
hoc', inquid, 'paccionem nullam faciam, set deo sensum
meum dirigente, ita me agam quod que sunt "dei
deo, et que regis regi reddam".' Presul vero Exonien-
F.17 sis, / ab apostolico novissime reversus, regi dixerat non

                ᵃ et tibi, om. A   ᵇ causa, A
    ᶜ Datum . . . Iunii, added in margin   ᵈ patissime, MS

you have so long borne such great discomforts from the exaction of the profession, concerning which we have written to our brother, Ralph, archbishop of Canterbury, bidding him at last to reconsider [his decision] and lay upon thee the consecrating hand without exacting any profession. If he listen to us, we shall give thanks to God. But if not, we bid thee, brother, by these presents, not to make him any profession, but, as is ordered in other letters, to come to the Council which we have planned by God's grace to celebrate on St Luke's day next at Rheims, in order that by God's help this question may be justly determined. Given at Clermont, on the 17th day of May.

The king also sent his ambassadors to the pope. But although they were charged with the will to petition successfully against the elect of York, they got no opportunity; and if anyone rejoiced in an imaginary success, he was bitterly disappointed when he found out later that he had been deceived. Now, the elect had mentally determined a date before which he would not leave Normandy to go to the pope against the king's good will, but beyond which he would not delay unless detained by imprisonment or illness. With this in mind he sent one after another of his companions and of his goods before him to France, as quickly as a safe opportunity occurred. But when he made a fresh application for leave, the king strictly commanded him not to receive consecration from the pope. 'About this', said he, 'I will make no bargain, but under God's direction, I will so act as to "render unto Caesar the things that are Caesar's, and unto God the things that are God's".' But the bishop of Exeter, who had just returned from the pope, told the king that there was no need to detain

esse opus detinere eum, sciebat enim quod ab eo non consecraretur.

Videns igitur rex quod eum longius retinere convenienter non poterat, quia dominus papa et archiepiscopum et illum ad concilium vocaverat, et ei mandaverat ne eos remoraretur, si uterque vel alter antea ad illum venire vellet; et propter verbum Exoniensis episcopi, licenciam abeundi concessit. Ille, non diutina dilacione procrastinans, Carnotum venit, ubi quos premiserat ᵃ exspectantes eum quasi capcionem evasisse gaudio magno gavisi sunt. Inde profectus quarto die Turonis Romam invenit. Ibi summus pontifex, et idem vir summe nobis dignus ᵇ nobilitate et excellencia sua, et curia, honorifice eum suscipientes, advenisse letati sunt.

Turonis, in metropoli ecclesia sancti Mauricii, in die festivitatis illius,¹ domino pape et curie comes iunctus, per dimidium annum ab eorum comitatu nec integra die est seiunctus. Dedit quoque deus illi graciam in conspectu regis Francie, episcoporum, principum, procerum, et cuiuslibet dignitatis personarum ad quos ille veniebat, vel qui undique ad papam confluebant.

Omnes eum diligebant, servicia sua devote offereba[n]t, et cognita causa illius inimicis eius inimici erant, et pro causa illius dominum papam et curiam diligenter interpellebant. Ad captandum eorum benevolenciam nemo magis promptus, nemo magis facetus morem cuique gerere, et quod maxime amicicias conciliat, iuxta illud Ecclesiastici, 'non' erat illi 'manus ad accipiendum porrecta, et ad dandum collecta',² set quod [ad] eum contra. Si quis forte aliquod ei servitium faciebat, non segniter aut parce retribuebat; si quis ei aliquid dabat, non pariter set uberius reddebat.

ᵃ promiserat, MS   ᵇ digne, MS

Thurstan, for he knew that he would not be consecrated by the pope.

The king saw that he could not decently keep him any longer, because the pope had summoned both the archbishop and Thurstan to the Council, and had commanded him not to delay them, if either or both of them wished to come to him before. And so, relying on what the bishop of Exeter had said, he gave him leave to depart. He made no delay and came to Chartres, where those whom he had sent before were waiting for him and greatly rejoiced as though he had escaped from prison. Three days later he found 'Rome' at Tours. There the pope, himself supremely worthy in our eyes for his nobility and excellence, and his court received him with honour and rejoiced at his coming.

He was in the company of the pope and his court at Tours, in the metropolitan church of St Maurice, on St Maurice's day [1] and remained with them for six months, without leaving them for a day. God also gave him grace in the sight of the king of France and the bishops, princes, nobles and persons of all ranks, whom he visited, or who flowed in to the pope from all quarters.

Everyone loved him. They devoutly offered their services, and when they had heard his case, his enemies were their enemies, and they diligently approached the pope and the court in his behalf. No man was readier to gain their good will, no man more polite and considerate; a thing which according to Ecclesiasticus [2] is a chief factor in friendships, a hand not 'stretched out to receive, and closed when thou shouldest repay'. On the contrary, if anyone did him a service he was neither slow nor sparing in repaying it; if anyone made him a present, he gave back, not as much, but more.

[1] 22 September   [2] Ecclus. 4 : 31

Veniente papa ad Blesense castrum, duo archidiaconi ecclesie nostre et scolasticus, qui cum electo nostro venerant, voce et litteris peticionem fecerunt ad dominum papam ut eum consecraret. At ille benigne respondit se fratribus suis inde collocuturum.

Cum autem Parisius venisset, idoneum visum est magistro nostro et suis iterum dominum papam requirere. Quo egrediente de monasterio sancti Martini de Campis, ubi missam cantaverant, clerici nostri, quorum supra memini, allaterati sunt illi, deo providente illis oportunitatem et spacium loquendi, quantum visum est illi satis est, omnibus remotis, casu ita contingente. Dominus noster Parisius remanserat sanguinatus. Illi vero veritatem dicendo, favorem eius captare volentes, sic aiunt: 'Audito, domine pater: dignitatem vestram ad hunc apicem promotam esse, multi gavisi sunt gaudio magno valde, clerici quidem maxime, quia quod diu monachi modo clericus Romane ecclesie presidebat, et pro generis nobilitate, dicentes summum sacerdocium summe nobilitati oportune concedere; habentes quoque fiduciam bonam in vobis de iusticia et patrocinio, eo quod et in prelacione archiepiscopali, et in legacione qua fungebamini, viriliter[a] digne deo, moderacio vestra officium debitum exercuerat. Eboracensis ecclesia nichil [h]esitavit bonum successorem a vestigiis bonorum predecessorum P[aschalis] el G[elasii] non deviare. Quocirca[b] paternitati vestre, cui per dei graciam universalis ecclesie cura commissa est, supplicamus, quatinus de consecrando electo nostro, Romane ecclesie servo, sicut ecclesie F.17v nostre / necessarium est, mature provideat.'

Ille vero ad omnia pene que dixerant, modeste, nec sine aliquo dolore sic reddidit: 'Fratres et amici,

---

[a] viri liceret, MS   [b] Quod circa, MS

When the pope came to the castle of Blois, the two archdeacons and the chancellor of our church, who had come with our elect, petitioned the pope, both by word of mouth and by letter, to consecrate Thurstan. He graciously answered that he would consult with his brethren about it.

But after the pope had come to Paris, it seemed good to our master [the chancellor?] and his friends to ask him again. So, as he came out from the monastery of Saint-Martin-des-Champs, where they had been saying mass, those clerks whom I mentioned approached him; God, as it happened, giving them the opportunity and room, sufficient, as it pleased him, for speaking without witnesses. Our lord had stayed in Paris to be bled. But they, trying to gain the pope's favour by speaking the truth, said, 'Many, our lord and father, greatly rejoiced when they heard of your promotion to the peak of dignity, but especially the clerks, because monks have long governed the Roman church, and now a clerk does; saying that it befits your birth, that the supreme priesthood should happily give place to supreme nobility; and having full trust in your justice and favour, because you did your duty as an archbishop, and in the legation which you held, except in so far as you might be worthy of God in parting from it. The church of York has never doubted that a worthy successor would not depart from the footsteps of his predecessors, Paschal and Gelasius. Wherefore we beseech your fatherhood to whom, by God's grace, the care of the catholic church is committed, to provide in due time for the consecration of our elect, the servant of the church of Rome, as our church needs.'

But he replied to almost all that they had said modestly and not without pain, 'Brethren and friends,

de promocione mea quicunque gavisus sit vel gaudeat,
ego nec gavisus sum nec gaudeo. Scio equidem Romane
sedis pontificatum omni honore excellenciorem esse. Set
tanti honoris honus est gravissiumum : gloria ista tribu-
lacio michi videtur et miseria : et nunc quidem quamdiu sum in partibus istis bene michi esse videtur.
Quando vero Rome ero, quot cardinales, tot principes ;
quot cives, tot domini erunt. Nec michi incognitum
est inter quos habito.' Hoc dicendo per vices respiciebat,
ne de Romanis quilibet approximaret. 'Honor', inquit,
'Vienensis ecclesie non multis possessionibus dives est,
verum michi sufficiebat ; et ideo maxime, quia quocunque tenderem nunciusque venirem ᵃ vix quemcun-
que alicuius nominis hominem in tota terra Burgundia
inveniebam, qui michi vel nepos, vel consanguineus,
propinquus, vel meus homo non esset. Erga ecclesiam
vestram et electum vestrum certe bonum animum et
bonam voluntatem habemus, quod in proximo concilio,
per dei consilium, et fratrum qui aderunt, opere
demonstrabitur.' Gracias deo et illi agentes discesserunt, et propter regem Francorum qui obviam ei veniebat, et propter Romanos qui sequentes appropiabant.
Et illos quidem satis dixisse, et illum bene dixisse videbatur. Parisius ad hospicium redeuntibus, et his magistro suo relatis, exhilaratus et confortatus est.

Post dies undecim ventum est Remis, tercia die
ante concilium. Eadem die venerat illuc Ra[dulphus]
Orcadensis episcopus, et quidam archidiaconus noster.
Sabbatum erat. Paulo post, in ipso lucis et noctis
confinio, mandavit dominus papa electo nostro, nichil
adhuc de hac re opinanti, ut cum clericis suis ad eum
veniret. Qui adveniens, et Orcadensem episcopum et
predictum archidiaconum cum ceteris secum adducens,

ᵃ The MS reads 'quorumcunque tendere, nunciumque venirem'.

whoever may have rejoiced or rejoices in my promotion, I neither have rejoiced nor do. I know that the bishopric of the see of Rome excels all else in honour; but the burden of so great an honour is heavy indeed; its glory seems to me tribulation and wretchedness. And now, all seems well with me so long as I am here; but when I shall be in Rome, every cardinal is a prince; every citizen, one of my masters. Nor am I unaware of what people I live among.' As he said this he looked back from time to time, lest any of the Romans should be approaching. 'The honour', he continued, 'of the church of Vienne is not rich in many possessions, but it was enough for me; especially because wherever I went, or arrived as an envoy, I scarcely found anyone of conse- quence in all Burgundy, who was not my nephew, or cousin, kinsman, neighbour, or one of my own men. To your church and your elect we have a good heart and good will as will be effectively shown, by the counsel of God and of my brethren who shall be present, at the next Council.' Our friends thanked God and the pope and so departed, both on account of the king of France, who was coming to meet him and of the Romans who followed him and were coming nearer. And it seemed that they had well spoken, and that the pope had given a good answer. When they returned to Paris, to their lodging, and reported to their master, he was cheered and comforted.

Eleven days later we came to Rheims, two days before the Council. There had come there the same day Ralph, bishop of Orkney and one of our archdeacons. It was Saturday. A little later, at twilight, the pope sent to our elect, quite unexpectedly, to come to him with his clerks. He came, taking with him the bishop of Orkney and the archdeacon and the others, and before

L

antequam audiret aliud vel diceret, ait : 'Ecce, domine,
iste est ecclesie nostre episcopus ; iste vero archidiaconus.' Quibus in occulo susceptis hiisdem verbis inquit :
'Deus augeat numerum vestrum !' Ceteros iam bene
noverat. Erant cum eis solummodo cardinales, qui
interrogaverunt clericos nostros ª si quid petebant. At
illi dixerunt : 'Romanam ecclesiam, dominum papam,
et vos, domini cardinales, de consecracione electi nostri
requirimus.' Post paulum more, apostolicus dixit electo
nostro : 'Vade, frater, prepara te, et anima et corpore,
crastino, deo annuente, consecracionem suscepturus.'
Prostratus pedibus et qui cum eo erant gracias agentes
recesserunt. Quam bene tam brevi spacio potuit, anima
et corpore se preparavit. Ipse vero ad papam mandatus
ante concilium consecrari non opinabatur.

    In crastinum venit in ecclesia metropoli beate Marie
consecrandus. Erant ibi archiepiscopi, episcopi, abbates, et cuiuscunque dignitatis et ecclesiastici ordinis
multi, qui et vocati ad concilium generale convenerant.
Certum habebat apostolicus quod Cantuariensis archiepiscopus, licet ad concilium vocatus, et pro contencione inter suam et nostram ecclesias, nec venerat nec
veniret, nec canonicam excusacionem mitteret, nec personas que pro eo agerent. Solus archidiaconus suus ᵇ
calumpniatus est illi, et nec canonice, nec composite.
Cui ille modeste dixit : 'Quod facio, semper salva
iusticia Cantuariensis ecclesie, si qua est, facio'. Ipse
vero consecrando et sanctissimus (?) ᶜ multa a rege comminatus est. Quapropter et ille quidem contumeliis
F.18 non illatis / non recessisset, si in ecclesia non esset ;
aliquibus tamen conviciis et exprobracionibus a Romanis
pulsatus exivit.

anything else was said either to him or by him, said,
'My lord, this is a bishop of our church and this other
an archdeacon'.   The pope gave them the kiss of peace
and said, 'God send more of you'.   He knew the others
already.   Only cardinals were present, and they asked
our clerks whether they had any petition.   But they said,
'We are asking the church of Rome, our lord the pope,
and you, lords cardinals, for the consecration of our
elect'.   After a short interval, the pope said to our elect,
'Go, brother, prepare thyself in mind and body, to be
consecrated, God willing, tomorrow'.   The elect fell
down before him, and he and his companions gave
thanks and retired.   He prepared himself as well as he
could in so short a time, both in soul and body.   But
when sent for by the pope, he had not been thinking of
being consecrated before the Council.

He came the next day to the metropolitan church of
Saint Mary to be consecrated.   There were there archbishops, bishops, abbots, and many dignitaries and
regulars who had been called and had come to the
General Council.   The pope was assured that the archbishop of Canterbury, though called to the Council, and
that over a dispute between his church and ours,
neither had nor would come, nor would send a canonical
excuse, nor persons to act on his behalf.   Only his archdeacon challenged [Thurstan], and that neither canonically nor eloquently.   Thurstan politely replied, 'What
I am doing is all saving the just rights of the church of
Canterbury, if it has any'.   But the archdeacon severely
threatened even the pope in the king's name if he were
consecrated.   And on that account he would not have
withdrawn without insults, had he not been in church;
but he was driven off by abuse and reproof from the
Romans, and went away.

Electus noster astantibus et assencientibus et coad-
iuvantibus tot et tantis personis, domini pape, saltem
tanquam beati Petri manibus, archiepiscopus consecratus est. Cui super humeros textus ewangelii apertus
impositus dum consecraretur, sicut mos est, cum a
domino papa respiceretur, viso versu obstupescens assistentibus ait : 'Eia videto, "Sicut novit me Pater, et e[go]
a[gnosco] P[atrem], et a[nimam] m[eam] po[no] pro
o[vibus] m[eis]"'.[1] Quo quidem pronostico visum est
multis illum obligatum teneri ut ascendat 'ex adverso',
et opponat 'murum[a] pro domo Israel', et stet 'in prelio
in die domini'.[2]

Archiepiscopus et episcopi Normannie, et qui de
Anglia ibi erant, nondum venerant. Quibus proficiscen-
tibus rex preceperat ut defenderent Eboracensi electo
per fidem quam ei debebat, et per iuramentum quod
ei iuraverat, ne ab apostolico consecracionem acciperet.
Quod si presumeret, in terram suam [non] reverteretur.
Set cum ipso die prope Remis venissent, exiit obviam
eis qui dixit, 'Eboracensis archiepiscopus consecratus
est'. Hoc audientes restiterunt, moram aliquam faciendo, conferentes ad invicem quid agerent, si ei com-
municarent, si illi loquerentur. Defendere frustra esset
ne fieret quod factum erat. Licet aliqui corde dis-
sensissent, propter timorem regis in palam omnium fere
sentencia eadem erat, illum non bene egisse : domino
suo et regi iuratam fidelitatem non bene servasse,
contra regnum fecisse, testabantur. Quidam vel veritate vel amoris similitudine pro eo dolebant in finem
archiepiscopatu carituro, et in vita regis huius nunquam Angliam intraturo. Super alios, Exoniensis

---

[a] apponat mirum, MS

[1] Jn. 10 : 15   [2] Ezek. 13 : 5

Our elect was consecrated archbishop in the presence, and with the assent and assistance of all these important persons, by the hands of the pope, as representing St Peter. And as the open gospel-book was laid on his shoulders, as is customary in consecration, while the pope was looking at it, he was astonished at the text and said to those standing by, 'Look, "As the Father knoweth me, even so know I the Father; and I lay down my life for the sheep" '.[1] From which omen, many thought he was bound to 'go up' and 'make up the hedge for the house of Israel', and 'stand in the battle in the day of the Lord'.[2]

The archbishop [of Canterbury] and the bishops of Normandy, and those who were there from England had not yet come. The king had told them, before they set out, to forbid the elect of York, by the faith which he owed him and the oath which he had sworn, to receive consecration from the pope. If he dared to do so, he should not return to his dominions. But as they were nearing Rheims on that very day, someone came out to meet them and said, 'The archbishop of York has been consecrated'. When they heard this, they stopped, and waited a while, consulting together what they should do; whether they should associate with the archbishop? whether they should speak to him? It was of no use to forbid him to do what was already done. Though some of them disagreed in their hearts, they were openly unanimous, through fear of the king, that the elect had done wrong: they bore witness that he had not well kept the fealty which he had sworn to the king, and had committed treason. Some grieved for him, from real or pretended affection, that he would lose his archbishopric after all, and might never return to England in this king's lifetime. The bishop of Exeter

episcopus rem aggravabat, dolens se deceptum fuisse et regem decepisse, et odio[a] persequebatur archiepiscopum, quod ausus fuit eum mendacem fecisse a papa consecratus. Deciso tandem ab omnibus se ab eius communione et collocucione suspendere, civitatem ingressi sunt.

Crastina sedit concilium, ubi, sicut consuetudo est, sede data cuique metropolitano cum suffraganeis suis, cum suo Orcadensi episcopo, qui supervenerat, noster assedit. Dunelmensis episcopus, qui venerat cum Normannis, non ausus est cum suo archiepiscopo sedere, nec ille clamorem faciendo eum cogere voluit, ne regem adversus episcopum, et magis adversum se exacerbaret. De episcopis Normannie et Anglie nullus aut rarus, et id clanculo propter metum regis, veniebat ad nostrum, vel colloquebatur antequam discederent. Ex parte regis ingressum tocius terre sue ei interdixerunt.

Que in concilio gesta fuerunt satis supersedendum arbitror. Quo post dies octo soluto, ceteris ad sua revertentibus, dominus papa, aliquantulum infirmatus, diebus xv. Remis remansit.

Redeuntes episcopi sui ad regem nostrum, qualiter de archiepiscopo nostro actum sit, et illi de Cantuariensi archiepiscopo narraverunt. Tunc rex aliquorum callida machinacione fidem spopondit, vel se spopondisse dixit, quod in vita sua T[urstinus] archiepiscopus Angliam non ingrederetur, si Cantuariensi professionem non faceret. Quod quidem tam prudentem virum nequaquam fecisse credibile est, set ideo dixisse et credi

[a] odium, MS

more than all the others, made the worst of the thing,
complaining that he had been deceived and had himself
deceived the king. He pursued the archbishop with his
hate, because he had been consecrated by the pope and
had made him a liar. When they had unanimously
decided to have no intercourse or conversation with
him, they entered the city.

On the morrow the Council sat: where, as the
custom is that a seat is assigned to each metropolitan
with his suffragans, ours took his seat with his suffragan,
the bishop of Orkney, who had joined him. The bishop
of Durham, who had come with the Normans, did not
venture to sit with his own archbishop; nor did the
latter choose to cause a disturbance by making him do
so, for fear of incensing the king against the bishop, and
still more against himself. Scarcely any of the bishops
of Normandy and England came to the archbishop or
conversed with him until the close of the Council; if
any did, it was secretly, on the king's account. They forbade him in the king's name to enter any of his dominions.

I think it unnecessary to report the acts of the
Council. It was dissolved after eight days. The others
returned to their homes; but the pope, who was indisposed, remained at Rheims for a fortnight.

The king's bishops returned to him and told him
what had happened about our archbishop; they also
told him about the archbishop of Canterbury. Then,
by some folks' cunning contrivance, the king pledged
his faith, or said he had done so, that archbishop
Thurstan should not enter England so long as he lived,
unless he made his profession to the archbishop of
Canterbury. We may well believe that so prudent a
man never did pledge his faith, but said it and wished it

voluisse ne ab apostolico eum recipere cum fidei lesione cogeretur, quamquam et in bonis tantum promissis fides sit tenenda, et in malis rescindenda, set quod sacramentum (?) fecit haut sana condicione, postmodum satis claruit. Decrevit quoque et in Angliam mittere, F.18v et de archiepiscopatu ᵃ / eum dissasire.

Interrogavit rex si adhuc palleum illi datum esset. Aliis se nescire dicentibus, qui prius regi dixerat quod a papa non consecraretur, et nunc illi dixit quod palleum non haberet donec per provinciam suam veniendi facultas ei donaretur. Quod eque verum fuit, nam die xii° post consecracionem ipsius palleum suscepit, set ei celare iussum est quam[diu] papa in Francia esset.

Archiepiscopus vero noster sollicite laboravit, per dominum Cononem Prenestinum episcopum et ceteros cardinales, requirens quatinus dominus papa colloquium regi Anglorum statueret, diem et locum illi premandans, in quo de formanda pace inter ipsum et regem Francorum summopere laboraret; quorum discordia diuturna multis et nimium damnosa et calamitosa extiterat; et bene summum pontificem decere inter tantos reges et filios suos spirituales pacem componere. Sperabat eciam si papa regi loqueretur, tum precibus tum blandiciis, vel aliquo modo, facilius eum posse reconsiliari. Quod iterum iterumque et sepe requirens, vix tandem obtinuit; cumque dominus papa de concilio rediens versus Normanniam veniret, mandavit regi velle loqui illi die et loco designato, et rex gratanter annuit.

Et cum esset Belvaci dedit archiepiscopo nostro litteras ad suffraganeos episcopos suos, que fuerunt exemplar istarum.

<hr/>

ᵃ archiepiscopo, MS

to be believed, for fear he should be compelled by the pope to receive Thurstan and so break his faith ; although faith should be kept in good purposes only, and should be broken in bad ones. But that . . . or saving the condition, was clear enough afterwards. He also determined to send to England and disseise Thurstan of his archbishopric.

The king inquired whether the *pallium* had been given him. Though the others said they did not know, the bishop who had previously said that Thurstan would not be consecrated by the pope, now said that he would not get the *pallium* until he was given leave to visit his province. This saying was no truer than the other, for he received the *pallium* on the twelfth day after his consecration, but was ordered to hide it so long as the pope should be in France.

But our archbishop worked hard, through Cuno, bishop of Palestrina and the other cardinals, demanding that the pope should appoint an interview with the king of England, at a place and on a date prescribed, in which he should use all his power to secure a peace between him and the king of France, whose long quarrel had brought damage and ruin on many people. It well became the pope to make peace between his spiritual sons the kings. He also hoped that if the pope spoke to the king, his prayers, compliments, or what not, might make a reconciliation with himself easier. He pressed his suit time after time and only just succeeded ; and as the pope, returning from the Council, approached Normandy, he sent word to the king that he wished to speak with him on a day and at a place appointed, and the king graciously consented.

While he was at Beauvais he gave our archbishop letters to his suffragan bishops to the following effect :

Littere eiusdem pape ad episcopos omnes Scocie,
subditos ecclesie metropoli Eboracensi

Calixtus episcopus, servus servorum dei, venerabilibus fratribus R[anulpho] Dunelmensi, R[adulpho]
Orcadensi, [Iohanni] Glescuensi, et universis per
Scociam episcopis, Eboracensis ecclesie suffrageneis,
salutem et apostolicam benedicionem. Ad hoc, disponente deo, sedis apostolice cura nobis commissa
est, ut ecclesiarum omnium sollicitudinem gerere
debeamus. Eapropter diutine destitucioni vestre
metropolis Eboracensis ecclesie paterna benignitate
compassi sumus, et venientem ad nos venerabilem
fratrem T[urstinum], ipsius electum, benigne suscepimus, atque in archiepiscopum, cooperante domino,
consecravimus; pallei quoque insigne, pontificalis
videlicet officii plentiudinem, secundum consuetudinem ᵃ apostolice sedis ei concessimus; non enim
fratribus nostris racionabile visum est, ut pro illa
confratris nostri R[adulphi] Cantuariensis archiepiscopi querimonia vacare diucius Eboracensis deberet
ecclesia, precipue cum frater idem frequenter ab
apostolica sede commonitus nullam ᵇ in causa hac
voluerit reverenciam exhibere. Vestre itaque fraternitati presencium litterarum auctoritate precipimus, ut
predictum fratrem nostrum T[urstinum] tanquam
metropolitanum vestrum diligere et honorare atten-
cius procuretis, eique in posterum omni occasione
deposita debitam obedienciam et reverenciam defera-
tis. Datum Belvaci xii. kalendas Decembris.ᶜ

Deinde venit ad castellum quod Calvum-montem
appellant, de diocesi Rotomagensis ecclesie. Rex Anglie venit ad quoddam castellum suum quod vocatur
Gisorcium, quod a Calvo-monte paulo longius duabus

ᵃ secundum consuetudinem *ins.* from A
ᵇ nullam, A ; nulla, MS
ᶜ Datum . . . Decembris *ins.* from A, i.e. *Reg. Magnum Album*, i. 51a

Letter of the pope to all the bishops of Scotland
subject to the metropolitan church of York

Calixtus, bishop, servant of the servants of God, to his venerable brethren, Ranulf, bishop of Durham, Ralph, bishop of Orkney, [John], bishop of Glasgow, and all the bishops throughout Scotland, suffragans of the church of York, greeting and apostolic blessing. The care of the apostolic see was, by God's providence, given to us that we should have 'the care of all the churches'. We have therefore taken fatherly pity on the long destitution of your metropolitan church of York; and have kindly received our venerable brother Thurstan, elect of that church, when he came to us, and have, by God's help, consecrated him archbishop. We have also granted him the *pallium,* the symbol of the fullness of the office of a bishop, according to the custom of the apostolic see. For it did not seem reasonable to our brethren that the church of York should be any longer void on account of the complaint of our brother Ralph, archbishop of Canterbury; especially since our said brother, though frequently admonished by the apostolic see, has refused to defer to it in this cause. We therefore order you by these presents to be the more diligent in loving and honouring our brother Thurstan as your metropolitan, and henceforth without fail to show him due obedience and reverence. Given at Beauvais, 20 November.

The pope then came to the castle of Chaumont[-en-Vexin], in the diocese of Rouen. The king of England came to a castle of his called Gisors, a little more than

leugis distat, ad ecclesiam quandam que est in medio
duorum castellorum, qui locus colloquio destinatus erat
in crastinum. Papa venit prior cum cardinalibus suis, et
episcopis, et abbatibus, et aliis personis de Francia, et
aliunde nonnullis. Rex vero paulo post cum filio suo
Willelmo, cum episcopis et abbatibus,[a] cum procerum
et militum multo comitatu ad papam regaliter venit.
A quo honorifice apostolico more susceptus est, et satis
F.19 alterutrum congratulati / sunt. Nam preter spiritualem
patris et filii relacionem, carnali consanguinitate pro-
pinqui erant, quorum avus et avia frater et soror fuerunt.[1]

Rex Francorum nec venit nec misit, set in Senonico
longe remotus erat. Dominus papa tamen cum rege
nostro satis sermocinatus est de pace inter eos facienda,
ostendens mala multimoda, vastitatem, paupertatem
multorum, et mendicitatem, miserias, et occasiones que
de discordia eorum provenerant, preter que deinceps,
si duraret, multa provenire timendum erat. Rex noster
iniuriam regis Francie, et suam enarrans iusticiam, sicut
prudens et modestus, placide et humiliter respondit:
'De discordia doleo, pacem desidero, nec in me remanet
quin libenter fecerim et facere velim quicquid regi
Francie dux Normannie debet'.

Cardinales, quia illis non adhibitis papa cum rege
secrecius agebat, hortatu domini Cononis, qui archiepiscopum nostrum multum diligebat, aliquantum in-
dignantes ab ecclesia exierunt, et, credo, timentes ne
de professione nostra temporaliter vel personaliter facienda aliquatenus regi consentiret. Quibus revocatis,
in publicum postea cuncta probata sunt. Habitis inter
se de statu et honore sancte ecclesie sermonibus, et de

---

[a] et . . . nonnullis, repeated in MS and subsequently 'vacated'

[1] Robert I of Normandy was the brother of Alice, wife of Renaud I,
count of Burgundy, great-grandfather of Calixtus II, though sometimes de-

two leagues from Chaumont, to a church midway
between the two castles, which was the place appointed
for the next day. The pope came first with his cardinals,
bishops, and abbots and other Frenchmen, and some
from other places. The king came shortly after with
his son, William, with bishops and abbots and a great
company of nobles and knights, in royal state, to meet
the pope, who received him honourably, as befitted a
pope, and the two exchanged hearty congratulations.
For besides their spiritual relationship of father and son,
they were carnally akin, since the king's grandfather
and the pope's grandmother were brother and sister.[1]

The king of France neither came nor sent, but was
far off, in the Senonais. However, our lord the pope gave
our king a long talk about making peace between them,
pointing out the many evils which had arisen from their
dissension : devastation, widespread poverty and begging, wretchedness, and causes of stumbling ; besides
which, if it lasted, it was to be feared that worse would
follow. Our king set forth the wrong done by the king
of France and his own righteousness, and answered
quietly and humbly, like a wise and modest man, 'I am
sorry about the quarrel, I want peace ; nor have I any
reason to avoid willingly doing whatever the duke of
Normandy owes to the king of France'.

The cardinals, since the pope was conferring privately
with the king and had not called them in, on the advice
of cardinal Cuno, who was very fond of our archbishop,
left the church somewhat vexed, and also, I think, for
fear the pope should yield to the king and consent to our
making a provisional or personal profession. They were
called back, and all further proceedings were publicly
approved. After some conversation about the estate and

scribed as his grandfather. The king and the pope were thus second cousins
once removed.

quiete ipsius et inquietudine secundum diversa loca,[1] et
aliquibus seriis et iocis honestis, de archiepiscopo nostro
sermo inceptus est. Papa et cardinales et plurimi qui
aderant satis illum laudabant, de sapiencia, honestate,
modescia, de amore erga dominum suum. Invehe-
bantur in Cantuariensem quod Eboracensis ecclesia
tamdiu fuerat pro non sibi debite professionis exaccione
pastoris regimine desolata, nec reverende memorie pape
P[aschalis et] G[elasii] nec preceptis illius in consecracione electi illius quicquam obediencie exhibuit, nec
ad concilium vocatus venit, nec qui vices eius agere
deberent misit, nec canonicam excusacionem mandavit.
Quapropter secundum dignitatem Romane ecclesie eum
consecraverat, nemini preiudicans, si quid super illum
se iudicandum existimat, et de hoc presentibus utriusque
partibus in presencia curie Romane causa audita diligenter eam faceret canonico et irrefragabili iudicio
diffiniri; nunc vero illum,[a] ut bonum regem, et sancte
Romane ecclesie filium et fidelem, deprecabantur [b]
supplicabant quatinus archiepiscopum suum, tanquam
beati Petri manibus consecratum,[c] cum pace et dileccione, pro dei et sancte Romane ecclesie amore et
honore, suscipiat, et in ecclesia sua tranquille permanere,
et opus dei operari permittat. Auditum enim habebat
quod ipse tocius terre sue ingressum illi interdixerat,
et de archiepiscopatu iam divestierat. Set apud dis-
trictum iudicem districte punietur, cuius culpa ecclesia
illa tamdiu pastore destituta est, et deinceps desti-
tuetur.

 Rex, excusato prius Cantuariensi archiepiscopo quod
pre infirmitate ad consilium venire non potuit, et
aliquibus regni sui consuetudinibus enarratis, sic ait:

---

  [a] illis, MS   [b] deprecanbantur, MS
     [c] consecracionem, MS

honour of holy church, and its rest or unrest in various places,[1] partly serious, and partly decently merry, our archbishop became the subject. The pope and cardinals and most of those present praised his wisdom, honour, modesty, and love of his lord. They abused the archbishop of Canterbury, because the church of York had been so long deprived of its shepherd owing to his demand for a profession not due to him; because he had shown no obedience to the late Popes Paschal and Gelasius nor to the commands of the former in the matter of the consecration of the elect of York; he had been called to the Council and had not come, nor sent anyone to act for him, or a canonical excuse. Wherefore, as befitted the dignity of the Roman church, [the pope] had consecrated him without prejudice to anybody who might consider he had a lawful claim against him, and would have it decided by canonical and irrefragable judgment, in the presence of both parties, the case being diligently heard by the Roman *curia*. The pope and cardinals besought Henry as a good king and a loyal son of the church of Rome, to receive his archbishop, as one consecrated by the hands of St Peter, with peace and affection for the love of God and the holy Roman church, and to suffer him to remain quietly in his church and do the work of God. For the pope had heard that the king had forbidden him entry into all his lands and had deprived him of his archbishopric. But that man shall be severely punished before a strict judge, by whose fault the church of York has been so long and shall be henceforth deprived of its shepherd.

The king first excused the archbishop of Canterbury as having been unable to come to the Council owing to illness, and explained some of the customs of his kingdom,

---

[1] Alluding to the schism

'Domine papa, domine pater, et, vos, domini cardinales, quod petitis, de recepcione videlicet Eboracensis
archiepiscopi, legitime facere nequeo, fidem enim spo-
pondi quod permissione mea regnum Anglie non intrabit,
nisi vel personaliter R[adulpho] archiepiscopo professus
fuerit; ita quidem quod nec ille, nec successores eius,
R[adulpho], neque successoribus suis ulterius unquam
profiteantur; et hoc litteris domini pape et nostris con-
F.19*v* firmatum esse volo et postulo; et sic, sine / lesura fidei
mee, cum amore meo, ad ecclesiam suam transire et quiete poterit permanere'.

Cui papa: 'Fili dulcissime, vice beati Petri, cuius
ego vicarius sum, quamvis indignus, ab hac promissione
te absolvo. Fides enim contra iusticiam minime est
observanda, et illa quidem professio indecens est et
iniusta.' Et ille: 'Aliter', inquit, 'inconsultis episcopis
et primoribus Anglie facere non possum. De archiepiscopatu non eum [a] divestivi.' Sophistice verum erat.
Nondum enim littere per quas spoliatus fuit illuc usque
fuerant prolate, set ad deferendum iam tradite, quod
eciam pape sic indicatum est.

Archiepiscopus [b] hiis non interfuerat, remotus in
partem. Venerunt quidam ad eum, sub optentu ami-
cicie fortasse, magis pro rege, persuadentes ei ut quod
predecessores eius fecerint, et ipse pro amore regis
modo personaliter faceret, et pro pace et quiete ecclesie
sue et successoribus suis in sempiternum habenda.
Quibus ille: 'Si hoc fecisse vellem, non necesse michi
fuisset dominum papam et Romanam ecclesiam requirere; set iamdudum ab archiepiscopo Cantuariensi
consecratus, possem in ecclesia nostra cum illa decora
vel indecora pace et quiete permanere. Qui de antecessoribus meis professi sunt, tristes et coacti fecerunt,

[a] est, MS   [b] Archiepiscopo, MS

and then said, 'My lord pope and father, and you, my
lords cardinals, I cannot lawfully do what you ask by
receiving the archbishop of York, because I have given
my word that he shall not enter the realm of England
with my leave, unless he makes his profession personally
to archbishop Ralph on the understanding that neither
he nor his successors shall ever make any further profession to Ralph or his successors; and I will have this
confirmed by letters of the pope and myself; and thus,
without any breach of faith, by me, he may go over to
his church with my approval and stay there in peace'.

The pope answered, 'Sweetest son, in the name of
St Peter, whose vicar I am, though unworthy, I absolve
thee from this promise. For faith is not to be kept
contrary to justice, and that profession is improper and
unjust.' The king replied, 'I cannot do otherwise without consulting the bishops and magnates of England.
I have not deprived him of his archbishopric.' This was
technically true. For the letters by which he was de-
spoiled had not yet been published, but had been handed
over for execution, as was also explained to the pope.

The archbishop took no part in these proceedings,
standing aside. Some people came to him, ostensibly as
his friends, but really on behalf of the king, persuading
him to do as his predecessors had done, and make his
personal profession for love of the king, and for the peace
and quiet of his church and his successors for ever. To
them he said, 'If I had chosen to do this, I need not have
called in the pope and the Roman church, but should
have long ago been consecrated by the archbishop of
Canterbury, and might be abiding in our church in
graceful, or disgraceful "peace and quiet". Those of my
predecessors who made their profession, made it in
sorrow, under compulsion and personally; so long as

M

et personaliter; du[m] de persona in personam Cantuarienses extorqueant, nil amplius que[runt]. Successoribus nostris exemplum non ero, quia nec ecclesie
nec persone profitebor, nisi canonico iudicio fuerit
terminatum. Dominus vero Cantuariensis archiepiscopus, qui nec ad concilium venit, nec ad colloquium
istud, a quo non nimium longe erat remotus. Si professionem istam quocunque modo lucrari putasset, que
eum tenebat invaletudo non detinuisset.'

Nec blandimentis, nec prece, nec absolucione dominus papa apud regem pro archiepiscopo nostro quicquam impetrans, animum suum tamen compressit,
nolens ei hac vice acrius insistere, nolens imperiose
agere, nec apostolica uti potestate; cogitans esse de-
cencius eminus iaculo pugnandum, quam modo comi-
nus gladio feriendum, et de amico congressu inimicum
fieri digressum.

Sic ergo regi et suis facta benediccione digrediuntur.
Multi vero asscripserunt ei cordis imbecillitati quod non
asperius et iustius egerat pro archiepiscopo a se nuper
consecrato, et hac de causa archiepiscopatu spoliato.
Et plerique[a] de Normannis et Anglis finiverunt, arbi-
trantes quod tota Chriscianitas in terra regis pro-
hibe[re]tur, si ipse Eboracensem archiepiscopum cum
pace non reciperet.[1] Ille autem quamvis de colloquio
quod plurimum continuaverat aliter quam sperasset
accidit, non tamen a spe penitus decidit, inter se dicens:
'Michi autem adherere deo bonum est, p[onere] i[n]
d[omino] d[eo] s[pem] m[eam]'.[2] Et dominus papa
blande et confortatorie locutus est illi, admonens ne
diffideret, ne desperaret, dicens Romanam ecclesiam
illi non defore necessaria ministrando, donec per dei
auxilium ad sua revocaretur.

<hr />

[a] plerisque, MS
[1] i.e. Normandy and England would be put under an interdict.
[2] Ps. 73 : 27

the Canterbury party can extort it from one person after another, they ask no more. I will not be a precedent for my successors ; I will not make a profession either to the church or to the person, unless the question is settled by a canonical judgment. But the lord archbishop of Canterbury, who has come neither to the council nor to this conference, though he was at no great distance, would not have been detained by his illness if he had thought he could by any means have obtained this profession.'

Neither by coaxing, nor by prayer, nor by absolution was the pope able to obtain anything from the king for our archbishop ; but he restrained his feelings, not wishing on this occasion to press harder, to command, or to use his apostolic power. He thought it more proper to fight with darts from a distance than this time hand to hand with the sword, and to turn a friendly conference to a parting in anger.

So he gave his blessing to the king and his followers, and they parted. But many people charged him with weakness in not acting more firmly and justly in behalf of an archbishop whom he had himself consecrated so lately, and who had on that account been robbed of his archbishopric. And most of the Normans and English ended by thinking that the Christian religion would be forbidden in all the land if the king would not peaceably receive the archbishop of York.[1] But though the conference, long as it had been, had turned out otherwise than he had hoped, he did not lose hope altogether, saying to himself, 'But it is good for me to hold me fast by God, to put my trust in the Lord God'.[2] And the pope spoke to him kindly and comfortably, bidding him not to lose confidence or despair, saying that the Roman church would not fail to supply his needs until by God's help he should be recalled to his place.

Dominus vero rex a colloquio reversus statim in
Anglia[m] misit qui archiepiscopum dissai[s]irent, in
hoc nobiliter et regaliter agens quod clericos qui cum
archiepiscopo erant nichilo spoliavit, intendens, licet
archiepiscopo iratus, legitime et canonice agentes.
Ceteri qui domi erant nimis tristes fuerunt et exterriti.
Orcadensis episcopus et predictus archidiaconus vix regi
reconciliari potuerunt quia consecracioni interfuerant,
quamquam vellent, et liquido possent, iurare se non
ideo ad concilium venisse.

F.20 Erant cum domino papa de Romanis Cono Prenestinus episcopus, Lambertus Ostiensis episcopus / post
illum papa effectus, Gresogonus cancellarius, Iohannes
Cremensis presbiter cardinalis, Petrus Petri Leonis
diaconus cardinalis, Gregorius diaconus sancti Angeli,
Petrus Ruffus diaconus cardinalis sancti Silvestri qui
fuerat nepos pape Paschalis, et alii presbyteri, et diaconi, et subdiaconi, et clerici, omnes fere contristati
quod adversus regem indulgencius egerat. Confortatus
a papa et cardinalibus exilium suum, tunc demum et
manifestum et verum, deo et sancto Petro, de cuius
ecclesia eiectus ad ipsum refugiebat, committere cepit.
Quod ei a principio adventus sui ad illos alacriter
fecerant, nunc quidem maiori complectebant amore et
copiosius honorabant. In consiliis, et causis, et iudiciis
erat inter illos quasi unus ex illis, et a nullis eorum fere
segregatus secretis. Clerici sui tanquam domini pape
clerici, famuli quasi de famulis ipsius. Plurimi vero
clam et[a] coram dicebant ei, et quasi precabantur, ne
quam pateretur indigenciam; si quid sibi vel suis
deesset, ne eos celaret, et de suo alii dono, alii mutuo
large offerebant.

Adventus domini Dominica prima[1] venerunt Ferrarias

---

[a] et clam, MS

[1] 30 November 1119

But the king, returning from the conference, immediately sent men to England to disseise the archbishop. He was noble and kingly enough not to deprive the clerks who were with the archbishop, acting lawfully and canonically, angry as he was with him. The others who were at home were very sad and frightened. The bishop of Orkney and the archdeacon already mentioned found it hard to make their peace with the king because they had assisted at the consecration, although they were willing to swear, as they clearly could, that they had not come to the Council for that purpose.

Of the Romans, there were with the Pope Cuno, bishop of Palestrina, Lambert, bishop of Ostia, his successor in the papacy, Chrysogonus the chancellor, John of Crema, cardinal-priest, Peter Pierleone, cardinal-deacon, Gregory, [cardinal-]deacon of St Angelo, Peter Ruffus, cardinal-deacon of St Sylvester, who had been Pope Paschal's nephew, and other priests, deacons, sub-deacons, and clerks, almost all grieved that the pope had acted too indulgently towards the king. Encouraged by the pope and the cardinals, Thurstan now began to cast his exile, now real and obvious, upon God and St Peter, out of whose church he had been expelled and with whom he took refuge. As they [the pope and the others] had eagerly done at his first coming to them, they now showed him more love and more abundant honour. In councils, trials, and judgments, he was, as it were, one of themselves and in almost all their secrets. His clerks were as the pope's clerks, his servants as the pope's servants. Many people privately and publicly said to him, indeed almost prayed him not to want for anything; if he or his needed anything they were not to hide it from them. Some of them freely offered gifts, others loans.

On the first Sunday in Advent [1] they came to

ad quandam abbaciam.   Eo rex Francie et regina,[a]
que erat pape proneptis, ad eum venerunt, qui devote
pro nostro exorabant archiepiscopo, et si episcopatus
aut archiepiscopatus in regno suo vacaret, concessu
domini pape se libenter ei concedere asserebant. Habitis
inter se sermonibus multimodis coram archiepiscopis et
episcopis et multis aliis, ut verba eius plene exprimam,
ita rex inquid: 'In causa Eboracensis archiepiscopi
Roma aut honorata erit aut multum dishonorata.   Et
certe in colloquio cum rege Anglorum habito pro archiepiscopo, vestris tanquam beati Petri manibus consecrato, et propter hoc quasi inexecrabili exterminato,
minus severe, et minus iuste actum [b] est.'

Erat ibi Gaufridus Rotomagensis archiepiscopus, qui,
negocium habens, ad dominum papam venerat.   Cui
paulo prius [c] coram rege et omnibus assistentibus sic
locutus est: 'Hoc fraternitati vestre iniungendo precipimus quatinus verbis nostris regi vestro aliquibus
vobiscum adiunctis sic dicatis.   In colloquio inter nos
nuper habito de recepcione [d] Eboracensis archiepiscopi,
quod iusticia et racio exigebat, et honor ipsius erat,
nichil apud eum nec precibus nec blandiciis obtinui.
Et quoniam supra dileccionem coniugium, adhuc illi
parcens nolui eum exasperare, nolui apostolica uti auctoritate; verum hoc illi mandamus, quod nisi ad presens
eum suceperit, et in ecclesia cui consecratus est cum pace
fecerit permanere, Romana ecclesia nullatenus potest
dimittere quin canonice severitatis iusticiam exequatur.'

Quod per obedienciam iniunctum archiepiscopus
dicere suscepit, estimo non dictum reliquit.   Cumque
de Ferrariis ad Senonicam urbem tenderent, placuit

[a] regine, MS   [b] auctum, MS
[c] primo, MS   [d] rescripcione, MS

Ferrières, to a certain abbey. There came thither the king of France and the queen, who was the pope's great-niece, and they besought him on behalf of our archbishop, and said that if any bishopric or archbishopric in the kingdom should be void, they would gladly give it him, if the pope permitted. After a long discussion in the presence of archbishops and bishops and many others, the king said (to give his words in full), 'In the archbishop of York's case the church of Rome will either be honoured or much dishonoured. And certainly, in the conference with the king of England on behalf of the archbishop, a man consecrated by your hands, as it were by the hands of St Peter and therefore sanctified for ever, and yet exiled, the matter was slackly and unjustly handled.'

Geoffrey, archbishop of Rouen, was there, having come to the pope on business. And the pope said to him, in the presence of the king and of all the others, 'We command and enjoin on you, brother, that taking other persons with you, you give the king the following message in my name. In the conference we lately had about the reception of the archbishop of York, I failed to get from him by prayer or by persuasion what justice and reason and his own honour, demanded. And because union is more important than affection, I spared him and would not make him angry: I would not use my apostolic authority. But we send him this message, that if he will not immediately receive him and permit him to abide in peace in the church to which he was consecrated, the church of Rome can by no means omit to execute justice with all the rigour of the canon law.'

The message which the archbishop was enjoined by his obedience to deliver, I judge he must have left unspoken. And, as they were going from Ferrières to

domino pape et curie dominum Cononem remittere, ut
sic in Francia, Anglia et Normannia legacionem haberet.
Ex quo nimirum archiepiscopus noster, et sui, valde
contristati sunt: illum etenim erga se quatuor istis,
iusticia, et veritate, et fide et dileccione quadratum
experti [a] erant. Set discedens dominum papam cum
lacrimis orabat ut archiepiscopum ita remitteret, sicut
ex iusticie racione et apostolice sedis honore decebat.[b]
Seorsum autem cum fratribus cardinalibus supplicabat,
manu eum in manus tradens, ne illi deessent; pro illo
domino pape suggererent; et quod de longinquo ille
non poterat, ipsi pro confratre suo presentes supplerent.
Quibus bene per omnia promittentibus ad regem Francorum, qui / non longe aberat,[c] reversus est.

F.20v

Cum autem Autisiodorum pervenissent, dominus
papa duos presbiteros cardinales, Petrum Pisanum, et
Gregorium Senem, Guidonem Pisanum archidiaconum,
ab urbe Roma ad se venientes, gaudiose suscepit. Hic
vero Petrus clericus erat bonus, castus et religiosus,
canonum et decretorum et legum scriptarum non
mediocriter peritus. Qui, audita ex ordine archiepiscopi
nostri exilii causa, pie condoluit,[d] et mutua collocucione
et rerum aliquarum inter eos collacione, et pro honesta
eius in curia conversacione, ei amore non modico in
brevi conglutinatus est. Id vero testimonii apud eos
qui eum noverant optinebat, ut nemo de illo diffideret
cui auxiliari promittebat.[e] Quem archiepiscopo nostro
et suis visum est dominum illis pro venerando Conone
reddidisse. Hic enim, quantum poterat, suggerendo,
supplicando, arguendo, oportune inoportune pro archiepiscopo nostro faciebat. Pisanus archidiaconus clericus
erat sapiens et honestus, et inter Romanos opinionis
bone; qui eum non modice dilexit. Postea vero Ti-
burtinus [f] episcopus effectus est.

[a] ex parte, MS   [b] decebat, dicebat, MS   [c] oberat, MS
[d] conduit, MS   [e] permittebat, MS   [f] Libertinus, MS

Sens, it pleased the pope and the *curia* to send back cardinal Cuno as legate in France, England, and Normandy. Our archbishop and his company were doubtless sad at this; for they had found him foursquare in justice, truth, faith, and affection. But as he left, he besought the pope with tears to send back the archbishop in such a way as befitted justice and the honour of the apostolic see. He also privately handed him over to his brother cardinals, begging them not to desert him, to speak for him to the pope, and, being present, to supply for their brother what he, at a distance, could not. When they gave favourable promises, he returned to the king of France, who was not far away.

When they had come to Auxerre, the pope received with joy two cardinal-priests, Peter of Pisa, and Gregory of Sienna, and Guy, archdeacon of Pisa, who came to him from Rome. This Peter was a good clerk, good, chaste, and religious, and more than usually skilled in canon and civil law. When he heard the details of the reason of our archbishop's exile, he kindly sympathised, and after conversing and comparing notes with him, and because of his honourable behaviour at court, soon became extremely attached to him. His reputation among his acquaintance was that of a man who could be implicitly trusted by anyone he had promised to help. The archbishop and his company thought that the Lord had given him to them in place of their revered Cuno. He did all he could for our archbishop, suggesting, petitioning, praying, and reasoning, in season and out of season. The archdeacon of Pisa was a wise and honourable clerk, and of good repute among the Romans, and he thought highly of him. He was afterwards made bishop of Tivoli.

Quamdiu dominus papa archiepiscopum nostrum secum retinuit, in missarum celebracionibus, in altarium consecracionibus eum proximum et collateralem, ut cardinalem vel capellanum, habebat; si duo altaria in ecclesia una consecraturus erat, alterum illi,[a] tradito uno vel duobus episcopis, consecrare precipiebat. Si vero ecclesiam dedicare debebat, quodcunque fieri iubet ordo intus et extra, cuncta illi usque ad consecracionem altaris, adiuncto aliquo quasi suffraganeo episcopo, facere iniungebat. In sollempnibus processionibus equitando factis, quando more apostolico coronatus fuit, sicut in die Nativitatis Dominice, Augustini, et die Epiphanie, Cluniaci, dominus Ostiensis, qui magister inter eos et dignior erat, eum sibi comparem esse voluit, et peracto[b] tante solempnitatis et dignitatis officio, archiepiscopus, sicut cardinales, bisancios aureos, quod presbiterium ab ipsis appellatur, a domino papa suscepit, quod cardinalibus et clericis suis, unicuique secundum quod ordinatum est, apostolicus die coronacionis sue distribuit.

Ad Purificacionem beate Marie fuit dominus papa Vienne, ubi archiepiscopus fuerat, nec adhuc alius[c] successerat, in qua tres septimanas faciens providebat et preparabat, qualiter secure posset et sponsam suam spirituali matrimonio sibi desponsatam, sanctam scilicet Romanam ecclesiam, nondum visam, visitare. Defuncto enim beate memorie papa Pascali, sicut supradictum est, Iohannes cancellarius in papam Gel[asium] elevatus est, set propter Alemagnicum regem, qui Romanam ecclesiam persequebatur, Rome se credere non ausus, per mare navigans urbi Ianue applicuit, demum Cluniacum pervenit. Exaugustus vero Henricus, Cesar Teotonicus, immo Cedar totus iniquus, sancte ecclesie inimicus, Burdinum archiepiscopum

---

[a] alteri, MS   [b] peracte, MS   [c] aliter, MS

As long as the pope had our archbishop with him, he kept him close by his side, like a cardinal or chaplain, in celebrating mass and in consecrating altars. If he was about to consecrate two altars in one church, he bade him consecrate the second assisted by one or two bishops. But if he had to dedicate a church, he enjoined on him, with some bishop as a sort of suffragan, to do everything which the Order requires, within the church and without, up to the consecration of the altar. In the solemn mounted processions, when the pope wore his crown, as on Christmas day at Autun, and on Twelfth Day at Cluny, the cardinal of Ostia, the *doyen* of the cardinals, chose him for his companion, and after this solemn function, the archbishop, like the cardinals, received from the pope the golden besants, which they call priest-money (*presbyterium*), which the pope distributes to his cardinals and clerks, to each according to rule, on the day when he wears his crown.

At Candlemas the pope was at Vienne, where he had been archbishop and no one had as yet succeeded him. He stayed there three weeks making provision and preparation how he might safely visit his spiritual spouse, the Roman church, which he had not yet seen. For after the death of Pope Paschal of blessed memory, John the chancellor was raised up as Pope Gelasius; but dared not trust himself in Rome on account of the king of the Germans, who persecuted the Roman church, but put to sea, landed at Genoa, and at last came to Cluny. For the ex-emperor Henry, a German Caesar, or rather Kedar, unjust, the enemy of the church, by means of some of his wicked partisans in Rome, set up

degradatum per quosdam Rome fautores maliciosos antipapam et anti-Petrum, aut potius anti-Christum, Rome constituit, propter quod in urbe et ecclesia dissensio et turbacio magna fuerat, nec tunc quidem penitus sedata erat. Ipse tamen Burdinus per dei amicos ab urbe pulsus Sutrie degebat, et merito heresis sue multis bonis egebat, et contra Jhesum Christum et suos nequicias et inquitates multas agebat, quem deus postea per proprium sal¹ destruxit.

Radulphus archiepiscopus non adhuc archiepiscopum nostrum persequi cessabat, nec a professionis exaccione /

F.21 destiterat; set in hac perseverans, regem compulit ut ad papam remitteret, temptans si quo modo apud ipsum et curiam efficere posset ut nostrum cogerent profiteri. Sciebant bonum Cononem ᵃ contra iniuriam conantem non adesse, cuius absencia facilius impetrare putabant.

Cumque dominus papa a Vienna recederet, cor lapideum habuit qui ipsius summi patris et multorum suspiria, gemitus, et lacrimas aspexit, si non ad condolendum et collacrimandum motus fuit. Relinquebat ecclesiam cui ᵇ a iuventute sua archiepiscopus priefuerat, relinquebat natalem patriam, nepotes, consanguineos,ᶜ et homines suos, nunquam redditurus ad illos. Illi vero simili dolore afficiebantur, videntes patrem suum et dominum eos deserere,ᵈ quem non ulterius sperabant videre.

Misit ergo cum muneribus Exoniensem episcopum, qui apud Valenciam dominum papam invenit. Quod audiens fidelis Cono confratribus suis cardinalibus scripsit, ut peticioni regis Anglie de professione Eboracensis archiepiscopi nullatenus consentirent; archiepiscopo quoque misit litteras que subscripte sunt.

ᵃ Canonem, MS   ᵇ qui, MS
ᶜ cum sanguineis, MS   ᵈ disserere, MS

[Maurice] Bourdin, a degraded archbishop, at Rome as antipope and anti-Peter, or rather Antichrist, which gave rise to great dissension and tumult in the city and church, which was not yet entirely subdued. However, Bourdin had been driven out of the city by God's friends, and was living at Sutri, and, as his heresy deserved, was much in want, and did much wickedness and injustice to Christ and his people. God afterwards destroyed him through his own weakness.[1]

Archbishop Ralph still continued to pursue our archbishop, and to exact his profession. With this object he forced the king to send again to the pope and try whether he could anyhow get him and his court to compel our archbishop to make his profession. They knew that the good Cuno was not there striving against wrong, and thought they would obtain their request more easily in his absence.

And when our lord the pope was to leave Vienne, that man must have had a heart of stone who beheld the sighs, groans, and tears of our holy father himself and of many others and was not moved to grieve and weep with them. He was leaving the church over which he had presided from his youth up as archbishop, he was leaving his native land, his nephews, kindred, and men, never to return. And they were afflicted with the like grief, seeing their father and lord desert them, and having no hope of seeing him again.

The king, therefore, sent the bishop of Exeter with gifts, who found the pope at Valence. On hearing this, the faithful Cuno wrote to his brethren the cardinals that they should by no means consent to the petition of the king of England about the profession of the archbishop of York. He also sent the archbishop the following letter :

[1] Taking *sal* to mean a flaw in a precious stone, as in Pliny

Littere domini Cononis [a] *cardinalis et legati ad*
Eboracensem archiepiscopum

Cono Prenestinus episcopus et sancte Romane ecclesie legatus, domino venerando et fratri in Christo dilecto T[urstino] Eboracensi dei gracia archiepiscopo, Spiritus Sancti Paracliti consolacionem. Audivimus quod rex Anglorum iterum misit nuncios suos ad dominum papam ut videntes per non videntes decipiat, scilicet ut dominus noster et alii fratres nostri vos ad hoc cogant, ut contumaci et presumptuoso suo adulterinam faciatis professionem [1]; et eciam, sicut a quibusdam amicis et familiaribus intelleximus, gaudet multum ipse rex de nostra absencia, quia iactat se per fratres nostros posse perficere omnia que in curia nostra voluerit; unde vestram monendo exoramus fraternitatem quatinus hoc nunquam fieri permittat. Eciam si 'angelus de celo' [2] aliud annunciaverit, quam id quod iusticie et auctoritatis est, nunquam faciatis! Memor eciam estote illius quod legitur in libro Regum de Nabad, viro glorioso, qui magis voluit mori quam vineam suam, hoc est paternam hereditatem, impio regi et idolatro Achabh ad ortum suum faciendum vel dare vel vendere. Omnipotens deus, dilectissime frater, qui est iustus iudex, faciat vobis et nobis de iniuria vobis illata iusticiam, et vos semper incolumes custodiat! De statu vero vestro et prosperitate, atque de curia vestra, et quomodo se habeat, et quid de Anglia vobis est nunciatum, nobis litteris vestris significate. Fratres nostros qui vobiscum sunt, clericos vestros, dulciter ex nostra parte salutate et confortate, ne desperent, quia domini est bellum, et ipse suos non derelinquit; et levius est victoria nisi iusticia et Christus est in causa.

[a] Coni, MS

Letter of the cardinal and legate, Cuno,
to the archbishop of York

Cuno, bishop of Palestrina and legate of the Roman church, to his venerable brother in Christ, Thurstan, by the grace of God archbishop of York, the consolation of the Holy Ghost, the Comforter. We have heard that the king of England has again sent his messengers to our lord the pope to deceive those who see by means of the blind, namely that our lord the pope and our other brethren may compel you to make an adulterous profession [1] to his contumacious and presumptuous [archbishop]. He also rejoices greatly, as we have heard from some of our friends and household, at our absence, because he boasts that by means of our brethren he can effect whatever he wills in our *curia*. Wherefore we pray and warn you, Brother, not to allow this ever to happen. Even if an 'angel from heaven' [2] should bring you any message inconsistent with justice and authority, do not ever do it. Remember what is read in the book of Kings about Naboth, that glorious man, who preferred to die rather than to give or sell his vineyard, his father's inheritance, to the impious and idolatrous King Ahab, to make a garden of it. May God almighty, brother, who is a just judge, do you and us justice for the wrong done to you and keep you safe for ever! Let us know by your letters of your health and welfare and of your *curia* and its state, and what news you have from England. Give our kind greetings to our brethren who are with you, your clerks, and encourage them not to despair, because the battle is the Lord's and He doth not desert his own; and victory is a poor thing unless justice and Christ are on our side.

[1] i.e. unfaithful to his spouse, the church of York   [2] Gal. 1 : 8

Parum videntes dixit dominus Cono propter predictum episcopum, qui cecus oculis nec litteratus erat,
set ideo rex noster, et antea et modo, illum legaverat
quod a fratre suo rege Willelmo ad papam Urbanum
et papam P[aschalem] sepe legatus fuerat, et strenuus
et vafer Romanos et eorum mores bene noverat. Sepe
tamen, eciam cum videret, Anglie imputatum est quod
penuria litteratorum in ea legabatur. Nunc autem
dupliciter, quod non litteratus et non videns, muneribus
regis ab archiepiscopo domino pape et curie divisis,
peticionem facit quatinus pro amore regis et pro pace
ecclesie in regno suo Eboracensem archiepiscopum
profiteri Cantuariensi preciperet, et legacionem super
F.21v Britannia in/sula,[a] illi concederet. Ut breviter dicam,
nec dona in graciam illi concepta, nec peticio est ex-
audita.

Invehebant [b] episcopo plures de curia et alii cecita-
tem sibi exprobrantes quod in nocumentum exulis
advenerat ; et quidam volebant illum in eundo vel
redeundo disturbare si scirent hoc illi placere. Noster
vero nichil mali illi accedere velle dicebat, quia mandata regis et domini sui exequebatur.

Ultra Valenciam papam prosecutus, alia quam pe-
tivit forsitan impetravit. Cui in dicessu dominus papa
precepit, ut diceret domino suo et regi fideliter inti-
mans quatinus Eboracensem archiepiscopum reciperet :
'Nunc,' inquit, 'pauper et exul nos sequitur, et Romana
ecclesia ei non deficiet, quando deo placebit, restituendo. Set sciat rex quod nisi ipse dominum suum dili-
gens, nec malum pro malo reddere volens obstitisset,
iam iuste severitatis districcio illata foret.' Discedens

Cardinal Cuno said 'blind' because of the bishop named, who was a blind man and no scholar; but the king had sent him as ambassador previously, and this time also, because he had often been sent by his brother King William to Popes Urban and Paschal, was energetic and cunning, and well knew the Romans and their ways. Yet, even when he had his sight, England was often reproached with the few scholars it had as ambassadors. Doubly so this time, since a man, no scholar, and blind as well, distributing the king's gifts as from the archbishop between the pope and the *curia*, was begging the pope, for love of the king and for the peace of the church in his realm, to order the archbishop of York to make his profession to the archbishop of Canterbury, and grant the latter the post of legate over all England. To be brief, the gifts were not graciously accepted nor the petition heard.

Many of the *curia* and others also, taunted the bishop with his blindness and abused him for coming to injure an exile; and some would have impeded his coming or return, if they were sure it would please Thurstan. But our archbishop said he would have no evil happen to him, because he was only carrying out the orders of his king and lord.

The bishop followed the pope beyond Valence, and got an answer that he had not bargained for. For, as the pope left, he commanded him to speak to his lord and king and faithfully tell him to receive the archbishop of York. 'He is now', said he, 'following us, poor and an exile, and the church of Rome will not fail him, and will restore him when it pleases God; but let the king know that unless the archbishop had protested, out of love for his master and being unwilling to return evil for evil, the sternest measure of justice would have been

N

episcopus extor[r]i nostro aliquid compassionis et humanitatis liberaliter exhibuit, existimans quod dominum papam usque Romam prosequeretur.

Sabbato in capite Ieiunii venit dominus papa Vapinoquum que est civitas in Provincia. Ibi iter archiepiscopi versus Romam interruptum est. Ibi enim, iudicio curie et multorum qui aderant, definitum est Eboracensem ecclesiam ab illa indecenti professione solutam et liberam esse, et hoc apostolico privilegio confirmari debere, et sic factum. Dedit quoque dominus papa litteras archiepiscopo nostro ad Turonensem archiepiscopum et Belvacensem episcopum, precipiens quatinus litteras quas regi Anglorum mittebat ipsi deferrent : que hic subscripte sunt.

Littere eiusdem pape ad archiepiscopum Turonensem pro archiepiscopo Eboracensi [a]

Calixtus episcopus, servus servorum dei, venerabili fratri G., Turonensi archiepiscopo, salutem et apostolicam benediccionem. Quia devocionis tue dileccionem et fidelitatis constanciam in beati Petri servicio sepius probatam agnovimus, eius tibi negocia potissimum duximus committenda. Siquidem prudenciam tuam pro venerabilis fratris nostri T[urstini] Eboracensis archiepiscopi causa, ex fratrum nostrorum consilio, nostra volumus legacione perfungi, in qua quanta nobis et Romane ecclesie iniuria irrogetur, ipse, ut credimus, non ignoras. Tuam itaque, frater karissime, sollicitudinem exoramus atque precipimus [ut] [b] illas, quas pro eodem fratre nostro T[urstino] [c] dirigimus litteras, in Normanniam ad regem Anglicum deferas, et prima earum tradicione [d] regem ipsum

---

[a] Collated with a copy in *Reg. Magnum Album*, i. 50a
[b] ins. A   [c] vel, MS
[d] prima . . . traditione, primo . . . traditionem, MS

taken against him.' As the bishop left, he showed our archbishop some compassion and kindness, thinking that he would follow the pope to Rome.

On the first Saturday in Lent [6 March 1120], the pope came to Gap, a city in Provence. There the archbishop's journey to Rome was broken. For it was there decided, by a judgment of the *curia* and many assessors, that the church of York was absolved and free from that improper profession, and that this should be confirmed by a papal privilege; and this was done. The pope also gave our archbishop a letter to the archbishop of Tours and the bishop of Beauvais, bidding them take to the king of England the letter which he was sending to him, as follows :

Letter of the pope to the archbishop of Tours on behalf of the archbishop of York

Calixtus, bishop, servant of the servants of God, to his venerable brother, G[ilbert], archbishop of Tours, greeting and apostolic blessing. Knowing by frequent proof the warmth of your devotion and the constancy of your fidelity in the service of St Peter, we have thought it best to entrust his business to you. On the advice of our brethren, we will that you act as our delegate in the case of our venerable brother Thurstan, archbishop of York, in which, as we believe, you are not unaware how great wrong is being done to us and to the church of Rome. We therefore pray your attention, and bid you take to the king of England, in Normandy, the letter which we are sending him on behalf of our said brother Thurstan, and that, as soon as you have delivered it, you and

vice nostra tu et confrater vester, G. Rotomagensis
archiepiscopus,[a] quem in huius allegacionis execucione tibi socium exhibemus, diligentissime convenire [b]
studeatis, eumque instancius deprecemini, ut in pre-
dicti fratris nostri restitucione ita matris sue Romane
ecclesie preces exaudiat quatinus verus filius eius
videatur.[c]

Que ad Belvacensem episcopum eandem sentenciam
continebant.[d]

Scripsit et domino Cononi mandans ut litteras quibus R[adulpho] archiepiscopo scribebat per aliquem
illi mitteret, si Eboracensis archiepiscopus per litteras
regi transmissas in ecclesia sua non susciperetur. Legacionem super Angliam voluit illi committere, quod et
antea optulerat, precipiens ei ut susciperet, set nunc
sicut et tunc pedibus eius provolutus misericordiam
postulavit ne ei iniungeret per quod regis animum iam
adversum se [e] . . . persone ipsius semper parceretur;
quod videntes dicebant ei quod supplicacionibus re-
F.22 torquebat, / et exilium sibi protelabat. Hoc tamen illi
a probis viris et fidelibus fidelitati et probitati eximie
innotabatur. Alias vero litteras scripsit regi, quibus
eum scire volebat quid R[adulpho] archiepiscopo interdicebat, et alias clero et populo Eboracensis parochie.

Advenerat Vapincum quidam clericus generosus et
probus, Gepennensis ecclesie prepositus, infra ordines,
immo ante omnes ordines eidem ecclesie electus episcopus, set consideracione hoc erat ei indultum, ideo quod
ad hoc magis obediencia erat coactus, quam se ingerens
vel intrusus; quoniam Te[u]tonicus rex, in Remensi

---

[a] vice nostra . . . quem, vicem nostram, et cum fratre nostro G. Rotomagensi archiepiscopo quem, MS
[b] convenire] om. MS
[c] om. A
[d] continuebant, MS
[e] The MS seems to have omitted a line here.

your brother, Geoffrey, archbishop of Rouen, whom we appoint your fellow in the execution of this legation, take good heed to summon and earnestly exhort the king, that by restoring our said brother, he may so hear the prayers of his mother the church of Rome, as to appear her true son.

The letter to the bishop of Beauvais was to the same effect.

He also wrote to cardinal Cuno, bidding him send to archbishop Ralph, by some messenger, the letter which he was writing to him, in case the archbishop of York should not be received in his own church by virtue of the letter sent to the king. He also wished to entrust to him [Thurstan] the office of legate over England, which he had previously offered him, bidding him undertake it. But now, as before, he prostrated himself at the pope's feet and besought him not to enjoin on him a duty which would expose him permanently to the wrath which the king now felt against him personally. Those who saw this told him that he was contradicting his petitions and prolonging his exile. But honest and loyal men took it as a mark of his own honesty and loyalty. The pope also wrote a letter to the king, letting him know what he had forbidden the archbishop of Canterbury to do, and another letter to the clergy and people of the diocese of York.

There had come to Gap a well-born and honest clerk, provost of the church of Geneva, who had been elected bishop of that church, though not in holy orders or in any orders at all. But this was pardoned him, because he had rather been compelled to it by his obedience rather than himself intruding or being thrust in. Because the king of the Germans, having been

concilio excommunicatus, unum de suis festinabat contra deum et dominum papam intrudere, qui excommunicato communicare[t], nec beatum Petrum nec Christum revere[re]tur. Cuius violencie iste melius resistere poterat, quia tocius regionis illius clericis diviciis et amicis potencior et forcior erat. Hunc electum precepit dominus papa archiepiscopo nostro in presencia sua, kalendis Maii, hostiarium, lectorem, exorcistam, acolitum; crastina vero subdiaconum ordinare, proximo Sabbato ab ipso papa diaconum ordinandum et presbiterum, et in crastinum episcopum consecrandum. Aderat ibi domnus Bernardus Sancti David episcopus. Sicut ibi tunc didicerunt, Romane ecclesie consuetudo est omnibus diebus Quadragesime et in ieiuniis Quatuor Temporum quinque ordinibus ordinare.

Scriptum privilegium domino pape allatum est. Quo perlecto, ipse manu sua scripsit. Deinde Ostiensis episcopus subscribens sic ait: 'Spacium proxime [post] dominum papam ad ascribendum domino Prenestino reservo, quoniam prior meus est'. Subscripserunt et alii quotquot aderant[a] presbyteri cardinales et diaconi privilegio subscripto cum ceteris litteris accepto.

Archiepiscopus rogavit dominum papam ut ei de sanctorum reliquiis et de balsamo donaret. Cui benigne annuens de utroque donavit, dicens: 'Et certe, si nostro sanguine opus haberes, non tibi conferre[b] denegarem'.

Usum vero pallei, quamdiu in exilio esset, ei concessit, illis diebus et officiis quibus in provincia sua, ex predecessorum suorum consuetudine, uteretur. Etenim extra[c] provinciam vel regnum, absque permissione

---

[a] adherant, MS [b] Stubbs; est ferre, MS
[c] Stubbs; juxta, MS

excommunicated in the council of Rheims, made haste
to thrust in one of his followers, in opposition to God and
the pope, who should communicate with an excom-
municate and reverence neither St Peter nor Christ.
The bishop elect was the better able to resist his violence,
because by his wealth and friends he was more powerful
and stronger than the clergy of all that region. The
pope bade our archbishop to ordain this elect on 1 May
door-keeper, reader, exorcist, and acolyte, and on the
morrow subdeacon. He was to be ordained deacon and
priest by the pope on the following Saturday and
consecrated bishop on the morrow. Bernard, bishop of
St David's, was then present. As those there then
learned, it is the custom of the Roman church to ordain
to the five minor orders on any day in Lent and on the
Ember days.

A written bull of privilege was brought to the pope,
who signed it with his own hand. The bishop of Ostia
then subscribed it and said, 'I leave the next place after
our lord the pope blank for the subscription of the bishop
of Palestrina, since he is senior to me'. All the other
cardinals present, both priests and deacons, also subscribed the privilege, which, with other letters, was
passed.

The archbishop asked the pope to give him some
relics of saints and some balm. The pope graciously
consented and gave both, saying, 'Yes, and if you had
needed my blood, I would not refuse it you'.

He also granted him the use of the *pallium*, during
his exile, for the days and offices in which, by the custom
of his predecessors he would have used it in his own
province. For a metropolitan may not use his *pallium*
outside his province or realm without the pope's

summi pontificis metropolite palleo uti non licet, unde
et in curia Romana aliquociens inter se contulerunt
R[adulphum] archiepiscopum excessisse, quod in alio
regno et in capellis et locis non decentibus palleatus
cantabat. Apostolica benediccione accepta, ipse et qui
cum eo erant clerici in osculo et lacrimis discesserunt.

Plerique vero cardinalium et episcoporum et clericorum qui ibi erant eos longe extra civitatem prosecuti
sunt, quibus abinvicem digredientibus utrinque singultu
et fletu pauci se continuerunt. Iam enim eo habitacione
et dimidii anni commoracione quasi confratres et con-
tuberniales esse videbantur. Regredientes per cunctas
fere civitates, castella, et oppida per que venerant ab
episcopis et ab abbatibus, clericis, et laicis cum gaudio
susceptus est, et se excusantes querebantur non eum ante
pro multitudine et sumptuosa procuracione domini pape
cum quanta debuerant honorificencia suscepisse. Tot
et tantos et tales in huius exilii transmigracione ei notos
esse et eos nosse contigit, in primis quidem, quod pre-
cipuum et maximum fuit, dominum papam et curiam
Romanam, deinde archiepiscopos, abbates, clericos,
F.22v monachos, principes, proceres, milites, / et cuiuslibet
generis et condicionis homines ; et apud eos deus illi
tantam graciam contulit, ut vere ex hoc exilii infortunio
et infelicitate fortunatus magis et felix debeat reputari ;
maius est enim quam quod sit cuiquam credibile, qui
non viderit, quam magnam infra sue exterminacionis
terminum benevolenciam sibi contraxit.

In Franciam perveniens, ad Blesensem comitissam,
corde eciam quam genere nobiliorem,[1] et ad filium suum
comitem Teobaldum divertit. A quibus hilariter et
accurate suscepto, quamdiu in terra eorum vel trans-
eundo vel perhendinando esse placuit, nichil ei defuit.
Sororem domini sui regis et nepotem, quasi dominam

permission. Accordingly in the *curia* they sometimes compared archbishop Ralph's transgressions, in singing mass in another realm and in chapels and unfit places clothed in his *pallium*. After receiving the pope's blessing, he and the clerks with him departed with kisses and tears.

But most of the cardinals, bishops, and clerks who were there followed them a long way out of the city, and when they parted few on either side refrained from sobbing and weeping. For now, after living and dwelling together half the year, they seemed to be colleagues and messmates. As they went back through almost all the cities, castles, and towns through which they had come, he was received with joy by bishops, abbots, clerks and laymen; and they excused themselves for not having received him with due honour before, complaining of the crowd and the expense of entertaining the pope. In the wanderings of his exile he came to know and be known by so many great and distinguished people: first and most important the pope and the Roman *curia*, then the archbishops, abbots, clerks, monks, princes, nobles, knights, and men of every sort and degree. And God gave him so much grace with them, that in the misfortune and misery of his exile he ought rather to be counted fortunate and happy; for the goodwill he acquired during the period of his exile is more than anyone could believe who had not seen it.

When he came to France, he turned aside to the countess of Blois, whose heart was even nobler than her birth,[1] and her son, count Theobald. They received him joyfully and with due honour, and he lacked for nothing while he journeyed or stayed in their land. He regarded the sister and the nephew of his king as his

---

[1] Adela, daughter of William I, married Stephen, count of Blois.

et dominum habebat, et ipsi eum valde diligebant, et de eius exilio fratri et avunculo suo minime favebant. Que fecerat, quod deferebat, non omnia eos celavit. Ad regem Francorum venire diffugit, prudenter agens, quia inter ipsum et regem nostrum gravis adhuc discordia durabat.

Cum vero Remis venisset querens dominum Cononem, Remensis archiepiscopus R., qui cognominatus est Viridis, alacriter eum suscepit, qui eciam illi et clericis et famulis quos secum habebat in victu et vestitu humanitatis obsequia dum exularet qualia sibi suisque se [e]xhibiturum liberaliter optulit. Cui nimirum gracias inde magnas egit.

Apud Suesionem domino Conone invento, ad alterutrum satis gratulati sunt. Interrogatis et responsis de prosperitate domini pape et cardinalium, et unde ab eis discesserat, quid profecerat, que quibus scripta detulerat, enarravit. Tunc, prout illis melius visum est, rem paraverunt. In proximo erat Pascha in quo rex Francie Silvanectis curiam magnam habere debebat tum pro solemnitate, tum pro filio suo ab archiepiscopis et episcopis et baronibus Francie facienda fidelitate. Ibi Turonensem et Belvacensem conveniret de proferendo litteras domini pape ad regem. Nolens archiepiscopus propter odium inter reges illi curie interesse, uno de suis clerico cum legato relicto, ipse ad comitissam rediit. Cum ea diebus aliquot demorato, de conversione domine, et dextere excelsi in ea mutacione est contrectatum, quod paulo post fuit ad finem tractum. Die Pasche apud Columbias primum cum palleo cantavit; tercia die venit ad castrum quod Domnum Martinum vocant, et legatus obviam illi; et relato quod nec Turonensis

lord and lady, and they loved him well and were less well-disposed to their brother and uncle respectively on account of his exile. He did not entirely conceal from them what he had done and what he carried. He avoided approaching the king of France out of prudence, because there was still strife between him and our king.

But when he came to Rheims in search of cardinal Cuno, the archbishop, R[alph], whose surname was *viridis*, received him with joy, and freely offered him and all his clerks and servants, during his exile, all the services in the way of food and clothing that he would have allowed himself and his own men. Thurstan surely gave him hearty thanks.

He found cardinal Cuno at Soissons, and they exchanged congratulations. After questions and answers about the welfare of the pope and cardinals and where he had left them, he told him how he had fared, and what letters and to whom he had brought away. They then made such preparations as they thought best. Easter was coming, when the king of France was to hold a great court at Senlis, both for the feast, and for the archbishops, bishops, and barons of France to do fealty to his son. He would there meet the archbishop of Tours and the bishop of Beauvais to arrange for the delivery of the pope's letters to the king [of England]. But the archbishop [of York] was unwilling to attend that court because of the strife between the kings; so he left one of his clerks with the legate and returned to the countess. He stayed with her for some days, discussing her entry into religion and the change, of the right hand of the Almighty therein, which was soon afterwards accomplished. On Easter day [18 April] at Colombes, he first sang mass in his *pallium*. Two days later he came to the castle called Dammartin and the legate met him;

nec Belvacensis propter multas occupaciones et impedimenta legacionem hanc mature perficere non poterant,
deputati sunt huic negocio duo religiosi, alter regu-
larium canonicorum abbas, alter alterius ecclesie prior.

Dum sic ageretur, archiepiscopus ad comitissam reversus, eam cum aliis episcopis et abbatibus usque ad
Ma[r]ciniacum produxit. Que, spretis seculi diviciis et
pompis, ibi monialis effecta est. Qua quidem, testimonio regis Ludovici et principum tocius Francie, nulla
prudencior, nec melius composita, nec magis virilis
virago, ex multa retro etate in tota Gallia extiterat.

Ipse vero quendam clericum suum reliquerat, qui
audito quid litteris domini pape rex respondisset, re-
deunti sibi renunciaret. Abbas et prior litteras domini
pape regi retulerunt, quibus quod eis iniunctum erat,
F.23 et quod sibi visum est oportere, racionabiliter / supple-
verunt. Earum exemplum est hoc.

Littere eiusdem pape ad regem Anglie pro eodem
archiepiscopo

Calixtus episcopus, servus servorum dei, karissimo
in Christo filio Henrico, illustri regi Anglie, salutem
et apostolicam benediccionem.

Causam venerabilis fratris nostri T[urstini], Eboracensis archiepiscopi, tanto facilius tecum ad pacem et
concordiam reducere sperabamus, quanto et manifes-
tius eum sincera te diligere dileccione comperimus;
unde in colloquio inter nos habito, tecum micius
egimus, et quod exigente iusticia precipiendum fuerat,
precum instancia optinere conati sumus. Verum si

and on their being told that because of much business
and other difficulties neither the archbishop of Tours
nor the bishop of Beauvais could readily perform their
mission, two regular clergy were deputed to the task,
one an abbot of regular canons, the other prior of another
church.

While this was going on the archbishop returned to
the countess and, with other bishops and abbots, brought
her to Marcigny, where, despising the riches and pomp
of this world, she became a nun. Than whom, witness
King Louis and the princes of all France, no more prudent, better constituted, or more virile woman had been
in all Gaul for ages.

He had left one of his clerks behind to hear what
answer the king had made to the pope's letter, and tell
him when he should come back. The abbot and the
prior brought the pope's letter to the king, and added a
reasonable account of what had been their instructions
and what they thought should be done. Here follows
a copy of the letter :

Letter of the pope to the king of England on behalf of the archbishop

Calixtus, bishop, servant of the servants of God,
to his dearest son in Christ, Henry, illustrious king of
England, greeting and apostolic blessing. We had
hoped it would be the easier for us, with your help, to
bring the case of our brother Thurstan, archbishop
of York to a peaceful and agreed conclusion, the more
clearly we saw that he was sincerely attached to
you. We therefore dealt the more mildly with you,
in the interview which we had, and attempted to
obtain by prayer, what we ought to have commanded
in the name of justice. But even though our prayers

necdum exauditi simus, adhuc tamen a spe nostra
nequaquam decedimus. Et spirituali et carnali affeccione coniungimur, et peticio nostra plena iusticie et
racione fulcitur. Quippe neque communis ecclesie
consuetudo permittit, ut archiepiscopus archiepiscopo
professionem exhibeat, que [a] soli Romano debetur
pontifici. Et egregius ille in regno vestro Christiane
fidei propagator, papa Gregorius, ad Augustinum
scribens, Cantauriensem [et] Eboracensem archiepiscopos pares post eundem Augustinum instituit. Cuius
auctoritatem domini predecessores nostri, felices
bone memorie Pascalis et Gelasius, ecclesie Romane
pontifices, imitantes, predictum fratrem nostrum
T[urstinum] professionem Cantuariensi archiepiscopo
facere penitus prohibuerunt.[b] Sane a fidei sponsione,
qua[m] in prefato colloquio pretendebas, nos te pre-
sentem [per] presentes apostolice sedis [auctoritate]
absolvimus. In ea caritate quoque Christus est.
Sicut filium karissimum te rogamus, et apostolica
tibi auctoritate precipimus, ut sepedictum fratrem
nostrum, T[urstinum] archiepiscopum Eboracensem,
nostris tanquam beati Petri manibus consecratum,
suscipias, et in commissa sibi Eboracensi ecclesia
quiete facias inposterum permanere; nec tot Christi
oves diucius proprii pastoris carere solacio paciaris,
ne ipsarum periculum a te districcius a summo Iudice
requiratur, qui eas luporum dentibus laniandas exponis,
dum ad earum custodiam pastorem [c] proprium accedere non permittis.

Misit et dominus Cono litteras suas, quibus mandando premonuit et quasi premunivit, necnon omnimodis [hortatus est, ut] [d] dominum papam audiret.
Auditis rex litteris domini pape et legati, se, prius habito

have not yet been heard, we have still in no way departed from our hope. We are joined to you both by spiritual and natural affection, and our petition is fully supported by justice and reason: indeed the common custom of the church does not permit an archbishop to make that profession to an archbishop, which is due only to the bishop of Rome. And Pope Gregory, the noble planter of the Christian faith in your land, writing to Augustine, appointed the archbishops of Canterbury and York equals after Augustine himself. Following his authority, our predecessors, Paschal and Gelasius, of happy memory, entirely forbade our brother Thurstan to make his profession to the archbishop of Canterbury. From the pledge of faith which you put forward in our interview, we absolve you directly by the authority of the apostolic see. It is an act of charity on Christ's part. We ask you as our dearest son, and command you by apostolic authority, to receive our said brother Thurstan, archbishop of York, consecrated by us as if by St Peter, and cause him to abide peaceably henceforth in the church of York, which is committed to him. Nor shall you any longer suffer Christ's sheep to lack the comfort of a shepherd, lest their danger be required by the supreme Judge of you, who are exposing them to the teeth of wolves, in that you do not allow the shepherd whose duty it is to keep them, to approach.

Cardinal Cuno also sent his own letter, in which he bade him, forewarning and almost preparing him, by all means to listen to the pope. After hearing the letters of the pope and the legate, the king first consulted his

cum suis consilio, dixit responsurum. Et cum hoc
semel et iterum et tercio procrastinaret, abbas et prior
dixerunt illi : 'Domine rex, utile et decorum consilium
accipite, sciens pro certo quod non pro hac re deinceps
litteras precatorias videbitis'. Tandem rex dixit se
velle legato colloqui et eius consilium sequi. Tamen
propter aliquas causas precedentes non sese invicem
amabant.

Abeuntes legato sic renunciaverunt. Ille bene ani-
mosus homo, se non curare regis colloquium respondit ;
et illi : 'Fortasse ex astucia dixit, quod vos nolle venire
credebat, quatinus ex hoc sumpta occasione domino
pape obicere queat ideo precepto suo non obedisse, quod
legatus suus loqui ei dedignatus, cum ipse velle consilium eius inde habere mandaverat, et pro tempore
adversum se aliquid pro amico suo agendum est. Ex
vestra collocucione per dei auxilium amico vestro archiepiscopo restitucio et pax provenire potest.'

Sic illis persuadentibus, eo adquiescente, destinatum
est colloquium apud Vernonem, Dominica post Ascen-
sionem, rege mandante quod archiepiscopus sic prope
esset, quod, si responderet, ad eos mandatus brevi pervenisse posset. Archiepiscopo de Marciniaco regresso,
clericus quem reliquerat cuncta illi per ordinem enume-
F.23ᵥ ravit. Quibus auditis deo et / domino pape gracias egit.
Dehinc ad legatum pervenit.

Prope erat dies colloquio decretus, ad quod venerunt rex et episcopi cum militum magna multitudine ;
legatus cum episcopo uno et aliquanta clericorum bonorum societate. Proposuit rex de litteris domini pape,

council, and then said that he would reply. And when he put off doing so, once, twice, and thrice, the abbot and the prior said to him, 'My lord king, take our profitable and honourable advice, and be assured that these are the last letters of request that you will receive on this matter'. At last the king said that he would talk with the legate and follow his advice. However, owing to previous causes, they were not on good terms.

The envoys went away and reported this to the legate. He, being a man of spirit, said he did not care to have an interview with the king. They replied, 'Perhaps he said this out of cunning, because he thought that you would refuse to come, in order to be able to make use of the occasion to answer the pope that he had not obeyed his order, because his legate had disdained to speak with him, when he had sent word that he wanted to have his advice. And on occasion a man must put himself out for his friend's sake. By God's help, an interview with you may result in restitution and peace for your friend the archbishop.'

So, by their persuasion and the legate's consent, an interview was arranged at Vernon on the Sunday after Ascension day [30 May], the king ordering that the archbishop should be near enough for him to join them when sent for, at short notice, supposing an answer was given. When the archbishop returned from Marcigny the clerk whom he had left told him all this from beginning to end. On hearing it he gave thanks to God and the pope, and then came to the legate.

The day appointed for the conference was near. To it came the king, the bishops, and a crowd of knights, and the legate with one bishop and a considerable number of worthy clerks. The king began with the

o

quod precepto ei obedire nequibat[a] propter fidei sue promissionem, nisi Eboracensis archiepiscopus Cantuariensi vel personalem vel temporalem faceret professionem, et papa regem ad fidem ledendam cogere non debebat. Ipse archiepiscopus iamdudum redierat in Angliam. Opposuit legatus professionem illam esse indebitam, nec exhibendam fidem, si verum esset, intra iusticiam precipitatam, nec tenendam, et dominus papa inde eum absolverat et absolvebat. Illi vero et ecclesie Romane iniuria magna illata erat quod archiepiscopus manibus eius consecratus ideo spoliatus exulabat. Eapropter saltem nunc demum ei obediendum erat, cum nichil nisi iusticiam perciperet, alioquin que sentencia sentiretur, et velociter, ei non reticuit.

Utrinque sermonibus multis placide et iracunde positis et appositis, rex tandem assensit quod de archiepiscopatu eum revestiret, tantum ut ad tempus ab ingressu Anglie abstineret, et hoc legatum exorabat ut concederet. Quod cum legatus id se facere nec velle nec debere responderet, insinuatum est regi, ut, ipsum archiepiscopum requirens, eum precaretur ut concederet, et de concessu suo apud legatum intercederet, mandans quod erga se melius ei inde contigeret.

Colloquio ipse non intererat, set castellum paulo ante ingressus, donec mandaretur alibi exspectabat. Unde requisitus per probos et honestos viros, quamquam ei absurdum et contra se videtur, volens cum bono malum vincere, propter amorem domini sui, concessit. Et, ut ipse concederet, domino legato humiliter supplicavit. Quam supplicacionem non sensatam nec

---

[a] nequinebat, MS

pope's letter; he could not obey the pope's command without breaking his word, unless the archbishop of York at least made personal and temporary profession to the archbishop of Canterbury. And the pope had no right to force the king to break his word. The archbishop had long ago returned to England. The legate countered that the profession was not due; the king should not have given his word needlessly while the matter was *sub judice*, nor should he keep it; the pope had absolved him, and still did absolve him from it. A great wrong had been done to him and to the Roman church, in that an archbishop, consecrated by his hands, had on that account been robbed of his see and exiled. For that reason he ought now at least to obey, when he would receive nothing less than justice; he told him plainly what sentence he would otherwise quickly incur.

After much discussion, sometimes calm and sometimes angry, the king at last agreed to reinvest him with the archbishopric, provided that he would refrain for some time from returning to England. This he besought the legate to grant. But when the legate answered that he neither would nor should do that, it was suggested to the king that he should send for the archbishop and beg him to grant it, and intercede with the legate to that effect, with a message that it would put him on better terms with the king.

The archbishop [of York] had taken no part in the conference, but had entered the castle a little before, and was waiting elsewhere to be sent for, until summoned by good and honourable messengers. Although it seemed to him absurd and unprofitable, wishing to overcome evil with good, he consented, out of love for his master, and humbly besought the legate to consent also. The legate protested that the request was neither sensible

sanam esse ei obiectans, tamen quia ei sic postulabat
consensit. Venerunt ergo uterque ad regem; legatus
pro parte ipsius archiepiscopi, ea quidem convencione,
quia rex predixerat ne faceret quod dominus papa ei
preceperat, usque ad festum sancti Michaelis celare se
dixit. Tunc vero rex et legatus amici facti, cum essent
prius aliquantulum inimici, et archiepiscopo licuit Normanniam ingredi et regredi. Digrediuntur rex et
legatus, et archiepiscopus in Franciam cum legato,
relictis quibusdam de suis qui de revestitura archiepiscopatus in Angliam afferrent. Quod rex suum
archiepiscopum recepit, bene fecit; quod vero ab Anglia
adhuc eum detinuit, non sibi in sinistrum recidit.

Ille enim per dominum Cononem et per archiepiscopos et episcopos et primores Francie de pace com-
ponenda inter reges studiose curavit; que non longo
post tempore, eo potissimum contrectatore et mediatore,
(et cui de Normannis rex Francorum magis inde credidit,)
multis hinc et illi[n]c allegacionibus, per dei graciam,
ad bonam finem perducta est. Quia ergo rex hac im-
pediente discordia a regno suo diu afuerat, pace composita, quamcicius commode posset, rebus in ducatu
bene dispositis, in regnum redire destinavit. Ad festum
sancti Michaelis voluit archiepiscopus in Angliam transire, sicut inter regem et ipsum convenerat, set rex
precibus et blandiciis et causa negociorum donec ipse
iret detinuit.

Qui et hac vice detentus, regi et archiepiscopo et
episcopis Normannie in aliquantis officiosus et utilis
extitit. Cum enim dominus Cono concilium, quasi
Remensis concilii anniversarium, de tota legacione sua
F.24 apud Belvacum convocasset, rex dimissionem / de suis

nor sane, but consented because the archbishop asked.
Both of them therefore came to the king, the legate on
behalf of the archbishop, said that he was concealing
the agreement until Michaelmas, because the king had
told him not to do what the pope had ordered. The
king and the legate then made friends, in spite of their
having been ill-disposed to each other before, and the
archbishop was permitted to enter Normandy and leave
it again. The king and the legate separated, and the
archbishop went to France with the legate, leaving
behind some of his company to bring news into England of his reinvestiture with the archbishopric. The
king did a good deed in receiving his archbishop, but
keeping him out of England was not counted against him.

For the archbishop took great pains to procure a
peace between the two kings by means of cardinal Cuno
and the archbishops, bishops, and nobles of France.
And this by the grace of God was brought to a good end
not long afterwards after bargaining on both sides,
mainly by his diplomacy and mediation, being the man
on the Norman side in whom the king of the French
had the most confidence. As the king had been kept a
long time out of his realm by this dispute, he decided
after making peace and regulating the affairs in the
duchy, to return to his kingdom as soon as possible. The
archbishop wished to cross to England at Michaelmas,
as had been agreed between him and the king. But the
king detained him by prayers and coaxing and for reasons
of business until he should go himself.

Being once again kept back, he was obliging and use-
ful to the king and the archbishop and the bishops of
Normandy. For cardinal Cuno having summoned a
council of his whole legation at Beauvais, as for the
anniversary of the council of Rheims, the king asked for

episcopis et abbatibus quesivit, set non nisi in am-
phibologia assecutus. Et cum die predicta concilium
sederet, nec de episcopis et abbatibus Normannie ullus
adesset, a legato et archiepiscopis et episcopis Remensis
et Senonensis provincie provisum est, eos ante solucionem
Concilii pro contemptu et inobediencia excommunicare
debere. Quo per aliquem notificato, rex archiepiscopum festinanter Belvacum misit. Quo viso legatus est
et ex parte subtristis. Intellexit enim propter quod
venerat. Set quid multa? Amicicia, precum instancia
tamen pro rege, pro se maxime, sentencia illa mutata
est. Siquidem Radulphus Remensis archiepiscopus
dixit ei: 'Certe, frater, si non venisses, Normanni
excommunicati forent'. Difficillimum esset eo tempore,
nec petitu nec obtentu dignum, quo archiepiscopus
noster petito a legato et episcopis Francie, non optento
recessi[sse]t. Siquidem in duplicis sue eieccionis exilio,
nemo omnium quos noverimus, apud excelsos et humiles,
apud religiosos et seculares, apud monachos et moniales,
largiendo, serviendo, honore preveniendo, tantam amiciciam venatus est.

Rex eciam per archiepiscopum legato mandaverat,
quatinus, si ei molestum non esset, ad se Gisorcium,
quod non longe distabat, veniret. Cupiebat enim loqui
illi priusquam transfretaret. Legatus adducto secum
Willelmo Catalauonensi episcopo, et Silvanectensi episcopo, et aliis personis, illuc advenit; ubi a rege graci-
arum accionibus legato exhibitis, et sermonibus plurimis
de deo, de santa ecclesia, de negociis, et iocis invicem
habitis, rex illi episcopos et abbates suos commendavit.
Ipsi vero et qui cum eo venerant omnibus fere dona
dedit. Legatus vero de archiepiscopo suggessit, intima-
vit, et inculcavit, ut sic faceret quod dominus papa
grates illi haberet. Quo bene se facturum pollicente,

the release of his bishops and abbots, but only obtained an ambiguous answer. And when the council sat on the appointed day, and none of the bishops or abbots of Normandy was there, it was determined by the legate and the archbishops and bishops of the provinces of Rheims and Sens that they must be excommunicated before the council closed for contempt and disobedience. On receiving notice of this, the king sent the archbishop to Beauvais in haste. The legate was a little sorry to see him, for he knew the reason for his coming. To be brief, the sentence was altered out of friendship, and owing to his earnest prayers for the king, and especially for himself. Indeed Ralph, archbishop of Rheims said to him, 'if you had not come, brother, the Normans would have been excommunicated'. It would have been a most difficult thing at that time, something neither to ask nor to have, for our archbishop to ask it of the legate and the bishops of France, and go away without obtaining it. Indeed, in the exile of his double ejection, nobody we know of won such friendship from high and low, religious and secular, monks and nuns, by liberality, service, and courtesy.

The king had also sent word by the archbishop to the legate, to come to Gisors (at no great distance) if it was not inconvenient to him. For he wished to speak with him before crossing. The legate came accompanied by William, bishop of Châlons, and the bishop of Senlis and others. The king thanked the legate, and after a long conversation about God, Holy Church, matters of business and mirth, commended to him his bishops and abbots. He also gave presents to him and almost all who were with him. The legate hinted, intimated, and urged that he should act in the archbishop's case, in such a way as to secure the pope's gratitude. When he had

data illi benediccione,[a] ad presens transiturum deo
commendans, in osculo et amicicia di[s]cessit. Post
dicessum eius rex coram episcopis Normannie et quibusdam Anglie sic ait: 'Melius fuisset nobis quingentas
marcas perdidisse quam Eboracensi archiepiscopo caru-
isse'. Cui aliquis de audientibus, etsi quidam viderent,
bene et urbane subiunxit: 'Dignum est igitur, ut inde
ei melius sit hic'.

Ad mare rex pedetentim tendit. Archiepiscopum
cum eo transire volentem et sperantem amicabiliter
adhuc deprecatus est quatinus in Normannia exspectaret quousque in Anglia in Natale domini archiepiscopo et episcopis collocutus esset, et unum de suis
clericis cum illo mitteret per quem remandaret. Ille
nec in hoc illi adhuc adversari volens, sicut petebat, se
facturum dixit, et usque ad mare cum eo perrexit. Set
antequam transfretaret remisit eum ad legatum qui
erat Carnoti propter negotium suum. Cui ibi invento
verba regis locutus.

Eo discedente filius eius, rex et dux iam designatus,
naufragio perierat, et universi qui nave eadem vehe-
bantur, quod eum vehementer contristavit. Nam preter
domini sui regis filium et dominum futurum multos
amicos amiserat. Rex autem nimirum gravi et immo-
derato dolore percussus, tandem per se, sicut sapiens
homo, et per comitem Teobaldum, qui cum eo venerat,
et per alios consolatus est.

Sicut promiserat proximo Natali Cantuariensem archiepiscopum et episcopos suos convenit. Litteras domini pape de recepcione Eboracensis ostendit, et nisi
reciperetur, que sentencia post modicum sequi debebat
F.24v edocuit. / Estimo regem aliqua precipitacione fidem

---

[a] benediccionem, MS

promised to do so, the legate blessed him, commended him to God for his coming crossing, and with a kiss of friendship, departed. When he had left, the king said, before the Norman bishops and some of the English, 'It would have been better to have lost five hundred marks than not to have had the archbishop of York'. One of his hearers regardless of being seen, well and politely added, 'After that, he deserves to be better treated here'.

The king moved gradually to the coast. The archbishop wished and hoped to cross with him, but the king begged him, as a friend, to wait in Normandy till he should have conferred at Christmas with the archbishop [of Canterbury] and the bishops, and to send with him one of his clerks by whom he could send back word. The archbishop, still unwilling to oppose him, said he would do as the king wished, and accompanied him to the sea. But before crossing, the king sent him to the legate, who was at Chartres, on business. He found him there and repeated the king's message.

As the king left Normandy, his son, the king and duke designate, and all who were with him in his ship, perished by shipwreck, which caused the archbishop much sorrow. For he had lost many friends as well as his lord the king's son and his future lord. The king, though smitten by deep and unrestrained grief, like a wise man, consoled himself, and was consoled by count Theobald, who had come with him, and by others.

On the following Christmas, as he had promised, he summoned the archbishop of Canterbury and his bishops. He showed the pope's letter about receiving the archbishop of York, and told them what sentence must quickly ensue unless they received him. I reckon that the king must have pledged his faith somewhat hastily,

spopondisse, condicionaliter tamen in licencia Cantuariensis archiepiscopi et permissione. Intelligens archiepiscopus sagittam hanc prius in se infigi, episcopi vero ignominiam regi reputantes[a] in regno suo Chriscianitatem interdici, ut eum revocaret et concesserunt et consiliati sunt.

Post octabas Theophanie nuncius venit Rotomagensis ad archiepiscopum cum litteris regis iubentibus eum venire. Qui gaudens de exilio revocatus, paratis que opus erat, triduo ante Purificacionem sancte Marie transfretavit. Deinde ad regem veniens eum Windesoris invenit; a quo et a regina quam nuper duxerat,[b] et aliquantis episcopis et proceribus, et de curia multis gaudenter susceptus.

Modicum ibi pernoctans ad sponsam suam presencia ipsius diu viduatam, Eboracensem scilicet ecclesiam, properavit. Cumque civitatem appropinquaret, tantus occursus factus est ei obviam exeuncium clericorum, monachorum, procerum, militum, virorum et mulierum, equitancium et peditum, ut quibusdam ex hoc ad mentem reduceretur, quod de beato Iohanne scriptum est : 'Occurrit beato Iohanni ab exilio revertenti [omnis] p[opulus] v[irorum] a[c] m[ulierum] c[lamancium] et d[icencium,] "B[eatus] q[ui] v[enit] i[n] n[omine] [Domini"'.] In ecclesia vero, sicut decebat archiepiscopum tamdiu pro libertate eiusdem ecclesie exulatum, Dominica qua cantatur, 'Esto michi in deum protectorem',[1] in amplexibus sponse sue cum exultacione et tripudio receptus est; et in tanta audiencia lecto et exposito de libertatis ecclesie reformacione apostolico privilegio, omnes congratulati sunt, et deo gracias reddiderunt.

In cathedra repositus, tercia die sollempnitatem beati

---

[a] reputantis, MS   [b] dixerat, MS

but not unconditionally, in the licence and leave given to the archbishop of Canterbury. The archbishop, understanding that the arrow would pierce him first of all, and the bishops, considering the disgrace to the king if his kingdom were placed under interdict, granted and advised that he should recall Thurstan.

After the octave of the Epiphany [13 January], a messenger from Rouen came to the archbishop with the king's letter bidding him come. Rejoicing in his recall from exile, he made the necessary preparations, and crossed the Channel two days before Candlemas [31 Jan.]. He then came to the king and found him at Windsor, and was joyfully received by him and the queen whom he had lately married, by many bishops and nobles, and many of the court.

He passed a few nights there, and hastened to his spouse, the church of York, which had long been widowed of his presence. And when he approached the city such a crowd came out to meet him of clerks, monks, nobles, knights, men and women, horse and foot, that some of them remembered what is written about St John [Chrysostom] : 'There came to meet St John as he returned from exile the whole people, male and female, crying and saying, "Blessed is he that cometh in the name of the Lord"'. But in the church, as befitted an archbishop who had so long been in exile for the freedom of that church, he was received with exultation and rejoicing in the arms of his spouse, on the Sunday on which is sung, 'And be thou my strong rock'[1] ; and when the apostolic privilege as to the restoration of the church's freedom was read and explained, in the hearing of so many people, all rejoiced together and gave thanks to God.

Two days later, enthroned once more in his chair,

[1] Ps. 31 : 3 ; the introit for Quinquagesima Sunday [20 February 1121]

Petri que Cathedra eius appellatur, in ecclesia ipsius beati Petri festive celebravit. Crastina vero die, que fuit capud Ieiunii, putrida membra, que pro merito peccatorum suorum mater ecclesia a se abicit, pastor pie feriens, cineres capitibus imponens, Sathane tradidit,[1] in interitum carnis, ut spiritus salvus fieret.

In proxima Cena Domini, crismate sollempniter consecrato, sex denarios de singulis ecclesiis parochialibus, et quatuor de capellis, quos[a] ex antiqua consuetudine quoque anno pro crismate reddebant, liberaliter remisit, et perpetuum remittendos decrevit. Precium quoque pro sepultura, vel pro unccione infirmorum, vel pro baptisterio[b] exigere vel accipere, nisi spontanee datum, omnimodis interdixit. Exemplar privilegii hoc est.

Littere eiusdem pape ad Cantuariensem archi-
episcopum pro Eboracensi electo

Calixtus episcopus, servus servorum dei, venerabili fratri Radulpho Cantuariensi archiepiscopo, salutem et apostolicam benediccionem. Licet te sicut fratrem in domino diligamus, Romane tamen ecclesie diuturnam iniuriam et contemptum preterire silencio non debemus. Siquidem dominus predecessor noster, sancte memorie Paschalis papa, missis ad te litteris precipiendo mandavit, ut venerabilem fratrem nostrum T[urstinum] Eboracensem electum, omni professionis exaccione deposita, consecrares. Eo defuncto, successor eius, dominus noster papa Gelasius, similiter de consecracione precepit, illud adiciens, ut cum electo pro cause decisione ipsius te conspectui presentares. Id ipsum et nos fecisse meminimus, set in causa illa nichil apud te dileccionis, nichil reverencie

---

[a] quorum, MS   [b] pro baptisterio] probasterio, MS

he celebrated the feast called 'St Peter's Chair' in St Peter's own church. On the morrow, being Ash Wednesday, the shepherd, religiously lopping the rotten limbs which Mother Church casts away from her as their sins deserve, he sprinkled ashes on their heads and delivered them unto Satan [1] to the death of the flesh, that the spirit might be saved.

On Holy Thursday [7 Apr.], after solemnly consecrating the chrism, he freely remitted and decreed to be remitted for ever, the six pence from each parish church and four from every chapel, which they rendered annually by ancient custom for the chrism. He also forbade the exaction of fees for burial, anointing of the sick, or baptism, or the acceptance of them unless freely offered. Here follows a copy of the privilege.

Letter of the pope to the archbishop of Canterbury on behalf of the elect of York

Calixtus, bishop, servant of the servants of God, to his venerable brother Ralph, archbishop of Canterbury, greeting and apostolic blessing. Though we love you as our brother in the Lord, we ought not to pass over in silence your long continued wrong to and contempt of the Roman church. Our predecessor Pope Paschal, of holy memory, sent you letters in which he ordered you to consecrate our venerable brother, Thurstan, elect of York, without exacting any profession. After his death, his successor, our lord Pope Gelasius, gave the same orders as to his consecration, adding that you should present yourself before him with the elect for the decision of the case. We remember that we ourselves did likewise, but in that case we could find in you neither affection nor

_____
[1] 1 Tim. 1 : 20

F.25

potuimus invenire. In Remensi concilio, ad quod invitatus a nobis fueras, questionem super eadem professione, qua[m] videlicet contra beati Gregorii constitucionem ab Eboracensi archiepiscopo exigis, decidere sperabamus; verum cum nec ipse ve/nires, nec personas que vices tuas agerent destinares, nos habito fratrum nostrorum tam cardinalium, quam archiepiscoporum et episcoporum, qui multi aderant, consilio, predictum fratrem nostrum T[urstinum] electum in Eboracensis ecclesie archiepiscopum consecravimus. Consecrato autem, quia exaccioni tue in professione illicita non consenserat, omnino non licuit ad sedem propriam remeare. In quo quantum ipse beatum [Petrum], et nos, qui[a] licet indigni locum eius in ecclesia optinemus, offenderis, tam Romana quam Gallicana ecclesia non ignorat. Etenim postquam idem frater a sede apostolica per manus nostre imposicionem archiepiscopus factus est, mox ecclesia spoliatus est quam electus annulo[b] optinebat. Pro tanta ergo et tam gravis contemptus pertinacia, nos tibi episcopale atque sacerdotale officium interdicimus, et in matrici Cantuariensi ecclesia divina celebrari officia prohibemus, nisi infra mensem unum post harum litterarum accepcionem predictus frater noster in Eboracensi ecclesia suscipiatur et manere quiecius dimittatur.

[*Littere eiusdem pape ad eundem regem Anglie pro eodem archiepiscopo Eboracensi*[c]]

Calixtus episcopus, servus servorum dei, karissimo in Christo filio, Henrico, vere illustri et glorioso Anglie regi, salutem et apostolicam benediccionem. Sepe iam dileccionem tuam pro venerabili fratre nostro,

---

     [a] quod, MS   [b] anna, MS
    [c] Added from below the following letter on f. 25

reverence. We hoped to decide the question about the profession which you demand from the archbishop of York contrary to the constitution of St Gregory, at the council of Rheims to which we had invited you. But since you neither came yourself nor appointed persons to act for you, after taking counsel with our brethren, both cardinals and archbishops and bishops, many of whom were present, we consecrated our elect brother Thurstan archbishop of the church of York. But he was not allowed to return to his own see after consecration, because he had not consented to your exaction of an unlawful profession. How far you have by this offended St Peter, and ourselves who, unworthy as we are, occupy his place in the church, is well known to the Roman church and the Gallican as well. For after our said brother had been made archbishop by the imposition of our hands, he was immediately robbed of the church which was conferred on him as elect by the gift of a ring. For such obstinacy in grave contempt, we forbid you the episcopal and sacerdotal office, and prohibit the celebration of divine service in the mother-church of Canterbury, unless our said brother is within one month received in the church of York, and allowed to abide there undisturbed.

*[Letter of the pope to the king of England
on behalf of the archbishop of York]*

Calixtus, bishop, servant of the servants of God, to his dearest son in Christ, the illustrious and glorious Henry, king of England, greeting and apostolic blessing. We remember having admonished you, by

T[urstino] Eboracensi archiepiscopo, verbis et litteris
monuisse meminimus, et nichil adhuc in eius negocio
de honore dei et ecclesie apud te valuimus impetrare,
unde graviori profecto correccione dignus fueras, set
quia duplici te dileccione complectimur, persone tue
ad presens in execucione iusticie duximus indulgen-
dum. Ceterum tamen fratris nostri, R[adulphi] Cantuariensis archiepiscopi, contemptum omnino diucius
tolerare non possumus. Et a dominis enim felicis
memorie P[aschali] et Gelasio, predecessoribus nostris,
et a nobis ipsis commonitus, nec electo Eboracensis
ecclesie, absque professionis exaccione manum imponere, nec pro eodem negocio nostre [se] voluit audiencie
presentare. Et ipsi igitur episcopale atque sacerdotale officium interdicimus, et in matrici Cantuariensi
ecclesia, necnon et Eboracensi, cum propria parochia
tota, divina omnia celebrari officia, et sepulturam
mortuis prohibemus, preter infantum baptisma et
moriencium penitencias, donec predictus frater noster
T[urstinus] Eboracensi ecclesie restitutus, manere in
ea quiecius dimittatur. Set eciam [cum] predictus
dominus noster Paschalis papa eum adhuc in eleccione
positum ab Eboracensi abesse ecclesia nullatenus
passus est, nos, consecratum iam per dei graciam
nostris tanquam beati Petri manibus, exulare prorsus
pati nec possumus nec debemus. [Datum Vapinci,
v. idus Martii.] ᵃ

[*Littere eiusdem pape ad clerum et populum Eboracenses pro eodem archiepiscopo Eboracensi*]

Calixtus episcopus, servus servorum dei, clero et
populo per Eboracensem parochiam constituto, salutem et apostolicam benediccionem. Matrem vestram,

ᵃ From margin

word and by letter, on behalf our venerable brother, Thurstan, archbishop of York, and have so far failed to obtain any of our requests in this case for the honour of God and the church; a thing which certainly made you deserve severe correction. But because you are doubly dear to us, we have thought proper in the execution of justice to indulge you personally for the present. However, we can no longer in any way endure the contempt of our brother, Ralph, archbishop of Canterbury. He was admonished by our predecessors Paschal and Gelasius, of happy memory, and by ourselves, and yet would neither lay his hands on the elect of York without exacting a profession, nor present himself to our audience about the matter. We therefore forbid him the episcopal and sacerdotal office, and prohibit in the mother-churches of Canterbury and York also, and the whole of their respective provinces the celebration of all divine service and the burial of the dead (excepting only the baptism of infants and the penance of the dying) until our said brother Thurstan has been restored to the church of York, and is allowed to abide there in quiet. Furthermore, whereas our said lord Pope Paschal in no wise suffered him, while still only elect, to be absent from the church of York, we neither can nor ought to let him be an exile, now that he has by God's grace been consecrated by our hands as though by those of St Peter. Given at Gap, on the 11th of March [1120].

Letter of the pope to the clergy and people of York on behalf of the archbishop

Calixtus, bishop, servant of the servants of God, to the clergy and people in the province of York, greeting and apostolic blessing. In virtue of our

P

Eboracensem ecclesiam, tanto tempore sponsi sui carere presencia paterne pietatis affectu dolemus vehemencius et gravamur. Et quidem in parte hac, licet vos inculpabiles existatis, quamdiu tamen alicuius violencia sponsum abesse contigerit, cum filii sponsi sitis,[a] et lugere vos convenit et merere, sicut et de ipsius gaudere presencia, iuxta illud evangelicum,[1] debebatis. Apostolica igitur auctoritate, tam in vestra matrice Eboracensi ecclesia quam in propria ipsius ubique parochia, sepulturam et alia omnia divina officia, preter infantum baptisma et moriencium penitencias, celebrari penitus prohibemus, donec venerabilis frater noster, T[urstinus] archiepiscopus, nostris tanquam beati Petri manibus consecratus, in ea suscipiatur, et manere quiecius dimittatur. Datum Vapinci, v. idus Marcii.[b]

F.25v Harum exemplaria (archiepiscopo [c] recepto tradere opus non fuit) in ecclesia nostra / adhuc bullata habentur. Quod, sicut prenotatum est, ad ecclesiam suam rediit Dominica in Quadragesima qua cantatur 'Esto michi in D[eum] p[rotectorem], et in [domum] r[efugii], u[t] s[alvum] m[e] f[acias]',[2] arbitrati sunt aliqui pacis esse pronosticum et quietis propter figuram quinquagenarii, cuius numeri annus iubileus erat. In tempore gracie dies quinquagesimus sacratus est, ideo quod d[i]e illo post resurreccionem domini spiritus sanctus super discipulos apparuit.

Nondum tamen, nec propter litteras quas sibi scriptas esse non ignorabat, passus est Radulphus archiepiscopus archiepiscopum nostrum habere de professione hac iubileum, nec proteccionem, nec refugium, nec salvacionem; et quod iste non est professus, ille eum apud regem non est infestare defessus ex occasione quorun-

---

[a] A; sponsis suis, MS
[b] Datum . . . Marcii. Added from A. Collated with another copy of this letter in the *Reg. Magnum Album* at York, i. 50*b*
[c] archiepiscopus, MS

paternal affection we are sorely grieved and pained that your mother, the church of York, is so long deprived of the presence of her spouse. And although you are without blame in this matter, yet so long as the bridegroom is taken away from you by force, it behoves you as children of the bridechamber to mourn and weep, as much as, according to the gospel,[1] you ought to rejoice in his presence. We therefore absolutely forbid, by apostolic authority, both in your church of York and everywhere in its province, burial and all other divine service to be celebrated, except the baptism of infants and penitence of the dying, until our venerable brother, archbishop Thurstan, consecrated by our hands as if by those of St Peter, be received in it and allowed to abide there in quiet. Given at Gap, on the 11th of March [1120].

The originals of these letters (which it was unnecessary to deliver now that the archbishop had been received) with their 'bulls' attached are still kept in our church. The fact that Thurstan returned to his church on the Sunday in Lent [Quinquagesima] on which is sung, 'Be thou my strong rock and house of defence: that thou mayest save me',[2] was thought by some to be an omen of peace and quiet on account of the number 'fifty', which is the number of the year of Jubilee. In the years of grace the fiftieth day [Pentecost] has been sanctified, because on that day after the Resurrection of the Lord the Holy Ghost appeared over the disciples.

Not yet, however, nor on account of the letter which he well knew had been written to him, did archbishop Ralph allow our archbishop to have a jubilee, nor protection, nor refuge, nor salvation from the profession; and since he had not professed, he did not cease to molest him before the king. In connection with certain

Matt. 9 : 15   [2] Ps. 31 : 3

dam privilegiorum Romanorum de dignitate et primatu Cantuariensis ecclesie, que monachi nuper invenerant vel cogitaverant,[1]

Ut faber extinctum prope follibus excitat ignem,

sic Cantuariensis acsensio[ni]bus (*sic*) regem accendit, et impulit quatinus nostrum cogeret profiteri. Quibusdam antea vero, sicut aliquociens regi persuadebant, regni decus esse magnum primatem habere, nec regnum quod coronam habeat esse sine primate. Quod veritate refelli potest. Regnum Lumbardorum unum tantum, Mediolanensem scilicet, habet metropolitanum, hic vero nec primas est, nec primatem habet. Episcopus Papiensis eciam, qui de provincia illius est et ei conterminus [a] palleo utitur, et crucem sibi preferri facit, neque metropolite subiectus est, quare nichil mirandum est duos metropolitas in regno uno alterum alteri non subesse. Set iuxta rusticorum proverbium, 'Qui asinum non vidit, de camelo miratur'. Treveris quoque in Teutonico regno prima sedes antiquitus fuit; set, sicut in curia pape Calixti episcopus noster et sui a quodam venerabili eiusdem civitatis archiepiscopo acceperunt, supra nullam modo primatum habet.

Mense Augusto premandavit rex archiepiscopo nostro quod ad presens videret quantum pro eius amore facere vellet. Ad festum sancti Michaelis convocavit colloquium magnum de episcopis et baronibus regni. Mandavit et archiepiscopo nostro ut cum personis ecclesie et clericis senioribus et sapientioribus illuc conveniret, quo, si quid ibi ageret, eorum assensu ratum firmaretur. Iam ei comminacionem tonitrus intonuerant aut

[a] cunterminus, MS

bulls of privilege concerning the dignity and primacy of the church of Canterbury, which the monks had lately found (or thought up),[1]

> As smith with bellows wakes the sinking fire,

so did the fire-raiser of Canterbury blow up the king's anger, and urged him to compel our archbishop to profess. They endeavoured to persuade by arguments as they had sometimes done before, that it is a great glory to a kingdom to have a primate, and that no kingdom possessing a crown is without one. That argument is refuted by the facts. The kingdom of the Lombards has only one metropolitan, him of Milan; but he is not a primate and has no primate. The bishop of Pavia also, who is of that province and adjoins the other, wears the *pallium* and has his cross carried before him and is not subject to a metropolitan. So there is nothing wonderful in there being two metropolitans in one kingdom, one of whom is not subject to the other. But as the country saying goes, 'The man who has never seen a donkey is astonished at a camel'. At Treves also, in Germany, there was of old a primary see; but, as our bishop and his men were told by a venerable archbishop of that city at the court of Pope Calixtus, he now has primacy over no other see.

In August, the king sent word to the archbishop that he should shortly see how much he was willing to do for him. At Michaelmas he summoned a great conference of the bishops and barons of the realm. He commanded our archbishop to come with the dignitaries of his church and his elder and wiser clerks, in order that whatever was done there might be confirmed by their assent. He was already receiving thunderous threats that he must

---

[1] Presumably the celebrated 'Lanfranc forgeries'

profiteri aut denuo exulare. Eo noster archiepiscopus
cum suis venit. Radulphum archiepiscopum pridie vel
nudius tercius ante infirmitas invaserat, qua detentus
colloquio interesse impotuit. Rex Cantuariensi agens
per episcopos et proceres archiepiscopo nostro mandavit,
quatinus Radulpho archiepiscopo pro pace ecclesiarum,
pro amore suo personaliter profiteretur. Quibus archiepiscopus : 'Quod ideo, quia contra iusticiam videbatur,
ante privilegium acceptum facere abhorrui, eo accepto
magis abhorrendum et periculosum estimo. Et dominus
meus rex a me exigere non debet, quod privilegium
meum infringens gladio anathematis scienter me per-
cuciam.' Quibus renunciatis, rex nec sine minis et
excercitacionibus remandavit, quatinus ei promitteret
se Cantuariensi [a] professurum, si apud apostolicum
assequi posset ut concederet ei, et ei preciperet. Set
nichil ab eo nec minis extorquere, nec blandiciis elicere
potuit, nisi quod si dominus papa contra privilegium
suum facere preciperet quod iuste debere intelligeret,
et ipse faceret.

　　Et mandavit ei quod, si sibi placeret, vellet cum
domino suo et rege familiariter loqui. Qui, rege man-
F.26 dante, ad eum / venit, contrascriptum privilegii sui in
manu sua. Quo regi ostenso et perlecto, astantibus
cum eis tantum R[anulpho] Dunelmensi episcopo et
Nigello de Albeneio, videns rex quod hoc [quod] precipiebat, apostolicus sub anathemate interdicebat, et
propter quedam amicitie et fidelitatis erga se habite
verba que ille [b] regi rememorabat, ipse pene lacri-
mari coactus est. Nigellus vero tunc et paulo ante
multum lacrimatus est, ideo quod archiepiscopo nostro

---

[a] Cantuariensem, MS　　　　　　[b] illi, MS

either profess or go again into exile. Our archbishop came to the conference with his friends. Archbishop Ralph had had an attack of sickness a day or two before, and so was unable to take part in the conference. The king, acting on behalf of the archbishop of Canterbury, sent orders through his bishops and nobles to our archbishop to make his profession to archbishop Ralph personally for the peace of the churches and his affection for the king. The archbishop rejoined, 'What I shrank from doing, before receiving my bull of privilege, because it seemed to me unjust, I regard, now that I have received the bull, as the more abhorrent and dangerous. And my lord the king has no right to ask me to infringe the privilege and knowingly expose myself to the sword of an anathema.' On receiving this reply the king sent back a demand, not without threats and pressure, that he should promise to make his profession to the archbishop of Canterbury if he could prevail on the pope to grant him leave and order him to do it. But all that he could get from him by threats or persuasion was that if the pope should order him, despite his privilege, to do what he should acknowledge to be justly due, he would do it.

The king then sent word that if he pleased, he might talk the thing over informally with his lord and king. On the king's message, he came to him with a transcript of his bull of privilege in his hand. When this had been shown and read to the king in the presence of Ranulf, bishop of Durham, and Nigel d'Aubigny and no one else; and he saw that the pope enforced his order by anathema and interdict; and also because of sundry expressions of affection and fealty to himself of which the archbishop reminded him, he was almost driven to tears. Nigel too wept copiously both then and earlier, because he saw

post recepcionem suam pacem habere sperante modo
omnia commota et conturbata esse cernebat, et ipse
vero in angaria ista pro ecclesia nostra fideliter stetit.
Rex modo pietate regali aliquantulum compunctus
consuluit archiepiscopo nostro, quatinus episcopis, qui
plurimi aderant, per aliquos de suis privilegium ostenderet. Quod cum illi, archiepiscopo remoto, coram
rege legere, vel ad legendum prebere voluissent, episcopi nec legere nec audire voluerunt, set unus ex illis
eructavit verbum non bonum, quia neque verum, nec
pro bono eiaculatum, scilicet quod apostolicus privilegium illud neque unquam viderat, neque fieri iusserat.
Cui quidam de nostris obiecit dicens : 'Domine, si vobis
placet, scio quod illud fieri precepit, et ego oculis meis
aspexi illud ei afferri ; quod allatum ipse perlegit, et
perlecto manu propria lineam unam faciens ipse sub-
scripsit'. Cui nichil illis contradicentibus nostri ad archiepiscopum suum discesserunt.

Ille vero et sui qui timide ad curiam venerant, et
illic contra inimicos meticulose egerant, deo et sancto
Petro pro illis agente confortati et hilares domum re-
vertuntur. Fuere tunc qui de controvercia harum ecclesiarum inter se conferentes dicebant Cantuariensis
archiepiscopi exaccionem iniustam videri, quociens enim
in Eboracensem ecclesiam acrius insurgebat, morbo
aliquo quasi virga dei tangebatur, reminiscentes illius
quo in Romano itinere vexatus est, et eius quam in
Normannia aliquamdiu passus est ; novissime autem et
huius, quo prepediente, colloquio, quod contra archiepiscopum nostrum convocari fecerat, adesse non valuit.
Illis quoque videbatur Eboracensem ecclesiam bonum
angelum a tot et a tantis insurgentibus in eam custodem
et defensorem habere.

that the archbishop had hoped to have peace after being received, but all was now upset and disturbed. Besides, in this forced service, he stood up faithfully for our church. The king now felt some compunction and advised our archbishop, by means of some of his company, to show the privilege to the bishops, of whom many were at court. But when they, without the archbishop, would have read it in the king's presence, or offered it to be read, the bishops would neither read it nor hear it. But one of them gave vent to a disgraceful speech (for it was neither true nor well meant), namely that the pope had never seen that privilege nor ordered it to be written. This was countered by one of our people, who said, 'Begging your pardon, Sir, I know that he ordered it to be made, and I saw it brought to him with my own eyes. He read it when it had been brought to him, and after reading it he drew a line with his own hand and subscribed it.' As there was no reply, our people went away to their archbishop.

But he and his friends, who had come to court with apprehension and had there fearfully opposed their enemies, now by the favour of God and St Peter, returned home encouraged and merry. Some people, discussing the dispute between the churches, said that the demand of the archbishop of Canterbury was clearly unjust; for as often as he pressed his attack against the church of York, he was struck down by some illness as if by God's rod. They recalled the sickness which came upon him during his journey to Rome, and that which he suffered some time ago in Normandy, and also this last, by which he was prevented from attending the conference which he had caused to be convoked against our archbishop. They too thought that the church of York possessed a good angel to keep and defend it from so many adversaries.

Sequenti anno, circa idem temporis, Radulphus archiepiscopus obiit, de cuius morte archiepiscopus noster et sui nichil gavisi sunt, iuxta id Salomonis, 'Noli gaudere de mortuo inimico'.[1] Siquidem illi sperabant eum pre infirmitate, pre tedio, pre diffidencia impetrandi, a sua impugnacione de reliquo cessare. Quis autem, et quando archiepiscopus substituendus esset certum non habeba[n]t.

Paululum ante Adventum domini venit quidam de urbe Roma litteras domini pape deferens utrique archiepiscopo Anglie ; set quod alteri non potuit, nostro sibi missas tradidit, precipientes ei quatinus, omni seposita occasione, concilio adesset quod per dei graciam Dominica qua cantatur 'Oculi mei semper',[2] in Urbe celebrare disposuerat. Non defuit qui [de]lator [a] regi diceret archiepiscopum litteras domini pape de voc[ac]ione ad concilium habuisse, quod ex regni consuetudine absque consciencia et licencia regis sucepisse non debuerat ; unde rex aliquantum commotus mandavit ei quatinus super hoc rectitudinem facturus in proxima Purificacione sancte Marie ad curiam veniret, et literarum baiulum ad se adduceret. Ipse vero nesciebat quis esset, neque quorsum acceptis ab eo litteris de/venerat.

F 26v

In predicta festivitate apud Gloecestriam rex de omnibus ecclesiasticis personis concilium magnum mandaverat pro archiepiscopo Cantuariensis ecclesie eligendo. Ante illam [diem] triduo archiepiscopus ad regem veniens satis letabundo susceptus est, nec de satisfaccione pro litteris acceptis, nec de portitoris earum adduccione rex archiepiscopum causatus est et ad festivitatem Gloecestriam simul venire [iussit].[3] In qua rex archiepiscopum satis laudatum multum honoravit, et episcopos eum honorare commonuit. In crastinum

---

[a] latore, MS

About the same time the next year, archbishop Ralph died. Our archbishop and his friends took no joy in his death: as Solomon says, 'Rejoice not when thy enemy falleth'.[1] They hoped that from weakness, weariness, and distrust in the success of his petitions, he would in future cease from attack. But who would replace him as archbishop, and when, they were uncertain.

A little before Advent, a messenger came from Rome with the pope's letters to both archbishops of England. But as he could not deliver them to the one, he gave ours the one addressed to him, ordering him without fail to attend the Council which he had arranged by God's grace to celebrate at Rome on the Sunday on which is sung, 'Mine eyes are ever looking unto the Lord'.[2] There did not fail an informer to tell the king that the archbishop had had the pope's letter of summons to the Council, which by the custom of the realm he should not have accepted without the king's knowledge and leave. Wherefore the king, somewhat moved, commanded him to come to court at Candlemas next to clear himself on this point, and to bring to him the bearer of the letter. But Thurstan did not know who the man was, nor whither he had gone when the letter had been delivered.

The king had summoned a great Council of all the clergy at Candlemas at Gloucester, to elect an archbishop of Canterbury. Two days before, the archbishop came to the king and was right joyfully received, nor did the king trouble him about receiving the letter or bringing its bearer, [but bade] him come to the festival at Gloucester.[3] There the king praised him and gave much honour, and admonished his bishops to do likewise.

---

[1] Prov. 24 : 17   [2] Third Sunday in Lent [18 March 1123]
[3] The text seems defective here.

inter episcopos et monachos Cantuarie de eligendo
archiepiscopo altercacio grandis existit. Episcopi enim
archiepiscopum nisi clericum habere nolebant, monachi
monachum deprecacionibus et persuasionibus apud regem contendebant. Set rege episcopis plus favente,
monachi, ad quos plurimum pertinebat eleccio, inviti
quidem, Willelmum de Corboleio, priorem Sancte Oside,
archiepiscopum tandem susceperunt. De quo quis esset,
archiepiscopus et Adeboldus prior Sancti Oswaldi, a
rege antea interrogati, satis eum de sciencia et honestate
et religione laudaverant. Episcopi archiepiscopum
nostrum eleccioni illi interesse non curaverunt, ideo
quod a professione subtractus quasi de illis non esse
videbatur.

Sciens rex inter Eboracam et Cantuariam alterne consecracionis consuetudinem, mandavit nostro requirens, si
episcopis electum suum archiepiscopum consecrare inter-
diceret. Cui ille respondit: 'Ex consuetudine ecclesiarum nostrarum consecracio illius michi debetur'. Set
internunciis inculcantibus quatinus regi mandaret si inter-
diceret; ille, cum his quos secum habebat consilio habito, regi remandavit pro amore suo nullo modo facere
interdictum, set hoc et ipsum et episcopos scire volebat
quod eum consecrare paratus erat; et se id facere offerebat, quoniam ex consuetudine a papa Honorio instituta
ecclesie sue competebat. Eadem die et electo mandavit
per Gaufridum Eboracensis monasterii abbatem, et per
Adewoldum priorem Sancti Oswaldi, et quosdam de nostris, archidiaconos et canonicos, presente Ricardo Londoniensi episcopo, quatinus eum consecrare volebat, sicut
debebat; et humilitatis [et] amicitie causa, hac vice,

On the next day there was a great debate between the bishops and the monks of Canterbury about the election of an archbishop. For the bishops were unwilling to have anyone but a clerk for their archbishop; but the monks pressed the king with prayers and blandishments for a monk. But as the king took the side of the bishops, the monks, having a better right to choose, at last unwillingly accepted William de Corbeuil, prior of St Osyth's, for archbishop. The archbishop and Adelwald, prior of St Oswald's, had been previously asked by the king who he was, and gave him an excellent character for learning, honour, and religion. The bishops were none too well pleased at our archbishop's being concerned in the election, because, now that he was relieved of profession, they did not regard him as one of themselves.

The king, being aware of the custom of alternate consecration by the archbishops of York and Canterbury, sent to our archbishop, asking whether he would forbid the bishops by interdict to consecrate their archbishop elect. He replied, 'By the custom of our churches I have the right to consecrate him'. But when the messengers pressed him to send word to the king whether he would forbid them, after taking the advice of those about him, he sent back a message to the king that for his sake he would not issue an interdict, but would have him and the bishops know that he was ready to consecrate, and offered to do it as befitted his church by the custom established by Pope Honorius. On the same day he sent word by Geoffrey, abbot of [St Mary's], York, and by Adelwald, prior of St Oswald's, and some of our archdeacons and canons, in the presence of Richard, bishop of London, that he was willing to consecrate him, as was his duty, and out of humility and friendship, on this occasion, saving the dignity of his

salva ecclesie sue dignitate, id se in Cantuariensi ecclesia facere offerebat. Quibus ille: 'Aliter modo res est
quam solebat: ecclesie divise sunt'. Ad hec nostri:
'Eiusdem regni et diadematis est utraque. Non est
divisio cuique ius suum habere. Ex iure autem utriusque
archiepiscopis eorum vicissim consecracio debetur; quam
facere, et vice contingente suscipere, ex parte archiepiscopi nostri et Eboracensis capituli offerimus.' Quo et
Londoniensi episcopo dicentibus quod ad presens sic
esse non poterat, ad archiepiscopum redeunt, sic re-
nunciantes: 'Quando electus fuit archiepiscopus vester,
minutus et aliquantulum paciens iacebat, set antequam
discessisset huiusmodi et alia cum eo verba locutus est'.

Regi vero archiepiscopus noster dixit se per litteras
domini pape ad concilium predicto termino vocatum,
et ab eo licenciam quesivit eundi: quem ipse aliquantulum iter[a] suum differre rogavit, donec Cantuariensis
ad requirendum palleum iret; ipse vero cum litteris
suis premitteret qui domino pape renunciarent eum
a rege detentum paulo post cum Cantuariensi venturum. Archiepiscopus tandem regi concessit; et rex,
sicut promisit, premisit, duos scilicet episcopos Normannie et clericum unum, quem, episcopis a concilio
recedentibus, Rome remanere iussit quousque archiepiscopi venissent. Archiepiscopo et electo rex precepit, quatinus prima Dominica Quadragesime apud
F.27 [W]odestoc / adessent, inde profecturi.

Interim Cantuariensis electus, peticione facta ut in
primatem tocius Britannie consecraretur, a Londoniensi

<hr>

[a] in, MS

church, he offered to do it in the church of Canterbury. The elect replied, 'Things are different now: the churches have been divided'. Our messengers answered, 'Both belong to the same kingdom and crown. There is no division in each church having its own rights. By the rights of both churches, it is the duty of the archbishops to consecrate each other in turn. We are offering, on behalf of the archbishop and the chapter of York, to consecrate and to accept consecration in our turn.' But when the elect and the bishop of London both said that was impossible for the present, they returned to the archbishop with the following report: 'When the archbishop was elected, he was humble and somewhat long-suffering, but before he left us he said this, and more to the same effect'.

However, our archbishop told the king that he had been summoned by the pope's letter to the Council at the aforesaid term, and begged him for leave to go. But the king asked him to put off his journey for a little, until the elect of Canterbury should go to ask for his *pallium*; he would himself send a messenger ahead with his letter to tell the pope that he had been kept by the king and would come shortly with the archbishop of Canterbury. The archbishop at last gave way to the king, and he sent, as he had promised, in advance, to wit two of the Norman bishops and one clerk, whom he ordered to stay in Rome when the bishops came back from the Council, and wait till the archbishops came. The king ordered the archbishop and the elect to be at Woodstock on the first Sunday in Lent [11 March], and set out from thence.

Meanwhile a petition was presented for the consecration of the elect of Canterbury as primate of all Britain,

episcopo et ceteris coepiscopis consecratus est,[1] Eboracensi ecclesie iniuria irrogata.[a] Quod quidem plerisque absonum visum est consecrari, ne dicam quod non debebat, in id quod non erat, nec adhuc est, nec ullus de antecessoribus suis fuerat preter unum, et ille quidem eo iure quo supradictum est; et in celebri et tam sacro officio divino, in quo spiritus sanctus invocari et cooperari debet, falsitas et ficcio abicienda sunt.

Sicut eis preceptum fuerat et die statuto, [W]odestoc uterque archiepiscopus affuerunt. Ibi rex nostro per episcopos et proceres mandavit ne Rome contra Cantuariensem aliquid iniuste peteret, neque in peticionibus iustis illi nocumento set adiumento esset, quod sic se facturum plene pollicitus est. Non enim rogabat, nisi quod et non rogatus ille faceret. Hinc iter Romanum aggrediuntur. Cantuariensis nostrum precedere voluit et speravit; nostro vero Sutrie invento, et de suis aliquos per alteram viam venientes exspectante, sex diebus ante illum Romam pervenit. Iam ante de eius eleccione Rome satis cognitum erat; que, quantum ad ipsum pertinuit, absque ambicione et spe facta fuit. Noster vero a domino papa et cardinalibus, cum quibus per dimidium annum conversatus fuerat, et per illos ab omnibus reliquis honorificentissime susceptus est. Demum venit dominus Cantuariensis habens secum dominum Bernardum episcopum Sancti David, et dominum Anselmum abbatem Sancti Eadmundi, et dominum Sigefridum Glestoniensem abbatem, postea Ciscertrensem (*sic*) episcopum, et alios bonos et honestos clericos et monachos. Venientibus ad curiam, dominus Ber-

[a] arrogata, MS

and he was consecrated [1] by the bishop of London and
his brother bishops, and a wrong was done to the church
of York.   Most people thought the consecration out of
taste, not to say, irregular, considering that he was not,
nor yet is, nor had any of his predecessors before him
[been so consecrated] except one, whose legal position
has been explained; and in so important and holy a
divine service in which the Holy Ghost must be invoked
and must take part, all falseness and pretence must be
cast aside.

On the day appointed, as they had been ordered,
both archbishops were at Woodstock.   There the king,
by his bishops and nobles, ordered our archbishop not
to make any petition unfair to the archbishop of Canterbury, and by just petitions not to injure him but rather
to help him, which our archbishop absolutely promised
to do.   For he was not asking anything which the pope
would not do without being asked.   They then set out
on their journey to Rome.   The archbishop of Canterbury wished and hoped to get there first.   But, finding
our archbishop at Sutri, waiting for some of his company
who were coming by another road, he got to Rome six
days before him.   His election was already well known
in Rome, being, so far as he was concerned, neither
wished for nor expected.   But our archbishop was
received by the pope and cardinals, who had had six
months of his company, and through them by all the
rest, with the highest honours.   At last came the archbishop of Canterbury, having with him Bernard, bishop
of St David's, Anselm, abbot of St Edmund's, and
Seffrid, abbot of Glastonbury, afterwards bishop of
Chichester, and other honourable clerks and monks.
When they came to the court, bishop Bernard, who was

[1] 18 February 1123

nardus, qui erat archiepiscopi prolocutor et pro-orator, premissa salutacione domino pape ab imperatore, a rege, ab episcopis Anglie, a capitulo Cantuarie, missas a singulis litteras seorsum obtulit, quas, illis resalutatis, cancellario suo recipere iussit. Dehinc post modicum dicens se litteras visurum, et per consilium fratrum responsurum, archiepiscopum cum suis ad hospicium secedere precepit. Erat ibi archiepiscopus noster cum suis, et Ieremias Rotomagensis ecclesie canonicus, quem rex archiepiscopos exspectare fecerat; qui, licet statura brevis, nec sensu, nec sciencia, nec eloquencia erat exilis,[a] et ipse valde archiepiscopum nostrum et suos diligebat et diligebatur.

Lectis litteris de archiepiscopi eleccione, de persone commendacione, de pallei requisicione, et precibus imperatoris et regis pro eo, cardinales et curia tota per dies aliquot conferentes et inter [se] disceptantes, tandem non esse canonicam, set illum de quatuor capitulis impetendum censuerunt, videlicet, quod non a quibus, neque de quibus, neque ubi debuit fuit electus, neque a quo debuit consecratus; quinto a quibusdam adiuncto, quod clericus monachis preerat. Hiis ergo obiectis et reiectis, volutis et revolutis, decisum est, papa quidem volente, eum palleum non habere, set ex indulgencia posse episcopatum unum obtinere.

Hoc vero archiepiscopo nostro minime celato, ipse dominum papam pro eo deprecatus est, dicens eum bonum clericum esse, et simplicem virum et religiosum; qui si modo repelleretur, fortasse rex ex iracundia ecclesiam diucius vacare sineret. De isto omni canonice et bene illi consuluisse existimabat; apud curiam

[a] ex illis, MS

the archbishop's spokesman and orator, after greeting
the pope, presented separately letters from the emperor,
the king, the bishops of England, the chapter of Canterbury, which the pope, returning their greetings, ordered
his chancellor to receive.   Soon after, saying that he
would look at the letters and answer by the advice of
his brethren, he bade the archbishop retire to his inn.
Our archbishop was present with his company, and
Jeremy, a canon of the church of Rouen, whom the
king made wait for the arrival of the archbishops.   He,
though short in stature, was lacking neither in learning,
sense, nor eloquence ; and he greatly loved our archbishop and his, and was loved by them.

When the letters about the archbishop's election, his
personal character, and the request for the *pallium*, and
the prayers of the king and the emperor on his behalf
had been read, the cardinals and *curia* spent some days
conferring and disputing among themselves.   They
finally decided that the election was uncanonical on
four grounds : that it was not made by the proper
persons, nor from the proper persons, nor in the proper
place, and that the elect was not consecrated by the
proper authority.   Some made a fifth objection, namely
that a clerk was presiding over monks.   After all
these objections had been made and refuted, and argued
backward and forward, it was at length decided, with
the pope's approval, that William should not have the
pallium, but might by indulgence hold a bishopric.

Our archbishop knew all about this and besought the
pope for William, saying he was a good clerk and a simple
and devout man, and that if he were now rejected the
king might be angry and allow the see to be void for a
long time.   In all this he considered that he was lawfully acting in William's interest.   He also devotedly

quoque devote pro eo intercessit. Ille autem, per suos
et per alios, dominum papam et curiam requirens,
F.27v per / dies quindecim non habuit [responsum], expecta-
cione suspensus, et tedio aliquantum affectus. Volens
ergo dominus papa imperatoris et regis, quas litteris
eorum acceperat peticionibus favere, curiam convenit,
humiliter et obnixe deprecans quatinus pro amore imperatoris, qui nuper ecclesie Romane reconciliatus erat,
et regis, eiusdem ecclesie filii et fidelis, a iusticie rigore
condescenderent, et Cantuariensi palleum dare concederent. 'Et quidem[a] Eboracensis, amicus noster, hoc
ipsum et efflagitat, et personam eius sciencia et vite
honestate valde commendat.' Patris et domini sui supplicacionibus non annuere durum esse reputantes, domino pape assenserunt. Mandatum est ei ad curiam
venire responsum accepturo. Tunc ipse papa in plena
curia sic exorsus est: 'De eleccione Cantuariensis archiepiscopi tractantes, aliqua in ea non canonice facta
invenimus'; et, predicta capitula enumerante, Cantuariensis ne verbum unum fecit; 'set quoniam', inquit,
'sedis huius pontifices canones fecerunt, et ipsorum est
eos, urgente necessitate, vel utili dispensacione, moderari.
Quia ergo personam illius, que per dei graciam honesta
est et religiosa, ecclesie profuturam confidimus, et pro
amore filiorum nostrorum regis et imperatoris, amici
quoque nostri Eboracensis archiepiscopi, eleccionem
illius confirmamus, palleum ei con[ce]dimus.'
Tunc noster illi gracias agens pedibus eius prostratus est. Similiter et Cantuariensis, et qui cum eo
erant; et tunc demum illi, sicut archiepiscopo, sedes
in loco digniori data est: et unum pro certo existimo

[a] quidam, MS

interceded with the *curia* on his behalf. But William, approaching the pope and *curia* through his friends and others, and having no reply for a fortnight, was kept in suspense and got very tired of it. The pope therefore, wishing to favour the petitions of the emperor and the king, contained in their letters, assembled the *curia* humbly and earnestly praying them for love of the emperor, who had lately been reconciled with the church, and of the king, a faithful son of the same church, to mitigate the rigour of the law, and grant the archbishop of Canterbury the *pallium*. 'Our friend, the archbishop of York', said he, 'is asking for this, and highly commends him personally for his learning and honourable life.' The court considering it hard not to consent to the petitions of its father and lord, gave the pope its assent. The archbishop was bidden to come to the *curia* and receive his answer. The pope then, in full court, began as follows, 'On considering the election of the archbishop of Canterbury, we found some points in it which were uncanonical'. He named the points and the archbishop of Canterbury answered not a word. 'But since', he went on, 'the bishops of this see made the canons, they also have the right, in urgent necessity or for administrative convenience, to modify them. Therefore because we trust that this person, who by God's grace is honourable and devout, will be profitable to the church, and for the love of our sons, the king and the emperor, and of our friend the archbishop of York, we confirm his election and grant him the *pallium*.'

Then our archbishop fell down at his feet to thank him: likewise the archbishop of Canterbury and his followers. Then at last he was assigned a more honourable seat as an archbishop. One thing I feel certain, that

quod nisi Eboracensis ª Cantuariensem adiuvisset, palleum tardius accepisset; si vero ei nocere voluisset, hac
vice omnino non habuissset.

Palleo accepto cepit adversus Eboracensem de primatu et professione quescio et contencio, quamquam
nec propter hoc venerant, nec vocati fuerant. Proposuit dominus Bernardus querelam et clamorem ex parte
Cantuariensis archiepiscopi et episcoporum Anglie adversus archiepiscopum nostrum, quod de [iure] Cantuariensis ecclesie subtraxerat; rogans et deprecans dominum papam et curiam Romanam quatinus audirent
que munimenta et privilegia de eius dignitate et primatu habebant; non tamen quod modo causaliter nec
iudicialiter agere vellent. Hiisdem enim verbis usus est.
Et noster archiepiscopus: 'Nec ego', inquid, 'veni ut
in causam vel iudicium ingrediar; ad concilium ve-
niebam, set dominus meus rex me detinuit'. Et dominus Bernardus, prave hoc intelligens, vel depravare
volens: 'Satis competenter paratus [sum]', ait, 'dominum regem defendere, eum non pro malo vos detinuisse'.
Ast dominus papa, aliquantulum indignanter, ad eum:
'Bone domine, non dixit, "pro malo eum detinuerit",
set quod "detinuit", et verum dixit, quoniam ita michi
mandavit'. Ieremias vero quod ᵇ rex eum detinuerat
donec cum Cantuariensi veniret. Cui Iohannes Cremensis: 'Benedicaris a deo! Tu enim in tempore
locutus es.' Et dominus Bernardus aliquanti percon-
fusus est venit (*sic*).

Iussa sunt legi privilegia predicta. Erant ᶜ quidem
Romanorum pontificum nominibus pretitulata,¹ set
stylum Romanum nichil sapiebant. Quibus perlectis,
et illo ad ultimum beati Gregorii ad Augustinum de

ª et *ins*. MS   ᵇ quem, MS
ᶜ Erat quidem Ro. pontifici, &c., MS

¹ These privileges are enumerated, and extracts given from them, in
Eadmer, *Hist. Nov.*, lib. 5, pp. 261-76.

had not the archbishop of York aided the archbishop of Canterbury, he would have been longer in getting his *pallium*. And if he had wished to injure him, he would not have got it at all.

After the receipt of the *pallium*, the question and contention arose again about the primacy and the profession, although they had not come on that account nor had been summoned on it. Bishop Bernard set forth the plaint and claim on behalf of the archbishop of Canterbury and the bishops of England against our archbishop, that he had infringed the privileges of the church at Canterbury, asking and praying the pope and the Roman *curia* to hear what muniments and privileges they had concerning its dignity and primacy; though they did not mean at this time to take judicial proceedings about them. Those were the words that he used. Then said our archbishop, 'I did not come to enter into judicial proceedings; I was coming to the Council, but my lord the king kept me back'. And bishop Bernard, misunderstanding this, whether wilfully or not, said, 'I am prepared to defend the king from the charge of wrongful detention'. But the pope, somewhat indignant, said to him, 'My good sir, he did not say "wrongfully detained", but "detained", and he spoke true, for [the king] sent word to me that he had'. And Jeremy [said] that the king had kept him back till he could come with the archbishop of Canterbury. John of Crema said, 'God bless you! You have spoken a word in season.' And bishop Bernard was put to some confusion.

The said privileges were ordered to be read.[1] They were headed with the names of popes of Rome, but had no trace of the style of the Roman chancery. When they had been read, ending with the letter of St Gregory to

distinccione duorum metropolitanorum Anglie, interro-
F.28 gaverunt quidam de Romanis Cantuarienses, si / privilegia illa bullas haberent: at illi dixerunt, bullata in
ecclesia reliquisse, et eorum exempla detulisse. Et
quia privilegiis aut cartis non bullatis, vel non signatis, non necesse est fidem adhiberi, sciscitati sunt, si
vellent iurare horum exemplaria bullata habere. In
partem cesserunt. Consultantes invicem dixerunt inter
se bullis carere. Aliquis tamen alicui per[su]adere
voluit ut pro causa ecclesie sue iuraret. Sanum quidem
consilium et legale. Cui nequaquam adquiescentes,
privilegia illa periurio bullare timuerunt. Consilium
eorum fuit ut coram redeuntes dicerent bullas consump-
tas vel perditas esse. Quibus sic dicentibus, alii sub-
riserunt, alii nares corrugaverunt, alii cachinnum emise-
runt, illudendo dicentes, mirum esse plumbum con-
sumptum fore vel perditum, et pergamenum durare.
Fortasse ficticium hoc esse cuiquam videatur, et qui
scripsit hoc nugator, set tam verum est quam ficticium
videtur. Dixerunt postea, forsitan eo tempore bullas
non fieri: set Romani a tempore beati Gregorii bullas
fuisse testati sunt, et adhuc [in] Romana ecclesia aliqua
ipsius privilegia bullata servari. Non habentes quid de
hoc aliud dicerent, turbati discesserunt, nec privilegia
illa cum credulitate, nec verba eorum in laude nec in
gracia recepta sunt.

Non tamen adhuc destituerunt professionem nostram
precio taxare. Erat nunc camerarius quidam subdolus
et nequam, familiaris et potens apud dominum, et
papam per illum efficere conati sunt, magna domino
pape et ipsi pollicentes, ut primatus Cantuariensis

Augustine about the separation of the two metropolitans of England, some of the Romans asked the Canterbury party whether the privileges had bulls attached. But they said that they had left the originals with their bulls in their church and brought copies of them. And because privileges are not valid evidence unless they have bulls attached or signatures, they were asked whether they would swear that the originals had bulls. They retired and consulting together, said that the bulls were wanting. One of them tried to persuade another to swear for the sake of their church. (What sound and canonical advice!) But they were by no means willing, and were afraid to supply the missing bulls by perjury. They made up their minds to come back and say that the bulls had either perished or were lost. When they said this, some smiled, others turned up their noses, and others laughed aloud; making fun of them and saying that it was a miracle that lead should perish or be lost and parchment survive. Some may think that this story is made up, and the writer trifling with him, but the thing is as true as it seems false. They afterwards suggested that perhaps bulls were not used so early. But the Romans bore witness that there had been bulls in St Gregory's time, and that some privileges of his with bulls were preserved in the church of Rome. Having no more to say, they retired in disorder; their privileges were disbelieved, and their speeches neither praised nor kindly received.

They did not, however give up hope of obtaining our profession by paying its price. The present chamberlain was a cunning and wicked man, intimate and influential with his master, and they tried to get a grant of primacy for the church of Canterbury by his means, making lavish promises to the pope and to him

ecclesie concederetur. De curia nullus eis favebat, tribus exceptis, et illis quidem modice inter ceteros auctoritatis. Omnium fere civium, nobilium, et proborum benevolenciam non habebat. Dominus papa mandavit archiepiscopo nostro, quatinus, si qua haberet munimenta, coram afferret. Ille vero respondit se nulla attulisse, quia non ad causam set ad concilium vocatus venerat; in qua solum Cantuarienses confidebant. De camera nostri aliquantum diffidebant, unde et quibusdam cardinalibus dixerunt: 'Nos non timemus curiam, set cameram'. Quibus ille: 'Per sanctum Petrum, si camera contra curiam vel motum unum mitti temptaverit, audiet que noluerit. Sicut dominus papa mandavit, si qua habetis munimenta, coram legere ne timueritis.' Tunc archiepiscopus noster: 'Litteras aliquas socii nostri, non rogati, secum fortuitu detulerunt, non bullatas, et privilegii nostri exemplum'. 'Et illas,' inquiunt, 'coram allatas, legite.' Consilio eorum ita fieri concessum est.

Altera die archiepiscopus noster veniens ante dominum papam et curiam predixit, quoniam sic eis placebat, litteras quasdam, quas socii sui detulerant, libenter ostendere, non quidem modo in causam intrare. Si enim ad hoc vocatus fuisset, et cleris et scriptis aliter et bene munitus venisset. De Cantuariensibus nec unus quidem aderat.

Lecta est igitur primo epistola beati Gregorii ad Augustinum quam[a] illi privilegiorum suorum novissime legerant. De quibusdam inter se disceptantibus illam nobiscum, nichil vero cum illis facere tandem eis visum est. Deinde epistola Honorii pape ad Paulinum Eboracensem et Honorium Cantuariensem archiepiscopos

<hr>

[a] qua, MS

personally. Only three of the *curia* were on their side, and those not highly considered there. He was not popular with the citizens, nobles, and honest people. The pope sent to our archbishop to bring any documents to him, if he had them. He answered that he had none, because he had been called to a Council and not a trial, which was the sole reason of the confidence of the Canterbury party. Our party rather distrusted the papal *camera*, which made them say to some of the cardinals, 'We are not afraid of the *curia*, but the *camera*'. They replied, 'By Saint Peter, if the *camera* tries to make any move against the *curia*, it will hear something it would rather not hear. As the pope has ordered, do not fear to read before him any documents you have.' Then our archbishop said, 'Our companions, without having been asked, happen to have brought with them some letters, without bulls, and a copy of our privilege'. 'Bring them', they said, 'and read them in public.' By their advice it was granted that this should be done.

On the next day our archbishop, appearing before the pope and the *curia*, began by saying that he gladly exhibited some letters which his companions had brought, because the court wished it, but that he was not now opening a case. For if he had been summoned for that purpose, he would have come differently, well equipped with clerks and documents. None of the Canterbury party appeared.

First, then, was read the letter of St Gregory to Augustine, which the Canterbury party had read last of their privileges. Some of them discussed this with us, but finally agreed that it did not support the other side's case. Then came the letter of Pope Honorius to Paulinus archbishop of York, and Honorius archbishop of

de palleorum missione ; et de vicaria inter metropolitanos consecracione. Post illam lecte sunt littere pape Urbani F.28*v* ad Thomam archiepiscopum de / redargucione professionis iniuste. Postea vero littere pape Pascalis et Gelasii et presentis Calixti ad Radulphum Cantuariensem et Turstinum Eboracensem, illi prohibentes ne professionem illam exigeret, huic ne exhiberet ; que suprascripte sunt. Novissime autem privilegium quod ipse papa Calixtus archiepiscopo nostro fecerat. Scrutinium de litteris istis factum est nullum, si bullas haberent ; omnes enim bene noverant. Auditis eorum et nostris munimentis, nisi quod uterque[a] pretenderat se non in causam venisse de controversia sua, inter Cantuariensem et Eboracensem iusto iudicio secundum voluntatem nostram decisum foret.

Videntes clerici qui erant cum Cantuariensi quod nichil proficerent, clericis nostris a rege minas inferebant. Quibus illi : 'Quia modo neque in iusticia neque in pecunia confiditis, ad minas conversi estis. Set potens est deus defendere nos, et rex nichil mali reddet immeritis cum archiepiscopo suo pro ecclesia sua resistentibus.' Archiepiscopo quoque dictum fuit quod non ideo quod archiepiscopus erat, iustum esse poterat quod antea sua ipsius attestacione iniustum fuerat. Denique uterque archiepiscopus simul ad curiam venerunt. Quibus, precepto domini pape, dictum est, quod quia se non in causam vocatos venisse predixerant, indefinita eorum contempcione recederent ; set [ad] eam definiendam, diem, si vellent, ille statueret.[b] Diem vero archiepiscopus noster accipere voluit. Cantuariensis autem, rege inconsulto, noluit. Accepta a domino papa licencia, ipse cum litteris istis rediit.

---

[a] MS repeats 'uterque'.   [b] statuerent, MS

Canterbury about sending *pallia*, and about the alternate consecration by the metropolitans. After that was read the letter of Pope Urban to archbishop Thomas reproving him for the undue profession. After that the letters of Popes Paschal and Gelasius and the present Pope Calixtus to Ralph, archbishop of Canterbury, and Thurstan, of York, which are written above, forbidding the one to exact and the other to offer the profession. Last of all the privilege which Pope Calixtus had made for our archbishop. The letters were not examined to see if they had bulls, since everybody knew about them. When both the Canterbury documents and ours had been heard, a just judgment could have been given betwixt the archbishops of Canterbury and York in our favour, had it not been that both sides had disclaimed any legal proceedings.

When the clerks with the archbishop of Canterbury saw that they were making no progress, they threatened our clerks with the king. They replied, 'Now that you no longer trust in justice nor in money, you have turned to threats. But God is strong to defend us, and the king will do no hurt to innocent men standing up for their church with their archbishop.' The archbishop also was told that his having become an archbishop did not make that just, which he had previously testified to be unjust. At last both archbishops came together to the *curia*. By the pope's orders, it was said to them that because they had claimed that they had not been summoned to trial, they must go away with their case undecided; but he would, if they wished, appoint them a day to decide it. Our archbishop wished to accept. But the archbishop of Canterbury refused to do so without consulting the king. So he took leave of the pope, and went off with this letter:

Littere eiusdem pape ad suffraganeos et clerum
provincie Cantuariensis

Calixtus episcopus, servus servorum dei, venerabilibus fratribus Cantuariensis ecclesie suffraganeis, clero et populo Cantuariensi, salutem et apostolicam benediccionem. Venientem ad nos suscepimus, et super causa eius una cum fratribus, episcopis et cardinalibus, diu tractavimus, et que minus canonice perpetrata fore repperimus, [correximus]. Nos autem quia de honestate persone, que per dei graciam religiosa est, et nulla prorsus macula[a] notatur infamie, valde confidimus, et magnum ex ea utilitatis fructum vestre ecclesie profuturum speramus, karissimi filii nostri Henrici regis et vestre peticionibus[b] annuimus, et quod de ipso factum fuerat confirmavimus. Palleum vero, pontificalis[c] videlicet officii plenitudinem, illi, iuxta consuetudinem ecclesie, concessimus. Ipsum itaque ad vos cum nostre gracie habundancia remittentes, universitatem vestram rogemus, monemus, atque precipimus, ut eum reverenter suscipiatis, affeccione precipua diligatis, eique tanquam patri et pastori vestro humilitate atque obediencia pareatis; quatinus per ipsius curam salutem in vobis omnipotentis dei gracia operetur, et vos de eo gaudium, et ipse de vobis coronam immarcessibilis glorie recipere mereatur.

Archiepiscopus noster, cum plenitudine gracie domini pape et tocius curie, et litteris hiis, ad regem digressus est.

Littere eiusdem pape ad eundem regem pro eodem
archiepiscopo Eboracensi

Calixtus episcopus, servus servorum dei, karissimo in Christo filio Henrico, illustri et glorioso Anglorum

[a] miracula, MS   [b] peticionis, MS   [c] pontificale, MS

Letter of the pope to the suffragan bishops and
clergy of the province of Canterbury

Calixtus, bishop, servant of the servants of God,
to his venerable brethren the suffragans of the church
of Canterbury, and to the clergy and people of Canterbury, greeting and apostolic blessing. We have
received [your archbishop-elect] as he came to us,
and have with our brethren the bishops and cardinals
treated at length of his case, and have corrected what
we found in it to be uncanonical. We, being satisfied
that he is an honourable man, and by God's grace
a devout one, and of unspotted reputation, and hoping
that his election will be highly profitable to your
church, accede to the petition of our dearest son King
Henry, and yours, and have confirmed what has been
done in his case. We have also granted him the
pallium, that is the fullness of pontifical office, according to the custom of the church. We therefore send
him back to you with the abundance of our grace,
and ask, admonish, and direct you all to receive him
reverently, love him exceedingly, and humbly obey
him as your father and shepherd; that by his care the
grace of almighty God may work salvation in you; and
that you may have joy in him, and he may deserve to
receive from you a crown of glory that fadeth not away.

Our archbishop went away to the king with the fullness of the grace of our lord the pope and his whole
curia, and the following letter.

Letter of the pope to the king for the
archbishop of York

Calixtus, bishop, servant of the servants of God,
to his dearest son in Christ, Henry, illustrious and

regi, salutem et apostolicam benediccionem. Ad
apostolorum limina et nostram presenciam venientem,
dilectum fratrem nostrum T. Eboracensem archiepiscopum, debita dulcedinis et caritatis affeccione
suscepimus, quod dum apud nos per aliquantulum
quoque[a] dierum spacium moraretur, multa nobis de
te bona sapienter et fideliter retulit, et pro tui regni
statu et exaltacione instantissime apud Romanam
ecclesiam intercessit. Qua de re nos et amplius te
diligimus et preces tuas, in quibus opportunum /

F.29   est, libenter admittimus. Pro ipso ergo dilectissimo
nobis fratre nostro egregiam magnificenciam tuam
rogamus, ut eum deinceps pro amore dei et nostro
maiori diligencia complectaris.

Veniente prius Cantuariensi archiepiscopo in Normanniam, quidam de sociis suis quedam aliter quam
res esset regis auribus instillaverunt, et de archiepiscopo nostro, quod eis fuerat in nocumentum. Secutus
paulo post Eboracensis, a rege gratulabunde et socii
sui suscepti sunt. Et domnus abbas Anselmus et
Ieremias, qui a rege Romam missi cum archiepiscopo
nostro redierant, rei veritatem ei plenius intimaverunt;
et quod Eboracensis Cantuariensi bene valuerat; tes-
tantes plene, quod si ei nocere studuisset, palleum ea
vice non detulisset. Noster vero nichil apud regem
conquestus est illos sibi, quantum potuerant, obstitisse,
cum de Gles[c]uensi et episcopis Scocie clamaret quod
se Eboracensi ecclesie subtrahebant; quod regis Anglie
dignitati adversabatur. Archiepiscopi, apud regem quantum ei placuit commorati, in Angliam repatriaverunt.

[a] quorum, MS

glorious king of the English, greeting and apostolic blessing. We have received our beloved brother, Thurstan, archbishop of York, coming to the thresholds of the apostles and to our presence, with the sweetness and loving affection that he deserves. During the few days of his stay with us, he has wisely and faithfully reported much good of you, and has earnestly interceded with the church of Rome for the welfare and exaltation of your kingdom. For which reason we love you the more, and freely accept your prayers so far as is suitable. We therefore ask your most excellent majesty in behalf of our beloved brother, that you will henceforth cherish him the more diligently for the love of God and of ourselves.

The archbishop of Canterbury arrived in Normandy first; and some of his company dropped into the king's ears a false account of the state of affairs, and asserted that our archbishop had done them harm. The archbishop of York and his company followed soon after, and were graciously received by the king. And abbot Anselm and Jeremy, who had been sent to Rome with our archbishop and had now returned, told the king the whole truth, and that the archbishop of York had done good service to him of Canterbury; fully witnessing that if he had tried to injure him, the archbishop of Canterbury would not have brought back his *pallium* this time. But our archbishop made no complaint to the king of the other party's having opposed him as much as they could when he complained that the bishop of Glasgow and the other Scottish bishops were withdrawing their obedience from the church of York, to the prejudice of the dignity of the king of England. So the archbishops remained with the king as long as he wished, and then returned home to England.

R

Proximo Septembre dominus papa Cantuariensi archiepiscopo ita scripsit.

Littere eiusdem pro eodem

Calixtus episcopus, servus servorum dei, G. Cantuariensi archiepiscopo, et universis suffrageneis eius, salutem, et apostolicam benediccionem. Quisquis a deo gloriam sempiternam et honorem indeficientem consequi desiderat, honore dignos venerari non negligat; unde universitati vestre mandamus et precipimus quatinus venerabilem fratrem nostrum T. Eboracensem archiepiscopum, honestum utique, sapientem, atque religiosum virum, pro nostri amoris reverencia diligatis, et ut impleatur in vobis illud apostolicum, 'honore invicem prevenientes',[1] mutue fraternitatis diligencia veneremini, nec ullam ei prerogativam,[a] quam predecessores eius habuisse noscuntur, in aliquio subtrahatis.

Sequenti anno misit dominus papa Iohannem Cremensem presbyterum cardinalem ut in Anglia legatus esset, quem dominus rex in Normannia propter aliqua negocia aliquamdiu detinuit. Adhuc eo illic morante, Calixtus papa in Adventu domini obiit,[2] et Lambertus Ostiensis episcopus, clericus sapiens et iustus homo, in papam Honorium substitutus est. Ipse vero legacionem a predecessore suo Iohanni iniunctam litteris suis confirmavit. Iste est quartus papa sub quo T. Eboracensis archiepiscopus passus est.

Archiepiscopus Cantuariensis, meliorem successum repperire existimans, apud novum papam clamorem renovavit de primatu, quem [b] super ecclesiam nostram habere debebat; petens ut causam hanc in Anglia a legato suo iuberet terminari, set non in presencia sua voluit. Legatus in Quadragesima in Angliam transivit.

a prorogativam, MS   b quod, MS

In the following September the pope wrote as follows to the archbishop of Canterbury:

The pope's letter on behalf of the archbishop of York

Calixtus, bishop, servant of the servants of God, to William, archbishop of Canterbury and all his suffragans, greeting and apostolic blessing. Whosoever desires to obtain from God eternal glory and unfailing honour, let him not neglect to reverence those worthy of honour. Wherefore we command and direct you all to love our brother Thurstan, archbishop of York, a wise and devout man, in reverence of our love; and, that the word of the apostle may be fulfilled in you, 'in honour preferring one another',[1] reverence him as brothers should, and do not in any way withhold from him any prerogative which his predecessors are known to have enjoyed.

In the following year [1124], the pope sent John of Crema, cardinal-priest, to be legate in England, but the king kept him some time in Normandy for matters of business. While he still delayed there, in Advent, Pope Calixtus died[2]; and Lambert, bishop of Ostia, a wise clerk and just man, replaced him as Pope Honorius. He confirmed by his letters the legation which his predecessor had enjoined on John. This is the fourth pope in whose time Thurstan, archbishop of York suffered.

The archbishop of Canterbury, hoping to have better success with a new pope, renewed his claim for the primacy which he ought to have over our church; begging him to order the cause to be determined in England by his legate. But he was not willing to have it tried in the pope's presence. The legate crossed to

---

[1] Rom. 12: 10　　　[2] 13-14 Dec. 1124

Circa Pentecosten[1] misit dominus papa utrique archiepiscopo litteras quatinus in proxima beate Marie Purificacione suam illi exhiberent presenciam, ille sicut de querela et clamore quos [a] fecerat acturus, noster vero sicut responsurus. Archiepiscopo nostro misse hic scripte sunt.

Littere domini Honorii pape prime ad eundem
Eboracensem archiepiscopum[b]

Honorius episcopus, servus servorum dei, venerabili fratri, T., Eboracensi archiepiscopo, salutem et apostolicam benediccionem. Ad hoc in celsa Romane ecclesie specula, disponente spiritu sancto, promoti sumus, ut ecclesiarum paci, et quod paterna vigilancia providentes conservare ius suum unicuique debeamus. Querelam siquidem [c] fratris vestri, G. Cantuariensis /

archiepiscopi de primatu adversus te et ecclesiam tuam accepimus. Dignum ergo duximus ut [d] tantarum ecclesiarum et tanti negocii causa in nostra presencia pertractetur, ideoque fraternitati tue mandamus, ut in proxima beate Marie Purificacione [e] ad nostram presenciam venias, de eodem negocio responsurus.

Datum Laterani, idibus Aprilis.[f]

Legatus tota fere Anglia circuita et perambulata usque prope Scociam, in Nativitate beate Marie concilium Londonie celebravit, quod in tempore regum utriusque Willelmi Romanus legatus nunquam fecerat. Una huius concilii dierum dominus Bernardus episcopus ab archiepiscopo nostro veniam postulavit, se peccasse confitens quod tantum contra ecclesiam nostram

---

[a] quod, MS
[b] Collated with another copy of this letter in Lansdowne MS 402, f. 104. The letter to the archbishop of Canterbury occurs there also.
[c] igitur, MS Lansd.   [d] in, MS   [e] Purificacionis, MS
[f] Datum . . . Aprilis, added from Lansd.

England in Lent. About Whitsuntide [1] the pope sent letters to both archbishops to appear before him at Candlemas next, the one to prosecute the plaint and claim he had made, and the other to answer. The letter sent to our archbishop follows :

First letter of Pope Honorius II
to the archbishop of York

Honorius, bishop, servant of the servants of God, to our venerable brother, Thurstan, archbishop of York, greeting and apostolic blessing. We have been raised, by the disposition of the Holy Ghost, to the lofty watch-tower of the church of Rome, that we may [watch over] the peace of the churches, and provide by our fatherly vigilance to preserve each man his rights. We have received the plaint of your brother William, archbishop of Canterbury, against you and your church about the primacy. We have therefore thought proper that a cause concerning such great churches and so important a matter should be discussed in our own presence. We therefore command you, brother, to appear before us at Candlemas next to answer on that matter.

Given at the Lateran, the 13th day of April.

The legate having gone about and through England almost to the Scottish border, celebrated a council in London on the Nativity of Our Lady [8 Sept.], a thing which no Roman legate had ever done in the time of either William. On one of the days of this Council bishop Bernard begged our archbishop's pardon, confessing that he had sinned in being so hot against our

[1] 17 May

institerat. Inde ambo archiepiscopi, provisis ad iter necessariis, in Normanniam transeunt Romam ituri. Legatus legacione sua expleta paulo post eo secutus est. Transierunt et Alexander Lincolniensis episcopus, et Iohannes Glesguensis, et Gaufridus abbas Sancti Albani, et abbas de Schireb', cum Cantuariensi archiepiscopo profecturi, non opinante archiepiscopo nostro quod rex de facienda professione vel subieccione ulterius eum angariaret, set totum iudicio vel disposicioni sedis apostolice reservaret. Mandavit ei tamen per episcopos et proceres, quatinus ecclesias sic esse dimitteret sicut sub patre suo fuerant; alioquin nec fidelitatem quam ei iuraverat bene servaret, et odium eius semper haberet. Ille, prius de periurio et infidelitate se excusans, dixit se gratanter dimittere ecclesias[a] sic stare, sicut sub patre suo, Aldredo vivente, ultimo Angligenarum Eboracensi archiepiscopo, steterant. Ait ille: 'Nequaquam'; set statu quo pater eius illas reliquerat. Et ille: 'Non possum hoc,' inquit, 'nisi privilegium meum destruendo, facere: et ad hoc uterque archiepiscopus vocati sumus, ut in audencia domini pape contencio nostra sedis apostolice iudicio terminetur'. Preter equitatem et consuetudinem fuit ut pro causa qua ad apostolicam sedem quisquam vocatus sic coartaretur, nec demum ut, pro eadem causa vocatus, regem sic alium coartare compulisset.

Quoniam sic inter archiepiscopos pax stabiliri non poterat, alia via per regem et alios mediatores cogitata est, ut Cantuariensis archiepiscopus de provincia sua magna Eboracensi archiepiscopo tres episcopatus concederet, Cestrensem, Pangorensem, et tercium inter

---

[a] ecclesiam, MS

church. Then both archbishops, having made the necessary preparations for the journey crossed to Normandy on their way to Rome. The legate followed them soon after, having fulfilled his legation. There also crossed Alexander, bishop of Lincoln, and John, bishop of Glasgow, Geoffrey, abbot of St Albans and the abbot of Sherborne, intending to go with the archbishop of Canterbury. Our archbishop did not think that the king would trouble him further about his profession, but that he would leave the whole matter to the disposition of the apostolic see. The king, however, sent him orders by bishops and nobles, that he should leave the churches as they were under his father; otherwise he would not be keeping well the fealty which he had sworn to him, and would always be hated by him. He, after rebutting the charge of perjury and breach of faith, said that he would let the churches stay as they had been under his father in the lifetime of Aldred, the last English archbishop of York. But the king said, No, but as his own father had left them. 'I cannot do that', said Thurstan, 'without destroying my privilege; and both of us archbishops have been summoned to have our difference determined in the pope's audience by the judgment of the apostolic see.' It was inequitable and contrary to custom that any man summoned to the apostolic see should be so coerced, and still more that one party so summoned should force the king so to coerce another.

Since peace between the archbishops could not be established in that way, another plan was thought of by the king and other mediators; namely that the archbishop of Canterbury should grant to the archbishop of York, out of his large province three bishoprics, those of Chester, Bangor and another lying between them [St

hos duos medium set pro vastitate et barbarie episcopo vacantem; hac quidem convencione quod Tur-
[stinus] archiepiscopus Cantuariensem archiepiscopum
solo verbo in primatem susciperet, successores autem
eius Cantuariensibus obedienciam seu reverenciam qualis primati debetur manu in manum promitterent, in
misericordia quidem et voluntate domini pape. Hoc
autem consilio multo, persuasionibus plurimis, pro
pace et quiete missionibus, rege quoque et legato ad
hoc obnixe laborantibus, vix ab utroque concedi ex-
tortum est. Nolebat enim noster, nec in minimo, subici illi, nec ille pro primatu de suo tantum partiri.
Existimo quod noster nullatenus concessisset, si Romanam ecclesiam non consentire non credidisset. Hec
conveniencia ab ipso legato descripta est ab eodem
Romam proferenda.[a] Rex de preterito penitens, de
futuro precavens ne Romanum legatum in regno suo
denuo reciperet, persuasit et precepit Cantuariensi
archiepiscopo quatinus legationem [peteret]. Precatus
est ut illi de hoc in consilium et auxilium fideliter
adessent, et illi annuere. Abeuntibus archiepiscopis
F.30 prohibendo imperavit, / si dominus papa concordiam
inter se provisam concedere et confirmare nollet, ne
inde placitarent; sin autem, ad ecclesias suas non
reverterentur.

Cantuariensis cum suis iter aggreditur; noster vero,
assumpto sibi fratre suo Ebroicensi [b] episcopo: quorum
societatem omine infausto et diro infortunio legatus
elegit. Siquidem multam pecuniam in cophinis, et
bulgiis, et loculis portabat; quod de illo proverbium
istud dici poterat: 'Depredari desiderat qui publice

[a] proferendo, MS
[b] i.e. Audoenus. The MS reads 'Eboracensi archiepiscopo'.

Asaph] which had no bishop because it was waste and barbarous. By the terms of this agreement Thurstan should accept the archbishop of Canterbury as primate by word of mouth only; but his successors should shake hands with the archbishops of Canterbury and promise them the obedience or reverence due to a primate, if the pope should mercifully permit them. But in spite of much debate, many arguments, many missions to secure peace and quiet, and the strenuous efforts of the king and the legate, it was only just possible to extort the consent of both archbishops. Our archbishop would not be subject in the very least; nor would the other give up so large a share to secure the primacy. I reckon that our archbishop would not have given way, had he not believed that the Roman church would refuse its consent. The agreement was drawn up by the legate himself to be produced by him at Rome.

The king, repenting what had happened, and taking care for the future not to receive another Roman legate in his kingdom, persuaded and directed the archbishop of Canterbury to [apply for] the legation. He prayed the others faithfully to support him with counsel and help; and they agreed. As the archbishops were leaving, he forbade them, if the pope should refuse to grant and confirm the agreement arranged between them, to go to law on the subject. But if they did, they should never return to their sees.

The archbishop of Canterbury and his company started on their journey. Our archbishop took with him his brother [Audoin] the bishop of Évreux, and, inauspiciously and by dire misfortune, the legate chose to travel with them. He took with him much money in boxes, bags, and purses; so the proverb, 'The man who openly carries treasure on a journey is asking to be

thesaurum in via portat'. Et ipse, quod quibusdam
in itinere odiosus erat, eapropter per avia, per aspera,
per ardua, per abrupta, per vias quibus de patria nostra
nemo Romam ambulavit. Vagabundi, disturbati, capti,
redempti adversa tanta noster et sui perpessi sunt,
ut si non illa pro repellenda professione indebita, ista
nimium et nimio fuissent. Iamque Cantuarienses Rome
tres septimanas fecerant cum nostri illuc pervenerunt,[a]
nec de negocio [b] aliquo quicquam temptaverant, legatum et archiepiscopum nostrum exspectantes. Cantuariensem vero non modice penitebat hanc concessionem
fecisse, iam audito incepto et modo pacis inter archiepiscopos provise. Aliquantum Romani indignabantur
regem se ad hoc ingerere, quod nichil eum attingere
videbatur. Legatus a nostris antea digressus paucis
post advenit.

Tunc Cantuariensis archiepiscopus primo voluit de
legacione requisicionem fieri, ceteri vero prius de pace
perficienda dignum duxerunt. Legatus igitur et verbo
et scripto allato concordie [modum] enarravit. Set
Willelmus archiepiscopus de tercio episcopatu sine
nomine nec mencionem se audisse constanter negavit.
Miratus est legatus et multi qui aderant et hoc audierant,
et ipse iurare obtulit pro veritate testificanda et pro pace
facienda sic esse conventum, et scripto presenti inde
facto coram rege et utroque archiepiscopo, et archiepiscopo Rotomagensi et episcopo Lexoviensi, et de
Anglia et Normannia nonnullis sic esse recordatum et
concessum. Similiter Eboracensis archiepiscopus. Ipse
tamen nichilominus in negando persistebat. Qui cum

---

[a] perveniant, MS   [b] denegacio, MS

robbed', fitted him exactly. Also, because there were
enemies of his on the road, he went to Rome by roadless,
rough, steep, and broken ways, by which nobody from
our country had ever travelled. Our archbishop and his
company, wandering, confused, captured and ransomed,
suffered such adversity, which would have been too much
and more than too much for them, had they not been for
the sake of repelling an undue profession. When our
party got to Rome, the men from Canterbury had been
there three weeks, and had taken no steps about their
business, waiting for the legate and our archbishop. The
archbishop of Canterbury sincerely regretted having
given way, now that the scheme and manner of the peace
arranged between the archbishops had been heard. The
Romans were indignant at the king's interference in a
matter which seemed to be no business of his. The
legate had left us shortly before and came shortly after.

Then the archbishop of Canterbury wanted the
request for the legation to be made first, but the others
thought establishment of peace more important. The
legate therefore explained the method of the agreement
both by word of mouth and by the document which he
brought with him. But archbishop William stoutly
denied having heard any mention of the third unnamed
bishopric. The legate was astonished, and so were
many who had been present and heard it; and the
legate offered to make oath that it had been so agreed
to testify to the truth and to make peace; that this
document about it was made in the presence of the king,
of both the archbishops, the archbishop of Rouen, the
bishop of Lisieux, and sundry others of England and
Normandy, and so recorded and granted. So also did
the archbishop of York. But he none the less persisted
in his denial. Those who were with him, though they

eo erant, licet veritatem non ignorantibus, archiepiscopo suo aperte contradicere molestum erat. Visum est quibusdam quod in quo consenciebant confirmaretur, reliquum vero testimonio regis et aliorum qui affuerant reservaretur. Set de dubio et contencioso privilegium firmare absurdum erat: ire vero et redire propter regis testimonium deferendum via longa et labor aliquantus. Ad audienciam domini pape perventum est. Ibi legatus, scripto relicto ex parte regis, dominum papam et curiam postulavit quatinus concordiam hanc concederent et confirmarent, et quod ita disposita et concessa fuerant iurare se presentavit. Dominus papa, accepto consilio, dixit, querela et responsione eorum auditis, in hiis quodeumque^a honestum esset regem exaudire, sicut filium et fidelem Romane ecclesie. Consilio inde habito, pensantes quod eos in causam trahere valebant, et ex altera parte regis prohibicionem, petiere inducias. Date sunt illis, et prohibicio regis non erat ignota Romanis. In angustiis erat Cantuariensis, hinc propter regis interdictum, quod transgredi formidabat; inde quod clamore suo uterque vocatus venerat, ipse ad agendum, ille ad respondendum, et nisi prosequeretur metuebat ne a causa defecisse et cecidisse iudicaretur. Noster vero non habebat nisi tacere, si non impeteretur. F.30v Set quid [de] hiis longius? Multorum intercessio/nibus, et de die in diem dilacionibus et suspensionibus vix obtentum est ut salva cuiusque causa eis regredi liceret. Nam de concordia descripta nec verbum deinceps audire voluerunt.

^a quia que, MS

knew the truth, could not decently contradict their archbishop openly. Some people thought that the agreement
should be confirmed so far as both sides agreed, the rest
being reserved for the witness of the king and the others
who were present. But it would have been absurd to
establish a privilege in a doubtful and contentious
matter; yet it would be a long and troublesome journey
to go and get the king's evidence and come back with it.
So it came to the hearing before the pope. Thereupon
the legate, abandoning the document so far as the king
was concerned, demanded that the pope and *curia*
should grant and confirm the agreement, and offered to
swear that those were the terms in which it was couched
and agreed. Our lord the pope, after taking counsel,
said that having heard their plaint and answer, that he
granted the king's prayer, as a faithful son of the church
of Rome, so far as he honourably could in this matter.
After consultation, reflecting that that this might drag
them into a lawsuit, and on the other hand considering
the king's prohibition, they asked for an adjournment.
That was granted, and the Romans were aware of the
king's prohibition. The archbishop of Canterbury was
in a strait, on the one hand on account of the king's
prohibition, which he was afraid to transgress, on the
other because they had both appeared at his instance,
he to sue, the other to answer, and feared that if he did
not pursue his claim, he should be adjudged to have
abandoned it and lost his case. Our archbishop need
only be silent if he were not sued. But why say more?
After many applications and adjournments and sus-
pensions of judgment, the parties were with difficulty
permitted to retire without a decision against either.
For thenceforward the court would not hear a word
about the written agreement.

De legacione iam antea dominus papa[a] archiepiscopum nostrum consuluerat, quid sibi de committendo
eam Cantuariensi archiepiscopo laudaret. Ille vero dixit
quod nesciebat cui melius illam committere posset. Erat
enim clericus bonus, et homo simplex et iustus. Propter
precem et preceptum regis noluit illum dehortari. Quod
si ex studio noluisset, archiepiscopus non legatus in
Angliam foret relegatus. Tandem requisicionibus cre-
bris, sicut inter dominum papam et ipsum convenit,
nec multis de cardinalibus, nec archiepiscopo nostro et
paucis de suo numero assistentibus, legacio illi super
Britanniam commissa est.

Quia modo archiepiscopus noster dominum Iohannem Glesguensem episcopum in curia videbat, de eo
tacere non fuit consilium. Clamavit ergo quod ipse
Iohannes in Eboracensi ecclesia sicut suffraganeus eius
dictus, et per litteras suas a papa Pascali consecratus,
postea nec propter litteras eiusdem pape Pascalis,
neque Calixti, quas ibi recitari fecit, quicquam obediencie vel reverencie voluit exhibere. Quibus litteris
intellectis ipse ideo ad aliquantulum ligatus intellige-
batur. Similiter et de episcopis Scocie conquestus est.
A principio adventus eorum a quibusdam domino pape
persuasum erat Scociam non esse de regno Anglie.
Volebant enim requirere palleum episcopo Sancti Andree, et sic archiepiscopum creari. Set archiepiscopus
noster et secreto et palam in curia ostendit Scociam
de regno Anglie esse, et regem Scottorum de Scocia
hominem esse regis Anglie: quod debuit dominus
papa sic esse credidit. Glesguensis episcopus querele[b]
archiepiscopi nostri respondit, se non vocatum venisse,

---

[a] p'p', add. MS   [b] querere, MS

Even before that, the pope had consulted our archbishop about the legation, and had asked his opinion about committing it to the archbishop of Canterbury. He replied that he knew of nobody to whom it could better be entrusted. For he was a good clerk and a simple and honest man. Because of the king's prayer and directions he was unwilling to give contrary advice. But if he had not deliberately chosen not to do so, the archbishop would not have been sent back to England as legate. At last, after many requests, as was agreed between him and the pope, the legation to England was committed to him, in the absence of many of the cardinals and of our archbishop; a few of his own company being present.

Because our archbishop now saw John, bishop of Glasgow, at the court, he was not minded to keep silence about him. He complained that John, being nominally his suffragan in the church of York, and consecrated by Pope Paschal by means of his letters, would not give him any obedience or reverence, either for the sake of Pope Paschal's letters or those of Pope Calixtus, which he there caused to be read. On the consideration of the letters, it was felt that John was bound in some degree. He made a similar complaint against the Scottish bishops. When they first came, the pope had been advised by some people that Scotland was no part of the realm of England. For they tried to demand a *pallium* for the bishop of St Andrews, and that he should thus be made an archbishop. But our archbishop showed the pope both privately and in open court that Scotland was part of the realm of England, and that the king of Scots was the king's man for Scotland; which the pope duly believed. The bishop of Glasgow answered our archbishop's plaint, saying that he had

set in legacionem domini sui regis Scocie; itaque
iudicio decretum est eum modo non debere cogi re-
spondere, set diem illi statuere et absentes per litteras
domini pape summonere. Cantuariensis et sui, quantum poterat, odio professionis denegate, contra nos
erant, totam Britanniam provinciam sibi usurpando
clamantes, unde dominus papa[a] subridendo et capud
movendo, uni eorum sic dixit: 'Frater indulgeat tibi'.
Fuit autem ibi quidam clericus sapiens et causidicus fa-
mosus, Gillebertus, cognomento Universis [sic] vel pocius
Universalis, iusticiam inversare contendens, a nostris
aversus et factus adversarius. Qui cum archiepiscopo
nostro secum venire promisisset, et per litteras suas
semel et iterum mandasset, postea Cantuariensi adhesit,
sperans se tanto copiosius accepturum quanto archiepiscopatus ille nostro copiosior diviciis abundat. Set,
deo pauperes adiuvante, nec illi profuit, nec nostro
obesse valuit, et spes sua eum aliquantum decepit,[b] et
a quibusdam in curia curio appellatus est. De quo
Lucanus[1]:

<blockquote>Audax venali comitatur Curio lingua.[c][1]</blockquote>

Sicut provisum fuerat, dominus papa archiepiscopo
nostro et Glesguensi episcopo diem statuit a proxima
Quadragesima in alteram,[2] Iohanni episcopo sic dicens:
'Frater, quibus beate memorie papa Calixtus te ligavit,
nos te non absolvimus'. Episcopos Scocie ad diem
designatum per litteras suas vocare disposuit.

Sic ergo factis negociis et infectis Cantuariensis
archiepiscopus legacione suscepta rediit, et Eboracensis
qualis meaverat, set aliquanto forcior et hillarior re-
meavit. Dominus papa misit has litteras pro eo ad
regem.

---

[a] Britanniam added in MS
[b] recepit, MS   [c] lingue, MS

not been summoned, but was an envoy of his lord the
king of Scotland. It was therefore decided he could not
be compelled to answer now, but should be appointed
a day and that absent parties should be summoned by
the pope's letters. The archbishop of Canterbury and
his company were against us as far as they could out of
hatred because of our refusal of the profession, and
claimed to themselves the whole province of Britain. At
this the pope smiled and nodded and said to one of them,
'Your brother must excuse you'. There was also there
a wise clerk, a famous advocate, Gilbert, surnamed
'Universe', or rather 'Universal', striving to reverse
justice, averse from us, and become our adversary. He
had promised to come with our archbishop, and more
than once confirmed this by letter. He afterwards
joined the archbishop of Canterbury, hoping to be better
paid, because that archbishopric is richer than ours.
But, since God helps the poor, it did him no good and our
master no harm. His hopes were deceived, and some
in the *curia* nicknamed him 'Curio', of whom Lucan
wrote :

> Bold Curio follows with his venal tongue.[1]

As had been arranged, the pope appointed a day
to our archbishop and the bishop of Glasgow in Lent of
the next year,[2] saying to bishop John, 'Brother, we do
not absolve thee from the bonds with which Pope
Calixtus bound thee'. He arranged to summon the
Scottish bishops by his letters on the day appointed.

When all this had been done, or undone, the archbishop of Canterbury went home with his legation, and
the archbishop of York as he had set out, but much
stronger and merrier. The pope sent the king the
following letter on his behalf:

[1] *Phars.* i. 269
[2] Literally 'the Lent after next'. The day must have been fixed before
3 March 1126. It would thus be 16 February 1127.

S

Littere domini Honorii pape ad eundem regem pro
archiepiscopo Eboracensi |

F.31   Honorius episcopus, servus servorum dei, karissimo [in] Christo filio Henrico, illustri Anglie et
glorioso regi, salutem et apostolicam benediccionem.
Quanto desiderio, quantoque devote humilitatis affectu
sanctam matrem tuam Romanam ecclesiam dilexeris
et honoraveris quamplurimis cognovimus argumentis;
quocirca te, tanquam specialissimum beati Petri
alumnum, apertis caritatis visceribus amplexamur, et
regnum magnificare largiente domino exoptamus.
Obsecramus autem in domino quatinus pro reverencia
beati Petri et nostra caritate carissimum nostrum T.
Eboracensem archiepiscopum venereris et diligas, et
nullis gravaminibus vel iniuriis inquietari permittas.

Rex adhuc in Normannia morabatur. A quo archiepiscopis per aliquot dierum spacium detentis, Cantuariensis [archi]episcopus prior ad ecclesiam suam reversus est; nec multo post noster rediens et apud Wit-
sand transfretans, per Cantorberiam transivit, ubi archiepiscopus eum voluit accurate suscipere et honorifice pro-
curare. Set noluit estimans eum et suos adversus ipsum
rancorem habere, quod eum minime fallebat. Dixit
autem archiepiscopo nostro et de archiepiscopi et legacionis officio per consilium suum velle plurimum agere.
Cui noster promisit se illi secundum sciencie sue facultatem fideliter consiliaturum et adiuturum; et si qua
ex consilio suo odia, blasphemie, damna, incommoda
illi provenirent, patienter et libens secum omnia pateretur. Sic quasi amice digredientibus noster in Natali
Apostolorum [1] domum digressus est.

Proximo Septembre rex in Angliam rediit. Adve-

---

[1] Presumably SS. Peter and Paul, i.e. 29 June

Letter of Pope Honorius to the king on behalf of
the archbishop of York

Honorius, bishop, servant of the servants of God, to his dearest son in Christ, Henry, illustrious and glorious king of England, greeting and apostolic blessing. We know by very many proofs with what devout and humble affection you have loved and honoured the church of Rome. We therefore embrace you, as a special nurseling of St Peter, with open bowels of charity and desire the increase of your kingdom by God's bounty. But we beseech you in the Lord that in reverence of St Peter and for love of us, you revere and love our dearest Thurstan, archbishop of York, and suffer him not to be disturbed by any grievance or injury.

The king was still staying in Normandy. He kept the archbishops for some days. The archbishop of Canterbury was the first to return to his church. Soon afterwards our archbishop crossed from Wissant and passed through Canterbury, where the archbishop was pleased to receive him with due respect and entertain him honourably: not willingly, because he thought that he and his company had a grudge against him, which did not escape our archbishop. But he told our archbishop that he wished to act mainly on his advice both as archbishop and legate. Our archbishop promised to advise and help him faithfully to the best of his knowledge, and patiently and gladly suffer with him any hatred, blasphemy, loss, and inconvenience which might arise from his advice. So they parted as friends, and our archbishop went home on the birthday of the Apostles.[1]

In the following September the king returned to

niente Natali domini archiepiscopus noster venit ad curiam regis, paratus inde Romam pergere propter placitum, quod prediximus inter ipsum et Iohannem Glesguensem episcopum et episcopos Scocie a domino papa in proxima Quadragesima statutum fuisse. Cantuariensis archiepiscopus mandavit regi quod curie sue non adesset, si Eboracensis ibi crucem sibi preferri faceret, vel ad eum coronandum manum mitteret. Quod rex graviter ferens, archiepiscopo sic mandavit, deprecans eum ut ad hospicium suum remaneret, ne in tanta sollempnitate et curia sua turbacio fieret. Erant tunc ad curiam David rex Scottorum et Conanus comes Britannorum. Archiepiscopus, hoc ex ore regis audire volens, ad eum ivit, et sic audivit; et ecclesie sue et sibi iniuriam irrogari, regi quoque dedecus fieri non tacuit, set: 'Modo', inquid, 'nolo curiam vestram per me turbari'. Recedens statim per suos archiepiscopum requisivit, si sic regi mandaverat. At ille recognovit, factum enim erat sibi intelligi hoc nichil ad eum pertinere.

Facto Natali domini Windesoris, ubi curia erat, crastina venit Londoniam, regem illuc quinta die venturum exspectans, et ad iter agendum se preparans. Eo rex adveniens, rege Scottorum secum adducto, quadam concordie provisione inter archiepiscopum nostrum et episcopos Scocie, concessu quoque regis David, nostro movere parato persuasit quatinus iter suum ad preens differens legatos Romam mitteret, petentes ex parte regi[s] et sua super hac causa dari sibi inducias usque ad alteram Quadragesimam, et interim inter eos concordandi licenciam. Quibus ita concessis archiepiscopus misit, et has inducias difficulter impetravit.

Londonie Cantuariensis archiepiscopus nostro collo-

England. When Christmas came, our archbishop came
to the king's court ready to set out for Rome for the plea
between him and John of Glasgow and the Scottish
bishops, which, as we said before, had been fixed by the
pope for next Lent. The archbishop of Canterbury
sent word to the king that he would not attend the
court, if the archbishop of York had his cross borne
before him there or had any hand in crowning him.
The king was annoyed, and sent to tell the archbishop
so, and requested him to stay at his lodging, lest there
should be any disturbance of the solemnity of his court.
(There were then at court David, king of Scots, and Co-
nan, count of Brittany.) The archbishop, wishing to hear
this from the king's mouth, went to him and heard it,
and did not refrain from saying that his church and he
were being wronged, and that it was a disgrace to the king.
'But', said he, 'I do not wish your court to be disturbed
by me.' He withdrew at once, and by his messengers,
demanded of the archbishop whether he had sent that
message to the king. He acknowledged that he had ; for
he had been assured that this need not affect him.

After spending Christmas at Windsor, where the
court was, he came next day to London, waiting four
days there for the king and preparing for the journey.
The king came, bringing with him the king of Scots, and
by planning a compromise between our archbishop and
the bishops of Scotland with King David's concurrence,
persuaded him, though ready to set out, to put off his
journey for the present, and send envoys to Rome, to
request on the king's and his own behalf, that the case
be adjourned to next Lent, with leave to settle the case
in the meantime. This being agreed, the archbishop
sent and, with difficulty, obtained an adjournment.

At London the archbishop of Canterbury wished to

qui voluit; noster vero, quia sic adversus eum egerat, loqui / ei renuit, neque postea usque in longum tempus

F.31v locutus fuit.

Decurso aliquot dierum intervallo, placuit Cantuariensi ex iure legacionis concilium convocare. Statuti sunt dies et locus, Ascensio[1] domini et Londonia. Mandavit itaque archiepiscopo nostro, et apostolica auctoritate precepit, quatinus concilio interesset; set prope diem, legati, quos Romam miserat, redeuntes, tale quid ei detulerunt per quod sicut nec voluit nec interfuit. Unde cum Cantuariensis apud regem conquereretur, quod quasi dedignatus erat ad suum venire concilium, rex ait: 'Et merito. Magnum enim dedecus ei in curia mea fecistis, michi vero non minus.' Et dominus papa pro iniuria et contumelia ista ad Cantuariensem ita scripsit:

Littere eiusdem Honorii pape ad eundem archiepiscopum Cantuariensem pro eodem episcopo Eboracensi

Honorius episcopus, servus servorum dei, Willelmo Cantuariensi archiepiscopo vere fraternitatis sincera dileccio. Tanto moderamine debet [episcopus] honorem et dignitatem suam in sui status prerogativa servare, ut in nullo fraterna caritas offendatur, vel reverencia minuatur. Ceterum, sicut accepimus, tu in plaga Septentrionali constitutus, nec maiorem nec parem sustinens, quos amare et honorare debueras opprimis, et ut quocunque modo eminencior apparere valeas elaboras. Karissimum namque fratrem nostrum, T. Eboracensem archiepiscopum, vehementer infestas, et refrigerata mutua caritate totis nisibus satagis oppugnare. Preterita enim sollempnitate Natalis domini ipsum, cui [cum] pro reverencia beati

[1] 12 May 1127

confer with ours, but the latter, because of his past opposition, refused to speak with him, and did not do so for a long time afterwards.

After some days it pleased the archbishop of Canterbury, by his right as legate, to convoke a Council. The date and place were fixed, Ascension day,[1] at London. The archbishop accordingly ordered our archbishop, and bade him by apostolic authority to take part in the Council. But, near the day appointed, the envoys whom he had sent to Rome, came back, bringing news which prevented him from attending the Council or wishing to do so. But, when the archbishop of Canterbury complained to the king, that he had, as it were, disdained to come to the legate's council, the king said, 'It serves you right. You treated him disgracefully at my court, and me too.' And the pope wrote to the archbishop of Canterbury about this insult and wrong as follows :

Letter of Pope Honorius to the archbishop of Canterbury on behalf of the archbishop of York

Honorius, bishop, servant of the servants of God, to William, archbishop of Canterbury, sincere brotherly love. A bishop ought to use such moderation in preserving his own honour and dignity in its excellence, as not to offend against brotherly love or fail in respect. But, as we have heard, that when you are in the North, you can bear no superior or equal, crush those whom you ought to have loved and honoured, and strive to appear more important than any one else. For you violently pursue our brother, Thurstan, archbishop of York; your brotherly love has cooled, and you make every effort to oppose him. Last Christmas, regardless of religion or charity, you shut him out, a man honourable not only out of

Petri et nostra, tum pro sue honestate persone honor est maximus deferendus, a corona regis, ubi pariter tecum esse debuerat, tanquam religionis et caritatis immemor exclusisti. Quocirca tibi mandamus ut de cetero honorem suum minuere non presumas. Si autem hoc veridica relacione versus aures nostras pulsaverit, tantum et tam immoderatum excessum non preteribimus impunitum. Dat' Laterani, idibus Marcii.

Unum est quod honoribus obicitur improborum[a] quod quasi in proverbium dicitur: 'Honores mutant mores'. Non enim in melius set in deterius mutare dictum est. Licet archiepiscopus noster Willelmum[b] modo Cantuariensem [archiepiscopum], antea sicut bonum et religiosum clericum et canonicum, amasset, et dicior et potencior eum honorasset; et ille, quod predecessoris sui Radulphi archiepiscopi causam adversus nos sepius improbans, nostram esse iustam comprobasset, ad hunc[c] promotus apicem, quod plurimum fuisse ipsius consilio et laudacione apud regem nec ille ignorabat; in exigendo tamen quod ante improbaverat perstitit, et nostrum acriter odio insectatus est, quod a defendendo non destitit ubi nunc temporis vera religio sedem habeat. Pauci vero[d] facile dinoscere possunt plura que[e] fuere adversa quam que scriptura ista continentur, set vel oblivione preterita, vel metu et tedio prolixitatis intermissa; quorum omnium causa fuit indebite professionis iniusta exaccio, et ad exhibendum potens et proterva coaccio. Contra que Tur[stinus] archiepiscopus pro defensione vel reparacione libertatis iuste et viriliter luctando imperterritus et indefessus perstitit. Quod si quis ad vocabulum alludere velit, non iniuria Turstinus nomen habuit, quia contra graves assultus et iacula tanquam turris stetit.

[a] in bonorum, MS   [b] Willelmus, MS
[c] hoc, MS   [d] ve, MS   [e] quod, MS

respect for St Peter and ourselves, but also in his own person, from the king's wearing of his crown, where he had as much right to be as yourself. We therefore order you not to dare to disparage him in future. If you shall be truthfully reported to us to have done so, we shall not leave your unrestrained excess unpunished. Given at the Lateran, the fifteenth day of March.

There is one objection made to the raising of bad men to honour, which is almost a proverb, 'Honours alter manners'. For the alteration is not for the better, but for the worse. Although our archbishop formerly loved William, now archbishop of Canterbury, as a good and devout clerk and canon, and honoured him when he was himself richer and more powerful; and William had often attacked his predecessor's, archbishop Ralph's case, and acknowledged ours to be just; yet being raised to this height, which he knew to be mainly due to our archbishop's advice and praise of him to the king; he yet persisted in demanding the profession he had previously scouted, and pursued our archbishop with fierce hate, because he did not cease his defence in the place where true religion now has its seat. Few people can easily perceive the many evils related in this treatise, but either forgotten or omitted from fear of wearying the reader, all of which were due to the unjust exaction of a profession, and the forcible shameless compulsion to make it. Against all these did Thurstan fearlessly and unweariedly persist in justly and manfully struggling, for the defence and restitution of freedom. And, if a play upon words is permissible, Thurstan was rightly so named, because he 'stood' like a 'tower' against attacks both hand to hand and from a distance.

Hec autem i[d]circo scripta esse decrevimus, ut pos-
F.32 teri / ecclesie nostre pontifices et clerici hiis qui de
partibus nostris professioni huic consenciendo, vel consilii seduccione, vel pacis amore, vel potestatis terrore,
et exilii formidine ad tempus cesserunt, quasi veniam
dantes, ne defunctis succensendo[a] improperent, eos vero
qui restiterunt imitentur et laudent.   Post epistolas
beati Gregorii, et Urbani pape redarguicionem, reve-
rendorum patrum Pascalis, Gelasii et Calixti prohi-
bitorias de exigendo privilegium, quarum legentes
tanto gravius quanto non inscienter prevaricari time-
ant, sit eciam illis confortacionis et vigoris exemplum
quod Tur[stinus] archiepiscopus pro persecucione et
exilio suo per Romanam et Gallicanam ecclesiam apud
omnimode dignitatis personas magis notus et dilectus
et celebrior factus est, adeo quod melius illi fuit; et
ipse quod restitutus maluit et sibi commodius repu-
tavit tantum exulasse, quam in ecclesia sua cum pace
et quiete integra permansisse usque ad annum ab
introitu eius in archiepiscopatum decimum tertium, a
consecracione vero illus octavum.   Hec ita gesta sunt
quinque annis et duobus mensibus.   Modo exul, modo
in patria since consecracione fuit, propter impedimenta
superius descripta.   A consecracione illius usque ad pre-
fatum Cantuariensis legati concilium annos septem et
menses fere totidem.   Potest autem incongrue libellus
iste quodammodo libertus intitulari, ideo quod ostendit
qualiter ecclesia nostra per Tur[stinum], eiusdem ecclesie quartum ex Francigenis archiepiscopum, a iugo
professionis illicite ad pristinam libertatem, deo auxiliante, revocata sit. 'Quanta audivimus et cognovimus,
ea patres nostri narraverunt nobis, filii qui nascentur
et exurgent et narrabunt filiis suis.'[1]

Tu autem, Domine, miserere nostri !

[a] successendo, MS

Our purpose in writing is, that future bishops and clergy may forgive those of us in these parts, who by bad advice, for love of peace, for fear of force, or dread of exile, gave way and consented to this profession, and not angrily reproach the dead; but imitate and praise those who resisted. After reading St Gregory's letter, Pope Urban's rebuke, and the prohibitions of the exaction of the profession by Popes Paschal, Gelasius, and Calixtus, and being the more afraid of transgressing them because they cannot plead ignorance, let them take comfort and example from the fact that archbishop Thurstan by his persecution and exile became better known and loved and more celebrated among men of all ranks in the Roman and Gallican churches, so that it was all the better for him; and when he was restored he preferred and deemed it better to have been so long in exile, than to have stayed in peace and quiet up to the thirteenth year from his entry on the archbishopric, and the eighth after his consecration. These last affairs took five years and two months. At one time he was an exile, at another at home but unconsecrated because of the difficulties mentioned. From his consecration to the Canterbury legate's council was seven years and almost as many months. This book might somewhat fancifully be christened 'The Freedman'; because it shows how our church was recalled from the yoke of an unlawful profession to its ancient freedom by Thurstan, the fourth French archbishop. Those things 'which we have heard and known; and such as our fathers have told us . . . that the children which were yet unborn . . . might shew their children the same'.[1]

But do Thou, O Lord, have mercy upon us.

[1] Ps. 78: 3, 6-7

INDEX

Printed in Great Britain by
Thomas Nelson and Sons Ltd, Edinburgh